the family handyman

ULTIMATE STORAGE SOLUTIONS

Contents

1 KITCHEN & BATHROOM

10 simple ways to organize your kitchen..........6
Easy-build rollouts.............................. 12
Two-tier spice drawer 18
Cabinet door rack 20

Kitchen hiding places.......................... 22
Simple kitchen shelf 24
Double your bathroom storage.................... 30
Kitchen & bathroom tips........................ 33

2 CLOSET & ENTRYWAY

Custom clutter buster..........................36
Triple your closet space!.......................43
Versatile clothes cabinets 49
Entry organizer.................................58
Twin closet shelves 65

Under-bed rollout drawer.......................66
Hide-the-mess lockers 68
Throw & go bins 73
Closet & entryway tips 77

SPECIAL SECTION: HACKS & SHORTCUTS

Simple bathroom cabinet........................80
Customized IKEA furniture 83

Fold-up workbench..............................90
Behind-the-door medicine cabinet 91

3 WORKSHOP

Ultimate tool corral 94
Rolling shop cart 101
Compact tool cabinet 103
Hardware organizer............................ 107

Space-saver workstation 110
Classic workbench.............................116
Workshop tips 121

SPECIAL SECTION: SHELVES

Floating shelves..128
Above-door display shalf 135
Showcase shelving..136

Lighted display wall 144
Modular masterpiece....................................154

4   OUTDOORS

Ultimate garden shed 164
Quick & easy shed 176
Mini shed..184

Garden storage closet 191
Outdoor tips...194

5   GARAGE

Ultimate garage cabinets..............................198
Super-sturdy drawers 208
Bin tower 214
Flexible garage storage................................218

Garage wall system 222
One-day garage makeover 228
Garage tips 232

SKILLS TUTORIAL

Circular saw 236
Jigsaw 241
Gluing wood 246
Spray painting..250
Caulk like a pro 253
Patching walls..255
Building face frame cabinets 257

Edge-banding plywood..................................261
Installing cabinets 264
Hanging shelves 267
Clamping tips...271
Driving screws...276
Using a hot-glue gun 281
Building cabinets with biscuit joints 285

Ultimate Storage Solutions

Project Editor   Mary Flanagan
Cover Photography   Tom Fenenga
Cover Art Direction   Marcia Roepke
Page Layout   Teresa Marrone

Text, photography and illustrations for *Ultimate Storage Solutions* are based on articles previously published in *The Family Handyman* magazine (2915 Commers Dr., Suite 700, Eagan, MN 55121, familyhandyman.com). For information on advertising in *The Family Handyman* magazine, call (646) 518-4246.

ISBN: 978-1-62145-417-5 (Paperback)
ISBN: 978-1-61765-691-0 (Hardcove)

A NOTE TO OUR READERS: All do-it-yourself activities involve a degree of risk. Skills, materials, tools and site conditions vary widely. Although the editors have made every effort to ensure accuracy, the reader remains responsible for the selection and use of tools, materials and methods. Always obey local codes and laws, follow manufacturer instructions and observe safety precautions.

The Family Handyman

Trusted Media Brands, Inc.

PRINTED IN CHINA

2 3 4 5 6 7 8 9 10 (Paperback)
2 3 4 5 6 7 8 9 10 (Hardcover)

Chapter 1

KITCHEN & BATHROOM

10 simple ways to organize your kitchen..........6

Easy-build rollouts............................ 12

Two-tier spice drawer 18

Cabinet door rack 20

Kitchen hiding places.......................................22

Simple kitchen shelf 24

Double your bathroom storage......................30

Kitchen & bathroom tips................................33

10 simple ways to organize your kitchen

For me, kitchen time is wasted time. I want to get the job done, get out and get on with life. So I designed these projects to give you efficiency, easy access and effortless organization. If you're like me, you'll appreciate the time savings. If you're not like me—if you actually enjoy your kitchen—you'll love the projects even more because cooking will be more convenient.

–Gary Wentz

WHAT IT TAKES

TIME: 1 to 4 hours, depending on the project

SKILL LEVEL: Beginner to intermediate

TOOLS: Drill, sander, table saw

Drop-down tablet tray

This tray will keep your tablet computer off the countertop. As it swings down, it also swings forward, so the tablet isn't hidden under the cabinet.

The mechanism is simple; just make and position the arms exactly as shown here and it will work smoothly. I cut the aluminum parts and rounded the corners with a grinder. When closed, the tray is held up by small cabinet door magnets. I clipped the plastic ears off the magnets and glued the magnets into place with epoxy. The liner in the tray is a foam placemat cut to fit. Don't worry, small magnets won't harm your tablet; it actually contains magnets.

CENTER HOLES 1/4" FROM ENDS

SHELF SUPPORT ACTS AS STOP

5-9/16"

3/4"

9/16"

3/8"

4-5/8"

6-3/8"

3"

4"

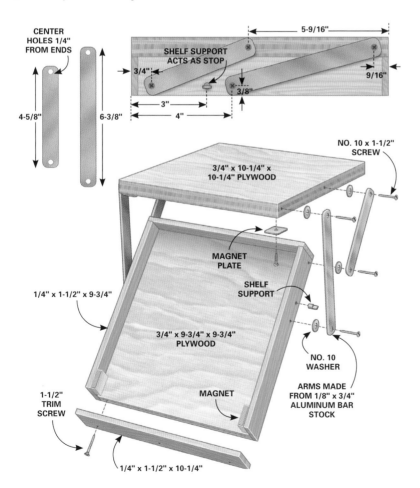

NO. 10 x 1-1/2" SCREW

3/4" x 10-1/4" x 10-1/4" PLYWOOD

MAGNET PLATE

SHELF SUPPORT

1/4" x 1-1/2" x 9-3/4"

3/4" x 9-3/4" x 9-3/4" PLYWOOD

NO. 10 WASHER

ARMS MADE FROM 1/8" x 3/4" ALUMINUM BAR STOCK

1-1/2" TRIM SCREW

MAGNET

1/4" x 1-1/2" x 10-1/4"

Instant knife rack

You can size this knife rack to suit any cabinet door and any number of knives. To build it, you just need a table saw and wood scraps. Run the scraps across the saw on edge to cut kerfs. Adjust the blade height to suit the width of the knife blades. You have to remove the saw's blade guard for these cuts, so be extra careful. Also cut a thin strip to act as an end cap. Glue and clamp the kerfed scraps together and sand the knife rack until the joints are flush. To mount it, use two 1-1/4-in. screws and finish washers.

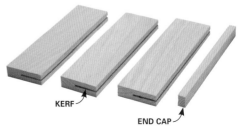

KERF

END CAP

Drawer in a drawer

Deep drawers often contain a jumbled pile of interlocking utensils. My solution is a sliding tray that creates two shallower spaces. Make it 1/8 in. narrower than the drawer box, about half the length and any depth you want (mine is 1-3/4 in. deep). When you position the holes for the adjustable shelf supports, don't rely on measurements and arithmetic. Instead, position the tray inside the drawer box at least 1/8 in. lower than the cabinet opening and make a mark on the tray. My shelf supports fit tightly into the holes, but yours may require a little super glue.

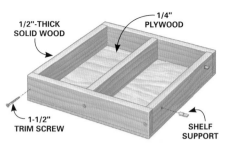

SHELF SUPPORT

Add a divider for upright storage

I don't know why the pan or tray you need is always the one at the bottom of the pile. But I do know the solution: Store large, flat stuff on edge rather than stacked up. That way, you can slide out whichever pan you need. Cut 3/4-in. plywood to match the depth of the cabinet, but make it at least an inch taller than the opening so you can fasten it to the face frame as shown. Drill shelf support holes that match the existing holes inside the cabinet. Finally, cut the old shelf to fit the new space.

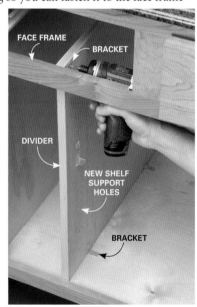

Fasten the divider with brackets

Screw two brackets to the cabinet floor; one to the face frame and one to the back wall of the cabinet (not shown).

Rollout storage panel

If you know how to mount a slab of plywood on drawer slides, you can take advantage of all the nifty shelves, hooks and holders sold at home centers. It's easy as long as you remember two critical things: First, make sure the drawer slides are parallel (see photo below). Second, make your cleats thick enough so that the slides will clear the cabinet door hinges. (I glued 1/2-in. plywood to 3/4-in. plywood to make my cleats.)

To install the panel in the cabinet, reassemble the slides. Hold the whole assembly against the cabinet wall and slide the panel out about 4 in. Drive screws through the cleats at the rear, then slide the panel out completely and drive screws at the front.

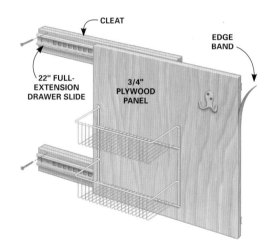

CLEAT

EDGE BAND

22" FULL-EXTENSION DRAWER SLIDE

3/4" PLYWOOD PANEL

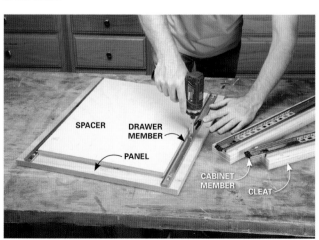

SPACER — DRAWER MEMBER

PANEL

CABINET MEMBER

CLEAT

Mount the slides

They have to be absolutely parallel for smooth operation. So place a plywood spacer between the drawer members as you screw them to the panel. Screw the cabinet members to cleats.

Convenient cutting board

The slickest way to store a cutting board for instant access is shown on p. 10 (see "Hidden Cutting Board"). But that only works for cutting boards less than 10-1/2 in. wide. For larger boards, mount a rack on a cabinet door. I used a sheet of 1/4-in.-thick acrylic plastic, but plywood would also work. You can cut acrylic with a table saw or circular saw as long as you cut slowly. Knock off the sharp edges with sandpaper. I also rounded the lower corners with a belt sander. For spacers, I used No. 14-8 crimp sleeves (in the electrical aisle at home centers). But any type of tube or even blocks of wood would work.

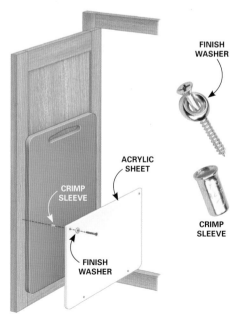

FINISH WASHER

ACRYLIC SHEET

CRIMP SLEEVE

CRIMP SLEEVE

FINISH WASHER

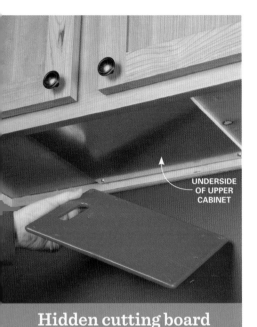

UNDERSIDE OF UPPER CABINET

Hidden cutting board

The secret to this project is "rare earth" magnets. The ones I used are just 5/32 in. in diameter and 1/8 in. tall. Browse online to find lots of shapes and sizes. Implant magnets at the corners of your cutting board and add more if needed.

Make the metal plate under the cabinet larger than the cutting board so the board will be easy to put away. Glue the sheet metal to plywood with spray adhesive. Drill holes near the corners and screw it to the underside of a cabinet.

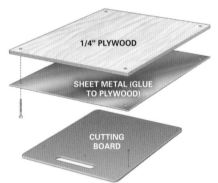

1/4" PLYWOOD

SHEET METAL (GLUE TO PLYWOOD)

CUTTING BOARD

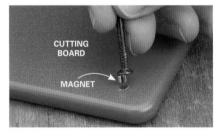

CUTTING BOARD

MAGNET

Magnetize your cutting board
Drill holes sized for the magnets and drop in a dab of super glue. Insert the magnets with a nail head. Slide the nail sideways to release the magnet.

Perfect place for lids

You can mount a drawer for pot lids under your pot shelf—or under any other cabinet shelf. Before you remove the shelf, put some pencil marks on it to indicate the width of the cabinet opening at its narrowest point (usually at the hinges). Your drawer front and slides can't extend beyond those marks (or you'll spend hours building a drawer that won't open). Then remove the shelf. If it's made from particleboard, I recommend that you replace it with 3/4-in. plywood and transfer the marks to the new shelf. If you can build a simple drawer box, the rest will be easy.

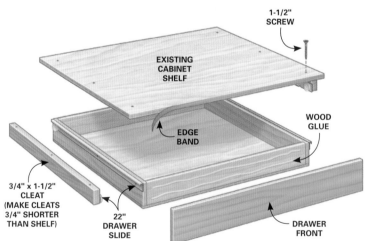

1-1/2" SCREW

EXISTING CABINET SHELF

WOOD GLUE

EDGE BAND

3/4" x 1-1/2" CLEAT (MAKE CLEATS 3/4" SHORTER THAN SHELF)

22" DRAWER SLIDE

DRAWER FRONT

Flip-down paper tray

This tray is perfect for pens and paper. When closed, it's mostly hidden by the cabinet face frame. To install the tray, screw on the hinges first. Then open the cabinet door above and clamp the tray to the underside of the cabinet while you screw the hinges to the cabinet.

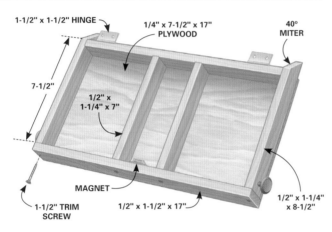

1-1/2" x 1-1/2" HINGE

1/4" x 7-1/2" x 17" PLYWOOD

40° MITER

7-1/2"

1/2" x 1-1/4" x 7"

MAGNET

1-1/2" TRIM SCREW

1/2" x 1-1/2" x 17"

1/2" x 1-1/4" x 8-1/2"

Building notes

■ The cost for each project will be more if you have to buy all the materials. If you have wood scraps lying around, you can cut those costs drastically.

■ All the wood projects shown here are finished with Minwax Wipe-On Poly.

■ Unless otherwise noted, all the materials for these projects are available at home centers.

■ If you want to cover plywood edges with iron-on edge band, find how-to help on p. 261.

■ Several of these projects require joining 1/2-in.-thick wood parts. You can do that with a brad nailer, but if your aim is a smidgen off, you'll blow a nail out the side of the part. Trim-head screws are safer. Their thin shanks won't split thin wood (as long as you drill pilot holes), and their small heads are easy to hide with filler (or ignore).

Add a shelf

Most cabinets come with only one or two shelves, leaving a lot of wasted space. So I added one (and sometimes two) shelves to most of my cabinets. All it takes is 3/4-in. plywood and a bag of shelf supports. The supports come in two diameters, so take an existing one to the store to make sure you get the right size.

Easy-build rollouts

You can build one in an hour, even if you're a beginner!

If you're tired of getting down on all fours and rooting through dark, jumbled base cabinets to find what you need, this project is for you. Rollouts make it easy to organize and access everything from your pantry items and cookware in the kitchen to the power tools and finish cans in your shop.

I've built many rollouts for my house and workshop, and believe me, the conventional way of building rollouts is tricky, time-consuming and frustrating. With the easier method shown here, you can build the rollouts on your workbench using just a few measurements taken from each cabinet.

Plan the rollouts

Before you build anything, decide what you'll be storing in each rollout. I lay out the items to determine the height of the drawer sides and to plan for clearance at the top (Photo 1). That will let you know how many rollouts are possible in each cabinet and exactly how high to place the cleats (Photo 10).

Buying the materials

Study Figure A to understand the construction. Since each cabinet is unique, the quantities of each material will vary. You'll have to measure your cabinets and plan your rollouts to figure out a materials list before you go to the home center. But the basic recipe is the same no matter what size rollouts you're building. Each unit

1 **Plan around your typical contents.** Stage the items you wish to store on rollouts until you're satisfied with the heights and quantity of the drawers. Note the clearance heights needed to get the spacing and positioning correct in the cabinet.

2 **Measure the opening.** Open the door(s) on the cabinet and measure between the narrowest part of the opening (including projecting hinge hardware) to size the rollouts. After measuring, remove the doors to make it easier to work and to prevent damage.

3 **Test-fit before assembly.** Cut the rollout base, drawer sides, front and back, and drawer slide mounts following Figure A on p. 14. Loosely assemble the parts in the cabinet to make sure everything is going to fit before moving on to assembly.

4 Assemble the parts. Glue and nail together the drawer with 2-in. brads. (Remember: The front and back go between the sides, not the other way around!)

Figure A
Anatomy of a simple rollout

If you have standard base cabinets, there are a few standard measurements and benchmarks to follow when building your rollouts. Standard cabinets have an inside depth of just under 24 in. With that in mind, use these rules of thumb to cut your parts:

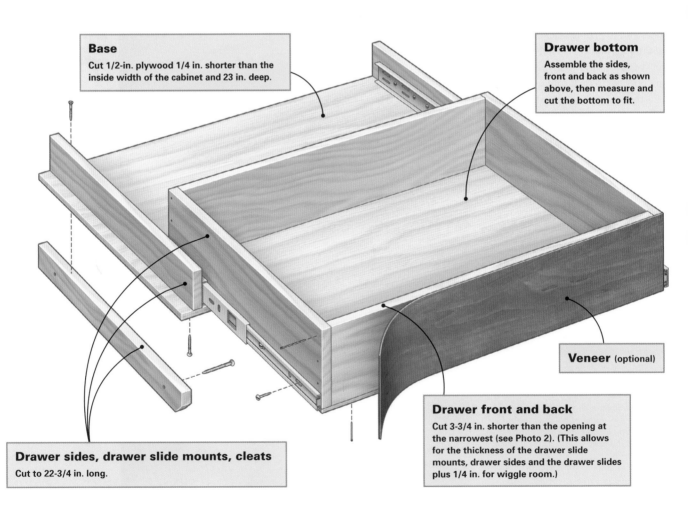

Base
Cut 1/2-in. plywood 1/4 in. shorter than the inside width of the cabinet and 23 in. deep.

Drawer bottom
Assemble the sides, front and back as shown above, then measure and cut the bottom to fit.

Veneer (optional)

Drawer front and back
Cut 3-3/4 in. shorter than the opening at the narrowest (see Photo 2). (This allows for the thickness of the drawer slide mounts, drawer sides and the drawer slides plus 1/4 in. for wiggle room.)

Drawer sides, drawer slide mounts, cleats
Cut to 22-3/4 in. long.

Travis's rollouts

"I love rollouts and have built several different versions for my shop and house. Here are just a few."

We keep our cookware right next to the stove: pans on the bottom, lids on the top.

Deep pantries make it notoriously difficult to access the stuff in the back. I filled our pantry with rollouts so we could get at everything.

This cabinet holds my biscuitry tools on the top, router accessories in the middle and routers on the bottom.

More rollout designs!
Go to familyhandyman.com
and search for "rollouts."

These three rollout/drawer hybrids hold the finishes and solvents in my shop.

requires a pair of 22-in. side-mount drawer slides (Photos 6 and 7). And each one will need 1/4-in. plywood for the bottom (Photo 5), 1/2-in. plywood for the rollout base (Photos 8 and 9) and of course, either 1x6s or 1x3s for the rollout frames. (We used clear pine for these, but you can use any wood as long as it's straight.)

Choose a 1x6 frame to corral bulky items like pans, linens or cereal boxes and a 1x3 frame for shorter items like canned goods, spices or utensils. (You can substitute 1x2s or 1x4s if you wish.) Both types get mounted on a 1/2-in. plywood base, which rests either on the cabinet bottom or on cleats that attach to the cabinet sides for elevated units. For each elevated rollout, you'll

5 Add the bottom. Use the bottom to square up the frame when you glue and pin it to the underside with 1-in. brads.

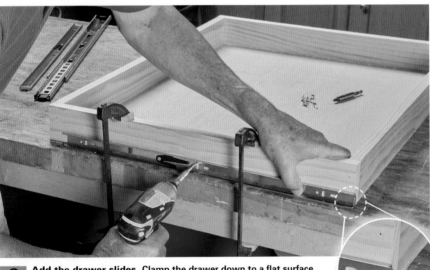

6 Add the drawer slides. Clamp the drawer down to a flat surface, rest the drawer slide flush with the front of the drawer and predrill the holes into the non-slotted holes with a self-centering drill. Then anchor the slides to the drawer with the included screws.

FLUSH

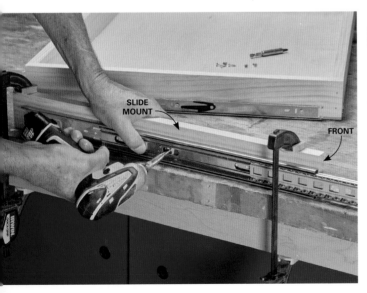

SLIDE MOUNT

FRONT

7 Mount the drawer slides on the slide mounts. Clamp the drawer slide mounts to the bench. Place the drawer slides flush with the end and then screw them to the drawer slide mounts.

need 40 in. of 1x2s for support cleats (Photo 10). Each rollout will also require 4 ft. of 1x3, which is used for drawer slide mounts (Photo 7). Rollouts need to be anchored to prevent tipping. Just screw bottom rollout bases to the bottom of the cabinet. Anchor upper rollouts with angle brackets (Photo 11).

Assembly and finishing

After you cut all the parts, dry-fit everything inside the cabinet to make sure it will fit and allow enough clearance to operate (Photo 3). I can't tell you how many times I've forgotten to account for the width of drawer sides, the thickness of slides or something else and had to knock everything apart and start over. Plus, dry-fitting will force you to think through the assembly so you can avoid making a mistake.

After you cut the parts and assemble the rollout drawer, apply your choice of finish before you put the drawer slides on and install the unit in the cabinet. We covered the front of our rollouts with a self-adhesive veneer to help them blend in with the cabinets. You can find some veneer options at home centers and woodworking stores, and many more online by searching for "self sticking veneer."

MEET THE EXPERT

Travis Larson, senior editor, has been tinkering with dozens of rollouts over the last 25 years.

8 Clamp the drawer assembly to the base. Engage the slides, then center the rollout drawer on the plywood base and clamp the drawer mounts in place at all four corners.

9 Screw the drawer mounts to the base. Flip over the assembly and predrill and anchor the slide mounts through the base with 1-5/8-in. screws.

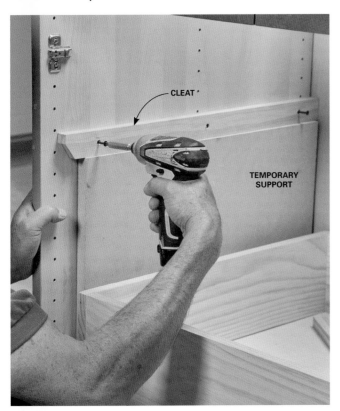

10 Fasten the cleats to the cabinet. Support elevated rollouts on cleats. Rest the cleats on squares of plywood cut to the right width while you screw the cleats to the cabinet sides with 1-1/4-in. screws.

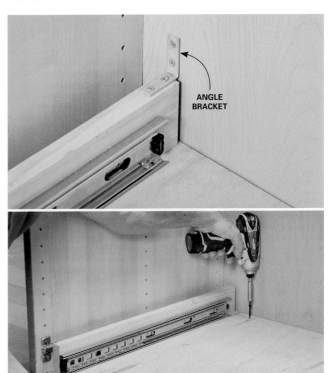

11 Secure the rollouts. Anchor elevated rollouts with angle brackets screwed to the cabinet back and drawer slide mounts (top photo). Anchor bottom rollouts by sinking a couple of 1-1/4-in. screws through the rollout base into the cabinet bottom, as shown in the bottom photo.

Two-tier spice drawer

Recently we remodeled our kitchen: new cabinets, countertops, appliances, the works. Yet the first thing we show off when people visit isn't the fancy new stove, but the inexpensive two-tier spice tray. When we open the drawer, we can slide the top tray all the way back into the cabinet to access the entire bottom layer; no need to lift out a separate tray or sort through layers of stuff. It's not only a space-saver but also a smart organizer since all the spices are in one place, face up. We used the same basic design to make a two-tier utensil drawer too.

Do a little measuring before diving into this project. You can install the 1-3/4-in.-thick tray (like ours) if your drawer is at least 4 in. deep on the inside. Also, these trays are most useful if your existing drawers have (or you install) full-extension slides on the main drawer.

WHAT IT TAKES

TIME: 3 hours

SKILL: Seasoned beginner

TOOLS: Jigsaw, miter saw, finish nailer, drill

1 **Cut away the top half of the drawer back.** Use a jigsaw to cut away a little more than half of the drawer back.

DRAWER BACK

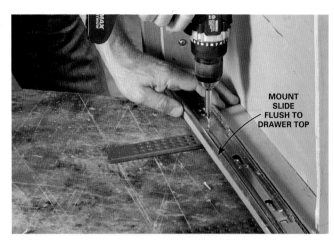

MOUNT SLIDE FLUSH TO DRAWER TOP

2 **Install the tray slides.** Secure full-extension drawer slides to the top inside edges of the drawer. Install them "backward" so they extend toward the back of the drawer. It's OK if they run an inch or so beyond the back of the drawer; most cabinets have extra space in back.

3 **Build the upper tray.** Since most standard drawer glides are 1/2 in. wide, build your tray 1 in. narrower (or a hair less) than the inside width of the drawer. Build your tray the same length as the inside drawer length. Install partitions according to your needs.

1/4" PLYWOOD BOTTOM

4 **Install the tray.** Attach the plywood bottom to the tray with nails or brads. Screw the tray to the drawer slides so the top of the tray is flush with the top of the drawer. Then reinstall the drawer.

Figure A
Spice drawer

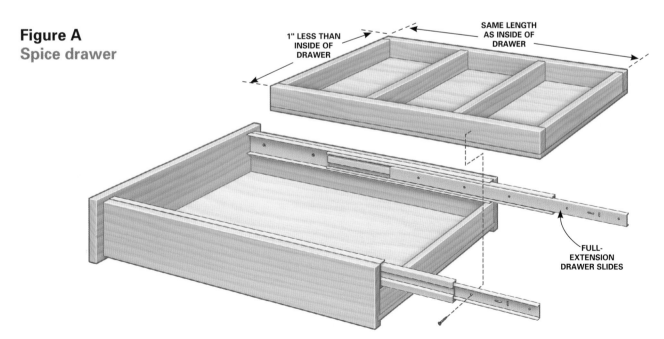

1" LESS THAN INSIDE OF DRAWER

SAME LENGTH AS INSIDE OF DRAWER

FULL-EXTENSION DRAWER SLIDES

Cabinet door rack

A super-simple solution for cabinet chaos

Some people think black holes exist only in outer space. Not true. There's probably one under your kitchen sink. Place detergent, cleaners or sponges under there and they disappear forever—or at least become really, really hard to find.

Here's a simple project to bring order to the chaos: a door-mounted storage rack. You can modify this basic idea to organize other cabinets too.

WHAT IT TAKES

TIME: 2 hours

SKILL: Beginner

TOOLS: Circular saw, miter saw or jigsaw, and drill

Planning and materials

As you plan your rack, consider building multiple racks. Building two or three doesn't take much more time than building one. Also think about (and measure!) the items you want your rack to hold. You may want to mount the upper shelf a little higher or lower than we did.

Most home centers carry everything you'll need, including 1/4-in.-thick wood strips in species like pine, oak and poplar. If you don't find thin material alongside the other lumber, look for "mull strip" or "mullion" in the millwork aisle. The wood quantities on our Materials List will yield a rack sized for most cabinet doors, but you may need a little more or a little less.

How to do it

Begin by looking inside your cabinet. With the door closed, this rack will project 3-3/4 in. into the interior. Make sure the installed rack won't bump into your sink, pipes, garbage disposal or other fixed object.

Materials list

1x4 x 6'
1/4" x1-1/2" x 6' strip
4 1" L-brackets
3/4" screws
2" screws
Finish washers
Spray lacquer

Measure the cabinet door and opening to determine the measurements of the sides and shelves (Photo 1). Mark the position of the upper shelf on the sides: We positioned ours 12 in. from the bottom, but you can adjust the location based on your needs. Secure the shelves to the sides using 2-in. screws and finish washers (Photo 2). Drill holes in the four cross slats 3/8 in. from the ends and fasten them to the sides with 3/4-in. screws.

With the rack assembled, we gave it two coats of lacquer. Lacquer is a durable finish, dries in minutes and comes in spray cans for quick, no-mess application.

Figure A
Cabinet door rack

1-1/2"
45-DEGREE MITER
1/2" MINIMUM
SLAT
1/4" x 1-1/2"
1x4
SIDE
L-BRACKET
1x4
SHELF
2" SCREW AND FINISH WASHER
1/4" x 1-1/2"

After the finish dries, screw the four L-brackets to the sides of the racks, making sure to position them so they won't interfere with the door hinges. Clamp the rack to the door, predrill mounting holes using the L-brackets as guides, and secure the rack to the door (Photo 3). Put a strip of tape 4 in. back from the front of the cabinet to indicate a "No Parking" zone for items stored inside.

1 **Measure to size the rack.** Measure the width of the door and cut the rack shelves 4-1/2 in. shorter than that measurement. Measure the height of the cabinet opening and cut the rack sides 1 in. shorter.

2 **Build the rack.** Mark the location of the top shelf on the sides. Drill screw holes and fasten the sides to the shelves using 2-in. screws and finish washers. Add the slats, apply a finish and screw brackets to the rack.

3 **Mount the rack.** Center the rack on the door and drill screw holes. Wrap tape around the drill bit to act as a depth guide so you don't drill through the door. Clamps aren't absolutely necessary for this step, but they're a big help.

Kitchen hiding places

Need to hide some valuables?
Take a look around your kitchen.

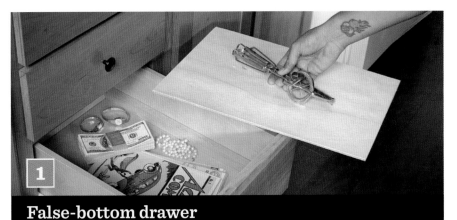

False-bottom drawer

Pick a deep drawer so the depth change won't be obvious. Cut 1/4-in. plywood 1/16 in. smaller than the drawer opening and rest it on a couple of wood strips that are hot-glued to the drawer sides. Then hot-glue some item you'd expect to find in that drawer to the bottom so you have a handle to lift the false bottom and reveal the hidden treasures.

Cabinet hidey-hole

Between almost every pair of upper cabinets, there's a 1/2-in. gap. Take advantage of that gap by hanging a manila envelope containing important papers or even cash. Hang the envelope with binder clips that are too wide to fall through the crack.

Toe-kick hideaway

There's an enormous 4-in.-tall cavity under all those kitchen cabinets behind the toe-kicks. It takes a few carpentry skills, but you can pull the toe-kicks free and make them removable. Most are 1/4-in. plywood held in place with 1-in. brads, and they're pretty easy to pull off. If you have a secondary 3/4-in. toe-kick, you'll have to cut it out at both ends. An oscillating tool works well for that task.

Stick both halves of round hook-and-loop self-adhesive tape to the toe-kick. Then push the toe-kick into place. The adhesive will stick to the cabinet base and leave half of the hook-and-loop tape in place when you pull it free. You can store a lot of items in this large, shallow space.

Counterfeit containers

Go online and type in "secret hiding places" and you'll be amazed by how many brand-name phony containers are available. Comet, Coca-Cola, Bush Beans—whatever. But you can craft a homemade version too. This mayonnaise jar had its interior spray-painted with cream-colored paint for plastic.

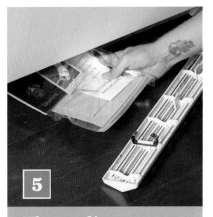

The appliance caper

Fridges and dishwashers have a snap-off grille in the front. Well, there's a lot of secret storage space under there. Ask yourself this: How many burglars will be thinking about cleaning your refrigerator coils? But before you stuff treasures under a fridge, take a peek to see where the coils are. On some models, a stack of cash might block the airflow. That will make the fridge work harder and could even damage it.

Simple kitchen shelf

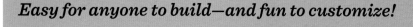

Easy for anyone to build—and fun to customize!

Lots of kitchens have a little wall space that would be perfect for a storage or display shelf. Plenty of bathrooms do too. This shelf is a great project for a beginning woodworker, and since it's so easy to adapt to different uses, a more advanced DIYer can have a lot of fun customizing it.

Tools and wood

You'll need a jigsaw, a drill and two accessories for the drill. The first is a No. 8 combination drill bit and countersink, which you can find anywhere drill bits are sold. The second accessory is a small sanding drum (Photo 3), which you can

find at home centers or online. The only other tool you might need is a nail set, for setting the heads of finish nails below the surface. Obviously, if you have a band saw and a miter saw, they will make this project a piece of cake.

You can build this shelf from just about any type of wood. Resist the urge to use the least expensive knotty pine, unless that's the look you're after. Knotty pine will be harder to work with and to paint well. Instead, get clear pine, poplar or any other knot-free board. If you're planning to paint the shelf, avoid oak. We used alder from a home center.

Cut out the shelf and brackets

Begin by cutting the shelf to length with a jigsaw (Photo 1). Then cut a piece 6 in. long from which you can cut the two brackets (Photo 2). Jigsaws often make a rougher cut on the top surface, so label that "top." The roughness will be hidden by the edging, even if the top of the shelf is visible after hanging it. But use a fine-tooth blade and set your oscillating feature (if your saw has it) to zero.

You can trace the curve for the brackets from the full-size pattern on p. 8, or even easier, use the bottom of a coffee can or a small plate. The exact curve isn't important. After the brackets are cut, smooth the sawn edges with a file, sanding block and the sanding drum in your drill (Photo 3) until the wood is smooth. You can stop sanding at about 150 or 180 grit.

Install edging strips on the shelf

Start edging the shelf by cutting the end strips to length. Instead of measuring, just hold the molding to the end of the shelf and mark it for cutting. It won't hurt if it's a hair too long. Mark one edge

Low-tech woodworking

This is a low-tech project. A jigsaw and a cordless drill are the only power tools you need, though there are more accurate and faster options. You'll also need some basic hand tools and two specialized accessories for the drill: a sanding drum and a combination drill/countersink bit. (See the text for more info.)

COMBO DRILL/ COUNTER- SINK

SANDING DRUM

Materials list

ITEM	QTY.
1x6 clear paint-grade softwood or hardwood	3'
7/16" x 1-1/4" pine stop molding	3'
1-1/4" drywall or utility screws	4
3/4" x 3/4" corner braces or brackets	2
Plastic or metal screw-in drywall anchors	2
Aerosol paint	1 can
Sandpaper	
Wood glue	

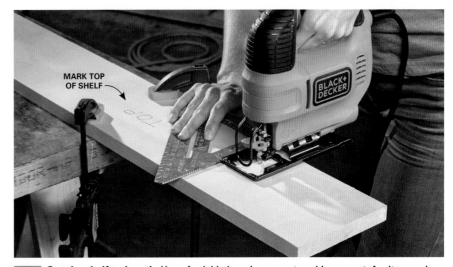

MARK TOP OF SHELF

1 **Cut the shelf to length.** Use a fresh blade and a square to guide your cut. A miter saw is the best tool for the job, but if you don't have access to one, you can substitute almost any other saw.

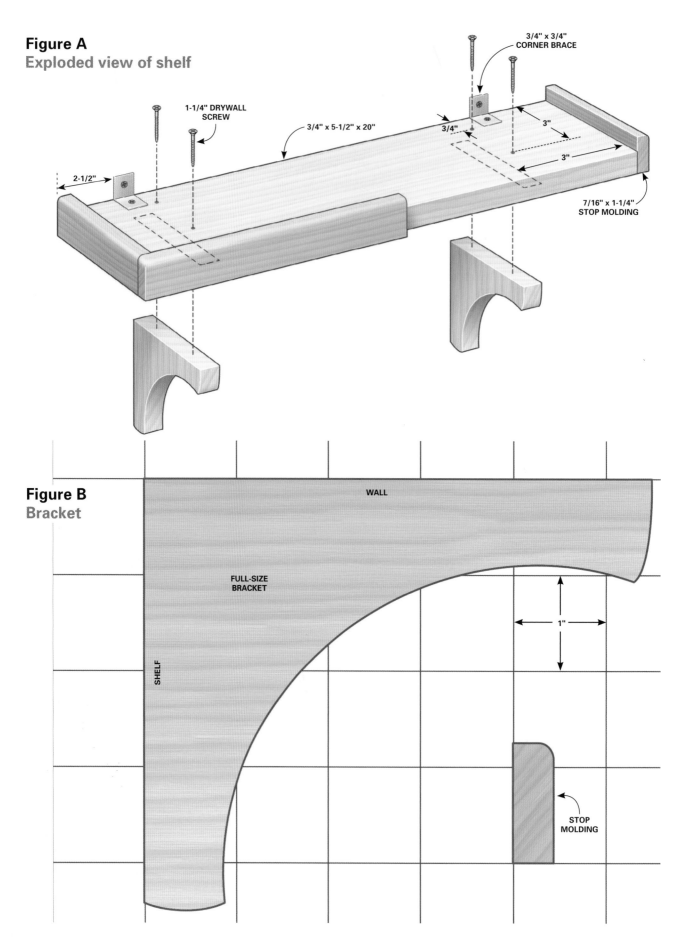

Figure A
Exploded view of shelf

3/4" x 3/4" CORNER BRACE

1-1/4" DRYWALL SCREW

3/4" x 5-1/2" x 20"

3/4"

3"

3"

2-1/2"

7/16" x 1-1/4" STOP MOLDING

Figure B
Bracket

WALL

FULL-SIZE BRACKET

1"

SHELF

STOP MOLDING

of the shelf as the front edge, then nail on the side strips (Photo 4), keeping the front edge flush. Make sure the rounded edge faces out. Put a thin bead of glue on the shelf edge before nailing, and keep the bottom edge as flush as you can. If the strips are a little long in back, you can easily sand or file off the excess, and if they stick out a little on the bottom edge, that can be sanded off too. Finally, nail on the edging strip in front.

Now set the nails and put a little painter's putty on them. When the putty is dry, sand the edging so the corners are smooth and the bottom edge is flush with the shelf. The bottom of the shelf will have a seam between the shelf and the edging. It's pretty much impossible to eliminate that seam permanently. Expansion and contraction of the wood will open it up even if you caulk or putty it, so don't be too much of a perfectionist. However, if your cut on the 1x6 is particularly rough, some putty there will help clean things up.

Screw the brackets to the shelf

The next step is to drill some screw holes in the shelf for attaching the brackets. The idea is simple: two screw holes on each side of the shelf so you can screw down into the brackets. Here's what to do. First, hold a bracket where you want it to be, but on the top of the shelf. Trace around the bracket, then do the same thing for the other bracket. Mark the screw locations and drill screw holes in the shelf from the top, using your combination drill/countersink bit.

Now hold a bracket in position on the bottom of the shelf, make sure the back edge is flush with the back edge of the shelf and that the screw holes are centered on the bracket. You can do it by eye, but if that's hard, put the two screws in their holes and use the points of the screws to guide you. Drive the screws by hand into the bracket (Photo 5), then repeat with the other bracket. Now is a good time to step back and admire your work, because you're almost done. But if for some reason you messed this part up, just drill new holes and fill the old ones with putty. You can shift the position of the brackets if you want.

2 Cut the curved brackets. For a curve like this, a smooth continuous cut is more important than following the line exactly. Any bumps or blips will be hard to sand out.

3 Sand the curves with a sanding drum. The trick is to go against the direction of rotation of the drill, with the drill going fast. If you make a gouge, angle the drum slightly to remove it.

4 Nail on the edging. The edging is a stock molding from home centers. It keeps stuff from falling off the shelf and covers the rough ends of the shelf.

5 Screw the brackets to the shelf. Notice that we've traced the shape of the bracket on the top of the shelf to help position the screw holes. We used a combination countersink/drill bit for the holes.

6 Spray-paint the shelf parts. You'll get better results by unscrewing the brackets and painting everything separately. A screw in the top of the bracket is a handy handle.

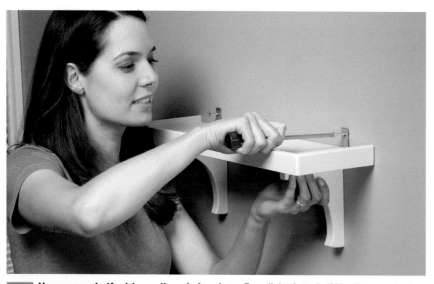

7 Hang your shelf with small angle brackets. For a light-duty shelf like this, you don't need to screw it to the studs. Just make sure the shelf is level and use drywall anchors in the wall.

Paint your shelf

Begin this part of the project by unscrewing the brackets. It's always easier to paint a project well if you can do the parts separately. Sand the pieces thoroughly to about 150 to 180 grit, removing sharp edges and corners, but not rounding them over too much. Wipe the sanding dust off with a rag and vacuum the parts thoroughly. Now set up your painting area. We highly recommend using spray paint for this project because it'll get you the smoothest finish.

Cover your work surface with paper or plastic, and set your shelf on strips or blocks to get it up off the surface. The shelf is pretty easy to paint, but go light on the edges to avoid drips. After the first coat of paint is thoroughly dry, sand it lightly with fine sandpaper, just enough to take off any roughness. Wipe and vacuum, then apply two final coats.

There's a trick to painting the brackets: Drive a long screw in one of the holes and use it as a little handle. That way you can spray the whole piece evenly in one shot (Photo 6). Then carefully set it down on a couple strips of wood to dry. When the paint is dry on all the parts, reassemble your shelf.

Hang your shelf

We recommend using small angle brackets to hang your shelf (Photo 7). Normally the top of a shelf is above eye level and the brackets are hidden, especially with items on the shelf. If your brackets are more exposed, give them a little spray paint to match the shelf, and paint the part that goes on your wall to match your wall. They'll be barely noticeable. Generally, though, this step isn't necessary.

To hang the shelf, use drywall anchors. Don't worry about hitting studs; there shouldn't be enough weight on this shelf to require it. Just put the shelf where you want it to go, make sure it's level, mark through the brackets where the anchors will go, and install the anchors. If it seems like you need a third hand to manage everything, you could draw a level line on the wall where the shelf will go. With the anchors in place, use the screws that came with the anchors to attach the shelf. Your shelf is complete! When you're ready to build more, check out the variations on the next page.

Customize your shelf

Go ahead—play with this project! It's easy to make your shelf as long as you want it to be. Just put more brackets underneath it, maybe one every 2 ft. or so. You could also scale it up by using 1x8 lumber, or even wider stock, as long as you also scale up the brackets. Some of our other favorite variations are shown below. However, we have one strong recommendation: If you're doing anything more than changing the size or color, first make a prototype out of inexpensive pine. Your plates, pot lids, cooking tools or whatever will be different from ours, so make sure they fit.

Pothooks and lids

This shelf has hooks screwed underneath to hold frying pans. We gave the hooks a dark finish by heating them with a torch as shown below. On our shelf, we cut off some of the threaded part of each hook with a bolt cutter because they were too long. The pot lids are held in place with two rows of 5/16-in. dowels. For heavier lids, use 3/8-in. dowels.

Blacken screw hooks with oil. Working outside, burn off the plating with a torch. Dip the hook into cooking oil and heat it until the oil burns off. You may need to repeat a couple times. This makes a hard, baked-on coating that resists wear. It's like seasoning a cast iron pan.

Plates and spoons

This shelf has a strip of molding (any kind will work) nailed on the top a couple inches from the back edge. This will keep plates from sliding off. The rod is 5/16-in.-diameter steel available at hardware stores. Cut it with a hacksaw and file the ends smooth. The trick is to drill the brackets before assembly, both at the same time, so the rod is perfectly aligned. The hooks are simple S-hooks, also a hardware item, opened up with a pair of pliers.

A wood strip makes it a plate rack. Tack a piece of molding to the top of the shelf to keep plates from sliding. Experiment with your plates to find the best location for the molding.

Double your bathroom storage

Two easy projects add storage and display space to a small bathroom

A larger mirror will make a small room seem larger.

Glass display shelves lend an open and airy feel to any room.

Bathrooms never have enough storage or shelf space. Finding a home for all your blow dryers, curling irons, toilet paper, and cans, soaps and bottles can be a challenge. Once you've filled your vanity, how do you squeeze more storage into a small bath? And what about your knickknacks?

Here are two simple projects to help you get the space you need.

PROJECT 1: Install glass shelves

Most bathrooms have one area you can count on for additional storage, and that's over the toilet. Open glass shelving is a great way to display decorative bathroom bottles or knickknacks.

There are zillions of glass shelving systems on the market.

Follow the directions that come with the system for the installation, but read on for help anchoring the shelves to the wall because you probably won't have studs exactly where you need them. We used masking tape to avoid marking the walls.

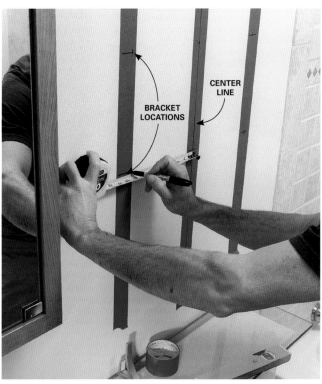

1 **Find location for brackets.** Apply a strip of 2-in.-wide masking tape above the center of the toilet and on both sides where the shelf brackets will be mounted. Draw a centerline with a level and mark the heights of the shelves on the center tape. Transfer the heights to the bracket tape with a 2-ft. level. Then measure from the centerline to mark the exact left and right locations for the brackets.

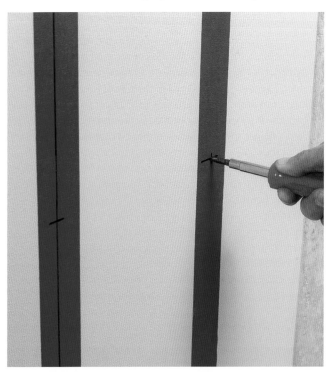

2 **Mark with a screwdriver.** Indent the drywall at the marks with a Phillips screwdriver and remove the tape.

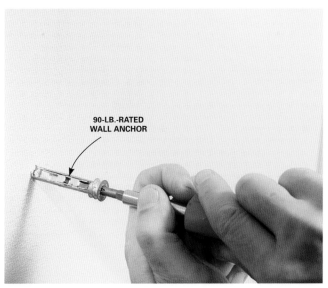

3 **Install anchors.** Drive hollow wall anchors through the drywall.

4 **Fasten the brackets.** Screw the brackets to the wall using the screws included with the anchors.

PROJECT 2: Install a larger medicine cabinet

You can find a wide variety of medicine cabinets and shelves at home centers and kitchen and bath stores. When sizing a medicine cabinet, measure the space you have available behind your sink, both height and width. Keep a few inches away from existing light fixtures (unless you want to move them). Buy a cabinet that fits within those dimensions.

Surface-mounting a large medicine cabinet is just a matter of centering it, leveling it and screwing it to the wall studs. Your old cabinet may be surface-mounted or recessed into the wall cavity between the framing. Remove a recessed unit by opening the door, backing out the screws in the side of the cabinet and pulling it out of the recess. You may need to cut around it with a utility knife if it's caulked or painted in around the edges.

Have a helper support surface-mounted cabinets while you back out the screws, or if you're alone, screw a temporary 1x2 support ledger under the cabinet as we show in Photo 1 to hold it while you unscrew it from the wall. You may need to move or replace the lighting beside or above the old cabinet. Now's the time to do it.

Hold the new medicine cabinet against the wall and adjust it up and down until the height is a good compromise for your family members, then mark the bottom and set the cabinet aside. Use the mark to draw a level line for positioning the 1x2 ledger (Photo 1). Then follow the photo series for installation details.

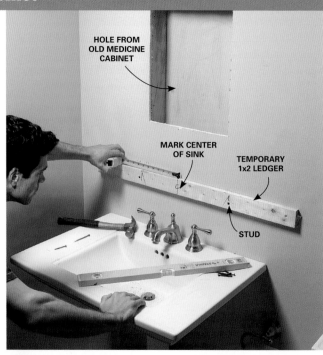

1 **Mark the studs.** Mark the height of the bottom of the cabinet and draw a line with a 2-ft. level. Locate the studs with a stud finder and mark the stud positions above the level line. Screw a temporary 1x2 ledger board through the drywall into the studs. Mark the center of the sink on the ledger, and then measure over from the center mark to the left and right studs.

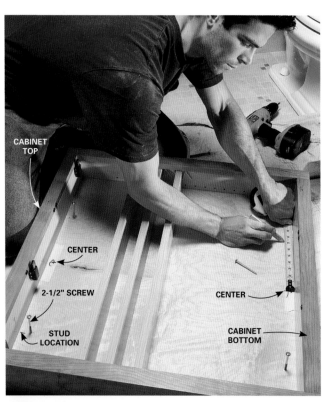

2 **Transfer stud locations.** Mark the center of the cabinet at the top and bottom and transfer the center-to-stud locations to the inside of the cabinet. Start 2-1/2-in. screws at those marks.

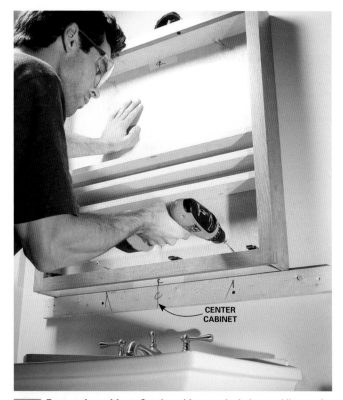

3 **Fasten the cabinet.** Set the cabinet on the ledger and line up the center of the cabinet with the center mark on the ledger. Drive the screws into the studs, then remove the ledger. Fill the screw holes with spackling compound and touch up the paint.

Kitchen & bathroom tips

Find extra space

A corner appliance cabinet hides coffeemakers, toasters and other small appliances while making efficient use of often-wasted corner space.

The above-refrigerator cabinet contains vertical partitions for storing trays, flat pans and cutting boards.

Double-decker drawers with sliding trays store two layers of knives, utilizing valuable drawer "dead air" space.

Swinging trash

Here's a space-saving solution to the kitchen or bathroom wastebasket problem. Screw wire shelf anchor clips to the inside of the door and hook the lip of a small wastebasket right on the hooks.

WIRE SHELF ANCHOR CLIPS

Keep your spray bottles in line

It can be hard to keep spray bottles from falling over and making a mess under your bathroom or kitchen sink. To keep them upright, hang them from a short tension rod (sold at discount stores) in your cabinet.

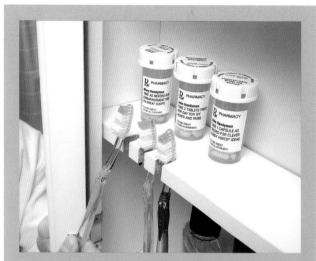

Hidden toothbrush organizer

If you keep your toothbrushes in the medicine cabinet stacked on a shelf, they probably fall out when you open the door. If you cut notches in the cabinet shelves, you'll solve this annoying nuisance. Use a rotary tool along with a woodcutting bit and sanding drum.

Under-sink organizer

To tame the clutter under our bathroom sink, I made this organizer from scraps of 3-in. PVC. I cut the pipe into short lengths and then glued them to 1/2-in. plywood with polyurethane construction adhesive. I spaced the pipe pieces to accommodate liquid soaps, shampoos and other bottles and left spaces between the pipe sections for odd-shaped spray bottles. Now things are organized and don't topple over every time we reach for something.

–Dan Nashold

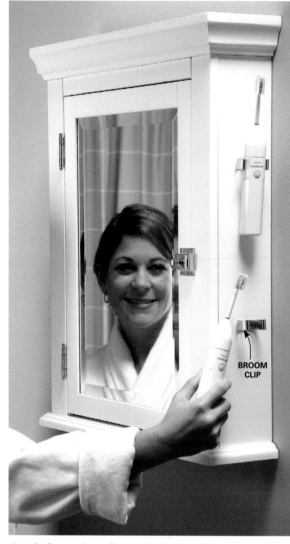

BROOM CLIP

Quick-grip electric toothbrush holder

Most toothbrush holders aren't big enough for electric toothbrushes. They end up falling out of the holder or taking up too much room on the vanity. Here's a clever storage idea: Make a holder for them using large grip-type clips (the kind you normally use for brooms or garden tools, available at hardware stores and home centers). Mount the clips on your medicine chest or on a piece of wood that you can hang on the wall. The clips work great to keep your toothbrushes secure!

Chapter 2

CLOSET & ENTRYWAY

Custom clutter buster 36

Triple your closet space! 43

Versatile clothes cabinets 49

Entry organizer 58

Twin closet shelves 65

Under-bed rollout drawer 66

Hide-the-mess lockers 68

Throw & go bins 73

Closet & entryway tips 77

Custom clutter buster

YOUR CLOSET CAN LOOK LIKE THIS!

From anarchy to order in a weekend! (melamine panels make it easy)

Walk through the closet aisle at any home center and you'll see lots of closet organizers—everything from wire shelving systems to ones that look like real wood cabinetry with all kinds of fancy accessories. And while these systems are designed to work in just about any type of closet, you can get a fully custom closet organizer—and possibly even save a few bucks—by building one yourself. Here's how we built ours using melamine panels, plus some tips on building your own.

What is melamine?

While real wood is strong and beautiful, building a closet organizer with it is expensive and time-consuming. Melamine products are an attractive and inexpensive alternative to wood or plywood. These boards, panels and sheets are made of particleboard with a tough, factory-applied melamine finish similar in appearance to plastic laminate. A 4 x 8-ft. melamine sheet is about half the cost of cabinet-grade plywood and available in a variety of colors. Be warned, however. Most home centers stock it only in white, which is what we used for our project.

PARTICLEBOARD CORE

BANDED EDGE

Predrilled panels save you time

At most home centers, you'll find 4 x 8-ft. melamine sheets. These full sheets are by far the most economical choice, but we bought 15-3/4-in. x 97-in. panels instead. These smaller panels come with banding on one or two edges and are available with or without predrilled shelf pin holes. So although we spent about three times as much as we would have on full sheets, we avoided hours of drilling and edge banding—plus the strain of transporting, lugging and cutting big, heavy sheets. Some home centers carry small melamine panels, but you may have to special-order them or shop online. Plan to cut 1/2 in. off each end to remove the ragged edges.

PREDRILLED SHELF PIN HOLES

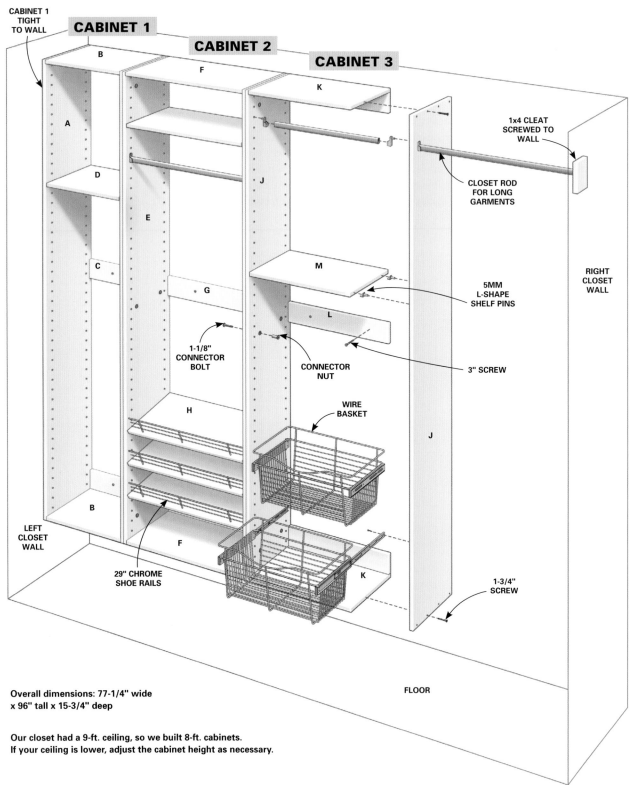

CABINET 1 TIGHT TO WALL

CABINET 1

CABINET 2

CABINET 3

1x4 CLEAT SCREWED TO WALL

CLOSET ROD FOR LONG GARMENTS

RIGHT CLOSET WALL

5MM L-SHAPE SHELF PINS

3" SCREW

1-1/8" CONNECTOR BOLT

CONNECTOR NUT

WIRE BASKET

LEFT CLOSET WALL

29" CHROME SHOE RAILS

1-3/4" SCREW

FLOOR

Overall dimensions: 77-1/4" wide
x 96" tall x 15-3/4" deep

Our closet had a 9-ft. ceiling, so we built 8-ft. cabinets.
If your ceiling is lower, adjust the cabinet height as necessary.

TECHNICAL ILLUSTRATION FRANK ROHRBACH III

Materials list

ITEM	QTY.
3/4" x 15-3/4" x 97" melamine panels (one banded edge with 5mm shelf pin holes already drilled)	6
3/4" x 15-3/4" x 97" melamine panels (one banded edge; no shelf pin holes)	7
Rev-A-Shelf 29" chrome shoe rails	3-pk.
Rev-A-Shelf 24" chrome wire baskets with full-extension slides	2
Rev-A-Shelf 14" valet rod	1
1-3/4" coarse-thread screws and plastic caps	102
3" No. 10 cabinet installation screws	6
1x4 ledger board	1
5mm L-shape shelf pins	56
1-1/8" connector bolts and nuts	12
36" oval closet rod (cut to length with hacksaw)	1
24" oval closet rods (cut to length with hacksaw)	2

Cutting lists

	KEY	QTY.	DIMENSIONS	NAME
CABINET 1	A	2	15-3/4" x 96"	Sides
	B	2	15-3/4" x 19-1/4"	Top and bottom
	C	3	4" x 19-1/4"	Hanging strips
	D	7	15-3/4" x 18-7/8"	Adjustable shelves
CABINET 2	E	2	15-3/4" x 96"	Sides
	F	2	15-3/4" x 29-1/2"	Top and bottom
	G	3	4" x 29-1/2"	Hanging strips
	H	4	15-3/4" x 29-1/8"	Shoe shelves; adjustable shelves
CABINET 3	J	2	15-3/4" x 96"	Sides
	K	2	15-3/4" x 24"	Top and bottom
	L	3	4" x 24"	Hanging strips
	M	3	15-3/4" x 23-5/8"	Adjustable shelves

WHAT IT TAKES

TIME: 1 to 2 days

SKILL LEVEL: Beginner to intermediate

TOOLS: Circular saw, cordless drill/driver, hammer, one or two pipe clamps, framing square, 6-ft. level, hacksaw.

Time and money

If you're an ace woodworker, you can probably build an organizer like ours in one day. If not, expect to spend a full weekend. You'll find everything you need to build it at most home centers. The melamine for our project cost about $250. But if you plan to add fancy accessories like we did, your final cost might be much higher.

Tips for building with melamine

Edge banding hides the ugly

The finished faces of melamine panels look great, but the raw edges don't. You might be able to build your organizer without having to apply any edge banding at all if you orient the raw edges so they're not visible once the organizer is installed. If that's not possible, you'll need to apply iron-on edge banding, which is available at any home center. Be sure to buy an edge trimmer. For edge-banding tips, go to p. 261 or familyhandyman.com.

Drill pilot holes

We assembled each of the three cabinet boxes for our closet organizer by first drilling pilot holes with countersinks and then driving 1-3/4-in. coarse-thread screws. These screws are designed to be self-drilling, but the particleboard in melamine has a tendency to crumble and blow out easily, so drilling pilot holes is worth the effort.

Choose your hardware first

If you're planning to install accessories similar to the ones we used for our project, be sure to buy them before you build the cabinets. Our wire baskets required a 24-in. opening, while the shoe shelf rails needed a 29-1/2-in. opening to allow for the width of the shoe shelves (with rails installed) plus the shelf pins.

Protect your hands!
Wear snug-fitting, rubber-coated gloves while working with sharp-edged melamine.

Prevent chip-out

You can cut melamine with a circular saw and regular woodcutting blade, but its brittle faces are prone to chipping out. To minimize this problem, use a 60-tooth, carbide-tipped blade and apply masking tape to the top side of your workpiece wherever you make a cut.

Make perfect cuts every time

One of the challenges of using a handheld circular saw is making perfectly straight and square cuts. For our project, we used a self-squaring crosscut jig for cuts across panels, and a longer jig for cutting long, narrow pieces like the hanging strips. These jigs also help reduce chip-out. The jig shown here is just a narrow piece of 3/4-in. plywood glued on top of a wider piece of 1/4-in. plywood, and it has a squaring fence on the bottom. To see how to make similar jigs, go to familyhandyman.com and search for "saw cutting guides."

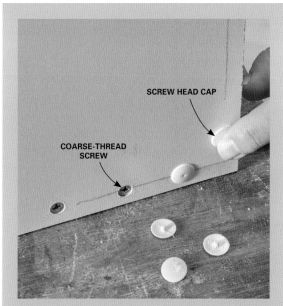

Hide the screw heads

The home center where we bought our melamine panels sells small bags of screws—labeled "melamine screws"—that are packaged with white plastic caps to hide the screw heads. You just press them on with a finger, then give each one a light tap with a hammer.

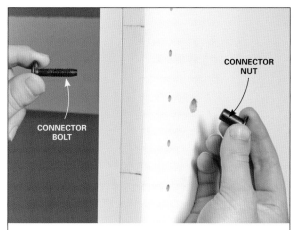

Connector bolts tie it all together

With the boxes screwed to the wall, drill holes and use connector bolts and nuts to join the sides of the cabinets. This will close any gaps between the boxes and stiffen up the entire assembly. Be sure the front edges of the cabinets are flush with each other before joining. If they're not, loosen the wall screws and adjust as needed.

A ledger board makes installation easy

Once assembled, each cabinet box weighs about 100 lbs. To make hanging them easier, screw a 1x4 or 2x4—called a ledger board—to the back wall of the closet down near the floor. Make sure it's perfectly straight and level. Mark the stud locations with masking tape. Then get somebody to help you lift each box onto the ledger board, which will hold it in position until you can screw it to the wall. Drive 3-in. washer-head screws through the hanging strips of all three boxes and into the wall studs.

Accessorize!

Instead of building drawers for our closet organizer, we decided to purchase Rev-A-Shelf wire baskets with full-extension slides. This company makes lots of different closet accessories, including the shoe shelf rails and valet rod that we installed. Other companies make similar accessories. Search for "closet accessories" or "closet hardware" online and you'll find a huge variety. We also installed oval closet rods with brackets that you insert into the cabinets' shelf-pin holes, which makes for super-easy height adjustments.

SHOE RAILS

BASKET DRAWERS

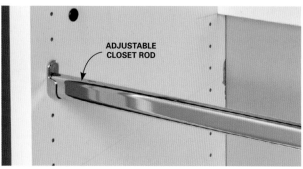

ADJUSTABLE CLOSET ROD

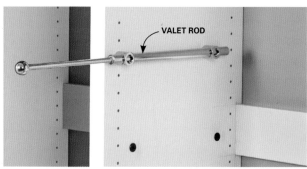

VALET ROD

Closet in a box

Want a closet organizer but don't want to measure and cut all the parts yourself? Your local home center sells precut closet kits that you just assemble and install. You'll likely pay a bit more for the convenience. A bigger downside is you won't be able to customize your closet exactly as you'd like.

Triple your closet space!

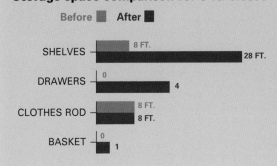

Three times the storage—and more!

Three times the storage in the same space may sound impossible, but just look at the numbers

Storage space comparison for 8-ft. closet

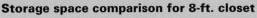

Before ■ After ■

	Before	After
SHELVES	8 FT.	28 FT.
DRAWERS	0	4
CLOTHES ROD	8 FT.	8 FT.
BASKET	0	1

If you have to dig through a mountain of clothes to find your favorite sweatshirt, it's time to take on that messy closet. This simple-to-build system organizes your closet with shelf, drawer and hanging space for your clothes, shoes and accessories. Buying a closet system like this would cost you at least $500, but you can build this one for about half that.

This system is really just four plywood boxes outfitted with shelf standards, closet rods or drawers. Here it is built for an 8-ft.-wide closet with an 8-ft. ceiling, but it'll work in any reach-in closet that's at least 6 ft. wide if you adjust the shelf width between the boxes or change the box dimensions.

1 **Finish now, save time later.** Prefinishing gives you a faster, neater finish because you'll have fewer corners to mess with. Apply two coats of polyurethane quickly and smoothly with a disposable paint pad.

2 **Preinstall drawer slides.** Attaching slides is a lot easier before the boxes are assembled. Position the slides using reference lines and a spacer. Remember that there are left- and right-hand slides, usually marked "CL" and "CR."

Time, money and materials

You can complete this project in a weekend. Spend Saturday cutting the lumber, ironing on the edge banding and applying the finish. Use your Saturday date night to clean everything out of the closet. That leaves you Sunday to build and install the new system.

This entire system was built with birch plywood. The cost, including the hardware for the drawers, shelves and closet rods, was around $300 (see Materials List). You could use MDF or oak plywood instead of birch. Everything you need for this project is available at home centers.

Cut and prefinish the parts

Start by cutting all the parts to size following Figure C on p. 48 and the Cutting list on p. 45. The corner box sides are slightly narrower than 12 in., so you can cut off dings and dents and still cut four sides from a sheet of plywood.

You won't be able to cut the shelves that fit between the boxes to length until the boxes are installed (the shelves need to be cut to fit), but you can rip plywood to 11-7/8 in. and cut the shelves to length later.

Once the parts are cut, apply edge banding (iron-on veneer) to all the edges that will be exposed after the boxes are assembled

(Figure A). Build a jig to hold the parts upright. Place a part in the jig. Then cut the edge banding so it overhangs each end of the plywood by 1/2 in. Run an iron (on the cotton setting) slowly over the edge banding. Then press a scrap piece of wood over the edge banding to make sure it's fully adhered. Trim the edges with a veneer edge trimmer. See p. 261 or visit familyhandyman.com and search "edge banding" for instructions.

Lightly sand the wood and your closet rod with 120-grit sandpaper. Wipe away the dust with a tack cloth, then use a paint pad to apply a coat of polyurethane on everything except the drawer parts (Photo 1). This inexpensive pad will let you finish each part in about 20 seconds. Let the finish dry, then apply a second coat.

Attach the hardware

It's easier to install the drawer slides and the shelf standards that go inside the boxes before you assemble the boxes. Use a framing square to draw reference lines on the drawer unit sides for your drawer slides (see Figure A). The slides are spaced 8 in. apart, centered 8-3/4 in. down from the top of the box. Keep the slides 3/4 in. from the front edge (this is where the drawer faces will go). Use a 7/64-in. self-centering drill bit to drill pilot holes and screw the slides into place (Photo 2).

Figure A
Closet storage system

C
1-5/8" SCREW
A
CLOSET ROD FLANGE
CLOSET ROD 18-1/4"
B

E
SHELF STANDARDS
S
D
G
F
8-3/4"
J
1-1/4" SCREW
8" ON CENTER
H
K
L
WIRE BASKET
13"
45° ANGLE

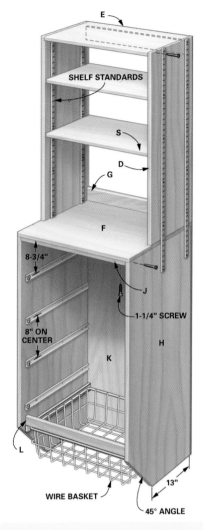

SHELF STANDARDS
B
18-1/2"
T
CLOSET ROD 18-1/4"
CLOSET ROD FLANGE
A
C

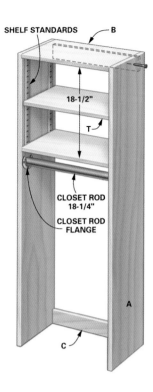

Figure B
Drawer construction

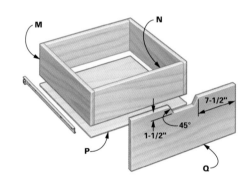

M
N
7-1/2"
45°
1-1/2"
P
Q

Materials list

ITEM	QTY.
4' x 8' x 3/4" plywood	3
4' x 8' x 1/2" plywood	1
4' x 8' x 1/4" plywood	1
8' closet rod	1
Edge banding (iron-on veneer)	2 pkgs.
20" drawer slides	4 prs.
6' shelf standards	10
Closet rod flanges	10
Wire basket	1
2-1/2" screws	1 box
1-5/8" trim screws	1 box
1-1/4" screws	1 box
1" screws	1 box
Wipe-on poly	1 pint

Cutting list

KEY	PCS.	SIZE & DESCRIPTION
A	4	3/4" x 11-7/8" x 52" corner box sides
B	4	3/4" x 11-7/8" x 18-1/2" corner box tops and bottom
C	4	3/4" x 2-1/2" x 18-1/2" corner box screw strips
D	2	3/4" x 13-7/8" x 34" shelf unit sides
E	1	3/4" x 13-7/8" x 22-1/2" shelf unit top
F	1	3/4" x 21" x 24" shelf unit bottom
G	2	3/4" x 2-1/2" x 22-1/2" shelf unit screw strips
H	2	3/4" x 20-3/4" x 44" drawer unit sides
J	1	3/4" x 20-3/4" x 22-1/2" drawer unit top
K	1	1/4" x 24" x 44" drawer unit back
L	1	3/4" x 2" x 22-1/2" drawer unit cleat
M	8	1/2" x 6" x 20" drawer sides
N	8	1/2" x 6" x 20-1/2" drawer fronts and backs
P	4	1/4" x 20" x 21-1/2" drawer bottoms
Q	4	3/4" x 8" x 22-1/4" drawer face
R	8	3/4" x 11-7/8" adjustable shelves, cut to length (not shown)
S	2	3/4" x 13-7/8" x 22" adjustable shelves for shelf unit
T	1	3/4" x 11-7/8" x 18" right corner box adjustable shelf
U	1	3/4" x 14-1/4" x 96" top shelf (not shown)

SHELF STANDARDS

METAL BLADE

3 **Gang-cut the standards.** Cutting 16 standards one by one with a hacksaw would take hours. Instead, bundle two or more together with tape and cut them with a jigsaw.

4 **Nail first, then screw.** If you have a brad nailer, tack the boxes together to hold the parts in position. Then add screws for strength.

You'll need your wire basket now (available at home centers). Attach the glides for the basket 3 in. below the drawer slides. If your basket is narrower than 22-1/2 in., screw a cleat to the box side so the basket will fit.

Now attach the shelf standards. You can cut them with a hacksaw, but an easier way is to use a metal blade in a jigsaw. Place two or more standards together so the numbers are oriented the same way and the standards are aligned at the ends. Tape the standards together where you're going to make the cut, then gang-cut them with your jigsaw (Photo 3).

Screw the standards to the inside of the box sides, 1 in. from the edges. Keep the standards 3/4 in. from the top (that's where the box tops go). Be sure the numbers on the standards are facing the same way when you install them—this ensures the shelves will be level.

Assemble the boxes

Use a brad nailer to tack the boxes together following Figure A and Photo 4. If you don't have a brad nailer, use clamps. Then screw the boxes together. Use 1-5/8-in. trim screws because the screw heads are small and unobtrusive (you can leave the screw heads exposed). Here are some tips for assembling the boxes:

■ Attach the screw strips to the box tops first, then add one side, then the bottom shelf, and then the second side.

■ Drill 1/8-in. pilot holes to prevent splitting. Stay 1 in. from edges.

■ If your cuts are slightly off and the top, bottom and sides aren't exactly the same width, align the front edges.

■ The boxes will be slightly wobbly until they're installed in the closet, so handle them with care.

■ The middle bottom box has a back. Square the box with the back, then glue and tack the back in place.

■ After the corner boxes are assembled, screw shelf standards to the side that doesn't abut the wall (it's easier to install the standards before the boxes are installed).

Build the drawers

Cut the drawer sides and bottoms (see Cutting List, p. 45). Assemble the sides with glue and 1-in. screws. To square the drawers, set adjacent sides against a framing square that's clamped to your work surface. Glue and tack the drawer bottom into place (Photo 5). Then set the drawer slides on the drawers, drill pilot holes and screw the slides into place.

Install the drawers in the box. Getting the drawer faces in their

5 Square the drawer boxes. If the boxes aren't square, the drawers won't fit right or glide smoothly. Drawers take a beating, so assemble them with nails and glue.

Labels: GLUE, FRAMING SQUARE, SPACER

6 Center the drawer faces perfectly. Stick the faces to the boxes with double-sided tape. Then pull out the drawer and drive screws from inside the box.

Label: DOUBLE-SIDED TAPE

7 Plumb the shelf boxes. The corners of your closet may not be plumb, so check the box with a level before you screw it to the studs. Mark stud locations with masking tape.

Labels: STUD LOCATION, LEVEL LINE

8 Install the center unit in two parts. The center unit is big and clumsy, so install the shelf unit first, then prop up the drawer unit with spacers and screw it to the shelf.

perfect position is tricky business. If the faces are even slightly off-center, the drawer won't close properly. To align them, place double-sided tape over the drawer front. Starting with the top drawer, center the drawer face in the opening (Photo 6). You should have about a 1/8-in. gap on both sides and the top. Press the face into the tape. Take out the drawer and clamp the face to the drawer to keep it stationary. Drive two 1-in. screws through the inside of the drawer into the face.

Hang the boxes in the closet

Now install the boxes. Start by drawing a level line in the closet, 11 in. down from the ceiling. This will give you just over 10 in. of storage space above the closet system after the top shelf is installed. Then mark the stud locations on the wall with tape.

Don't assume your closet walls are plumb—they're probably not. So you can't just place a box in a corner without checking for alignment. Hanging the boxes is a two-person job, so get a helper. Start with the corner boxes. Align the top of the box with your level line on the wall. Have your helper plumb the box with a level while you drive 2-1/2-in. screws through the screw strip into the wall at the stud locations (Photo 7). Attach the other corner box the same way.

Find the center of the wall, then make a mark 12 in. on one side of the center mark. That's where your shelf unit will go. Again, have your helper plumb the box while you align it with your marks and screw it to the wall.

Prop up the drawer unit on spacers so it's tight against the shelf unit. Align the edges, then clamp the boxes and screw them together (Photo 8). Drive screws through the screw strip into the wall.

Then place the top shelf over the boxes. This shelf barely fit into place. If yours won't fit, you'll have to cut it and install it as two pieces. Make the cut near one end, over a corner box, so it's not noticeable. Screw the shelf to the box tops with 1-1/4-in. screws.

Then attach shelf standards along the sides of the shelf and drawer units (Figure A). Cut the adjustable shelves to length to fit between the corner boxes and the middle boxes. Finally, screw the closet rod flanges into place, cut the closet rod to size and install the rods.

Figure C
Closet system cutting diagrams

This shows only the 3/4-in. plywood. The 1/2-in. and 1/4-in. plywood sheets are for the drawers and back.

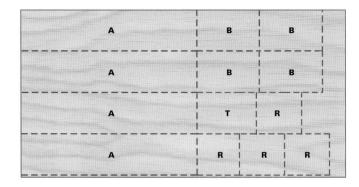

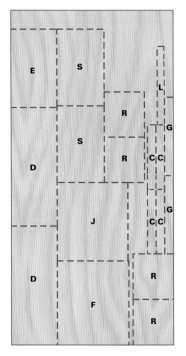

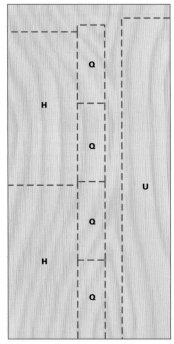

Versatile clothes cabinets

Add extra clothes storage space to any room with these attractive cabinets

It seems like no matter how much closet space you have, there's never quite enough. But building attractive clothes cabinets like these allows you to expand storage into your bedroom or a spare room and gain the extra space you need. You can build one storage tower or connect several together. Each tower consists of a drawer base, a wall cabinet with doors, and two side panels with holes for adjustable shelves. We'll show you how to build the cabinets and assemble the towers. And we'll also include details for adding a clothes hamper drawer, a pullout pants-hanging rack

and shoe storage between the two towers.

Even though the style is simple, building these cabinets requires close attention to detail and accurate cuts. If you can cut plywood precisely and have the patience to carefully assemble the parts, you shouldn't have any trouble building this project.

We used 3/4-in. maple plywood for everything but the drawers and the backs of the cabinets. For these we used good-quality shop-grade plywood. You could substitute less expensive plywood for the cabinet boxes to save a little money.

Tons of storage for all your clothes

The large, deep drawers hold sweaters and other bulky items. Full-extension ball-bearing slides allow easy access.

The wall cabinet has space for extra bedding or off-season clothes.

The shoe shelves can store shoes, purses and hats, or small baskets for socks and underwear.

Cut and prepare the plywood

The most important step in the building process is cutting the parts accurately. Use the Cutting List and Figure E (p. 57) as a guide. Our plywood was a full 3/4 in. thick, and the sizes shown are for 3/4-in. plywood. If yours is slightly thinner, cut the shelves, doors and drawer parts after you've assembled the cabinet boxes so you can adjust the fit.

A stationary table saw with an accurate fence and outfeed tables would be ideal for this job. But you can get great results with a portable saw too. You'll need a top-quality blade designed to crosscut plywood. We splurged on a 90-tooth 10-in. blade and were amazed at the glass-smooth, splinter-free cuts we got.

After all the parts are cut, separate out the uprights and shelves that receive solid wood nosing. Then cover the raw plywood edges of the remaining 3/4-in. plywood parts with edge-banding veneer. For the cabinet boxes, you only need to cover the front edges. On the doors and drawer fronts, you'll want to cover all four edges.

WHAT IT TAKES

TIME: Two or three weekends

SKILL: Intermediate to advanced

TOOLS: Standard carpentry tools plus a table saw, miter saw, compressor and pin nailer, and a 35-mm Forstner bit

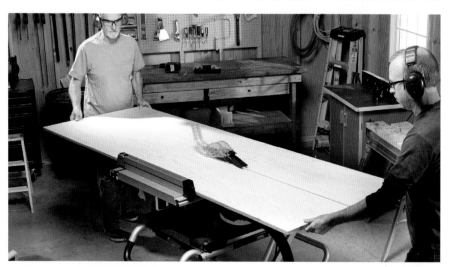

1 **Rip the plywood.** Round up a helper and rip the plywood sheets into strips according to Figure E on p. 57. Choose the best-looking plywood for the tall end panels because these are the most visible.

STOP GAUGE

CROSSCUT SLED

2 **Crosscut the plywood.** A crosscutting sled is the best tool for accurately cutting the plywood strips to length. Take the time to build a sled if you don't have one. Clamp a stop to the crosscutting sled to cut same-size parts accurately.

3 **Cover the raw plywood edges.** Finish the edges of the cabinet parts and the shoe shelves with edge banding. We're using self-adhesive edge banding, but iron-on edge banding works well too. Center the edge banding and press or iron it on according to the manufacturer's instructions.

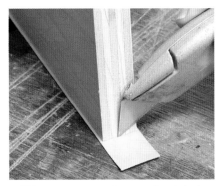

4 **Trim the ends.** Place the banded edge down on the work surface and use a sharp utility knife to trim the ends flush.

5 **Trim the edges.** Use a veneer edge trimmer to slice off the excess edge banding along the sides. A double-edge trimmer like this one trims both edges at once. Single-edge trimmers cost about half as much and work well. They just take a little longer. Use sandpaper to remove any overhanging edge banding to create a perfectly flush edge.

Build the cabinet boxes

The cabinets are simple plywood boxes with drawers or doors added. The key to accuracy is to make sure that the edges of the plywood remain perfectly aligned as you assemble the boxes and that the cabinet box is square. Photos 6 – 8 show how.

CENTERLINE

6 **Install the slides first.** It's easier to attach slides to the cabinet sides before the cabinet is assembled. Draw lines to indicate the center of the slides. Then center the screw holes on the line and attach the slide with the included screws.

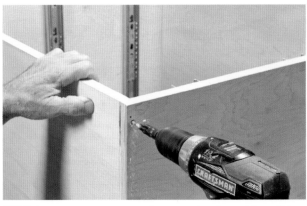

7 **Nail, then screw parts.** To prevent the plywood from sliding around when you're drilling pilot holes, tack the parts first with a brad nailer. Then drill countersink pilot holes and connect the parts with screws.

8 **Attach the back.** If you're careful to cut the back perfectly square, you can use it to square the cabinet. Apply a bead of glue and set the back onto the cabinet. Make sure one edge of the back is flush with one side of the cabinet box and fasten it with 1-in. nails. Adjust the cabinet box until the other sides align, then partially drive a nail to hold it. Check the cabinet for square, then finish nailing on the back.

Figure A: Clothes storage tower

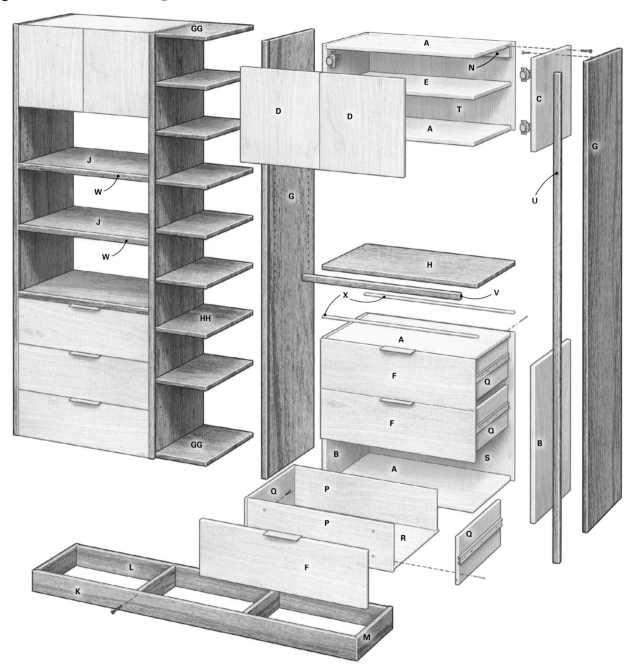

Build the drawers

The most critical part of the drawer-building process is to make sure the finished drawer is between 1 in. and 1-1/16 in. narrower than the inside dimensions of the cabinet to allow for the drawer slides. To determine the exact dimensions of the front and back of the drawers (parts P), measure between the cabinet sides and subtract twice the thickness of the drawer plywood. Then subtract another 1-1/16 in. Photos 9 – 14 show how to build and install the drawers.

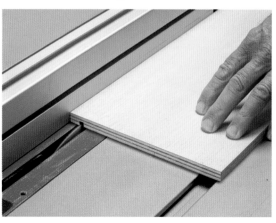

9 **Groove the drawer parts.** Set your table saw fence at 1/2 in. and raise the blade 1/4 in. above the table. Cut a groove in the drawer sides and fronts. Move the fence away from the blade about 1/16 in. and make a second pass to widen the groove. Check the fit of the drawer bottom plywood. It should be snug but not too tight. You may need a third pass. After the grooves are cut, rip the backs to width.

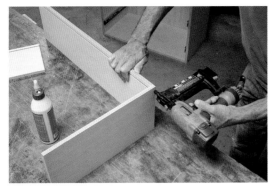

10 Build the drawer boxes. Glue and nail the sides to the front and back. Use glue sparingly to avoid squeeze-out mess. Use 1-1/4-in. nails and aim carefully to prevent them from shooting out the sides. Make sure the grooves line up—it's easy to get a part upside down.

11 Slide in the bottom. Check the fit of the drawer bottom and trim the width a little if needed. Don't force the plywood or it may push the drawer sides apart.

12 Nail the drawer bottom. Measure diagonally to make sure the drawer is square. Then drive 1-in. nails through the drawer bottom into the drawer back to hold it in place.

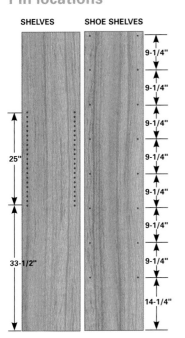

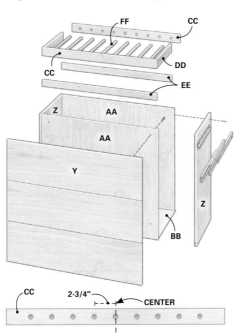

13 Attach the drawer slide. Draw a line 3-3/4 in. from the top edge of the drawer. Center the drawer slide on the line, keeping the front edge lined up with the front of the drawer. Attach it with two screws. Add the remaining screws later to secure the drawer slide in place after making any adjustment.

14 Install the drawer fronts. Mount each drawer front with hot glue, then pull it out and secure it with four screws driven from inside the drawer. Set the bottom door flush with the bottom of the cabinet. Then use two stacks of two pennies as spacers between the drawer fronts. The top drawer should be 1/8 in. below the top of the cabinet.

Figure B
Pin locations

SHELVES | SHOE SHELVES

9-1/4"
9-1/4"
9-1/4"
9-1/4"
9-1/4"
9-1/4"
9-1/4"
14-1/4"

25"

33-1/2"

Figure C
Super-size drawer or pants rack

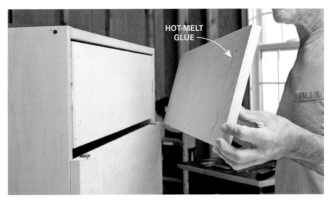

FF
CC
CC
DD
EE
Z
AA
AA
Y
Z
BB
CC
2-3/4"
CENTER

Figure D
Drawer slide centers

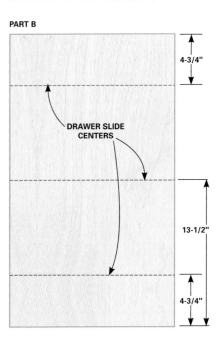

HOT-MELT GLUE

PART B

4-3/4"

DRAWER SLIDE CENTERS

13-1/2"

4-3/4"

Hang the doors with Euro hinges

This type of cabinet construction is perfect for Euro-style hinges. You simply mount a plate to the cabinet and drill a 35-mm (1-3/8-in.) recess in the door to accept the hinge. The Blum 120-degree clip hinges we're using are adjustable up and down, in and out, and side to side, making final door fitting a breeze. Photos 15 – 21 show how to install the hinges and hang the doors.

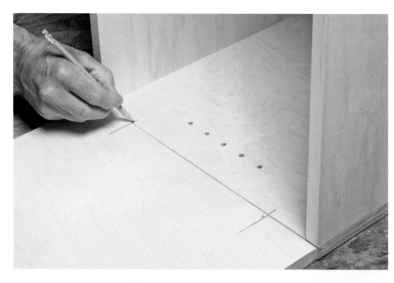

15 **Mark the hinge locations.** Mark the hinge position on the doors, 3 in. from the top and bottom. Then align the door with the cabinet and transfer the marks to the cabinet side.

16 **Start the hinge holes.** We built this plywood jig as a guide for starting hinge holes. You can also buy a jig, or simply mark the center of the hinge and use a center punch to create a starting hole. For these Blum hinges, the center of the hole is 7/8 in. from the edge of the door. Start drilling the hole with the 35-mm (or 1-3/8-in.) Forstner-style bit.

17 **Complete the hinge hole.** Remove the guide so you can judge how deep to drill. With most bits you can drill until the top of the bit is flush with the surface. The recess should be 1/2 in. deep. Drill a hole in a scrap first to check the depth before drilling a door.

18 **Mount the hinge.** Press the hinge into the recess and align it with a square. Use a self-centering bit to drill pilot holes for the hinge screws. Then attach the hinge with the screws provided.

19 **Mark for the hinge plates.** Draw lines 1-7/16 in. from the front of the cabinet to locate the center of the hinge plates. If you're using a different hinge, check the instructions to find the correct distance.

20 **Attach the hinge plates.** Center the hinge plates on the marks and line up the center of the screw holes with the second mark. Drill pilot holes with a self-centering bit and attach the plates with the screws.

21 **Hang the door.** Clip the hinges to the plates to hang the doors. Don't bother to adjust the hinges until after the cabinet is mounted to the wall.

Super-size drawer

Replacing three drawers with one huge drawer allows you to hang pants or store two clothes hampers. The big drawer is just a deeper version of the small drawers. But to keep it from sagging, we mounted the drawer on file-cabinet drawer slides instead. To simulate three drawers, we grooved a single sheet of plywood by running it through the table saw with the blade raised 1/4 in., and used this for the drawer front. To convert the drawer for pants storage, just build the dowel rack and rest it on cleats.

Super-size laundry drawer

Figure C shows the parts for the deep drawer. Center the cabinet part of the file-drawer slide 4-3/4 in. from the top of the cabinet, and the drawer part of the slide 1 in. down from the top of the drawer. Finish by mounting the grooved drawer front.

Pullout pants rack

Use Figure C as a guide to build this rack from 2-in. strips of plywood and 5/8-in. dowels. Screw cleats to the front and back of the drawer, 2-1/4 in. from the top, to support the rack.

Build the side panels

The side panels have 1-in.-wide solid wood edging on one side and shelf-pin holes on one face. If you'll be adding shoe shelves between two towers as shown in the photo on p. 49, then drill holes for these shelf pins too. Be careful to attach the nosing to the correct edge of each panel. Since the shelf-pin holes are not an equal distance from top and bottom, the two sides are not interchangeable, but are mirror images.

22 **Drill the shelf-pin holes.** We're using a store-bought jig, but you can also use a length of 1/4-in. pegboard as a template for drilling the holes. Mount a stop on your 1/4-in. drill bit to drill the holes 3/8 in. deep.

23 **Glue and nail the nosing.** Spread a bead of glue along the plywood edge. Align the wood edging flush to the inside edge of the panel and attach it with 1-1/4-in. nails.

Install the cabinets in your room

After all the cabinets and side panels are built, you'll want to stain and varnish or paint them before installing them in your room. Remove all the drawers, doors and hardware to make finishing easier. Carefully sand all the parts. We used a random orbital sander and 120-grit sandpaper. Then we stained the side panel and shelves and finally brushed two coats of polyurethane on all the parts. After the finish dries, reinstall the hardware and carry the cabinets, side panels and base into your room. Mark the studs in the location where you'll install the cabinets. Photos 24 – 27 show the installation steps.

24 **Level the base.** Installing the towers is easier if you start out with a level base. If your floor isn't level, slide shims under the base to level it. Then screw it to the studs. Cut off the shims and cover the gap with molding if necessary. You can make your own molding by ripping 3/8-in.-wide strips from 3/4-in. maple, or buy base-shoe molding.

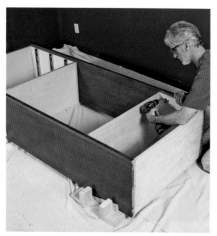

25 **Assemble the towers.** Arrange the cabinets and side panels on the floor. We built simple 2x4 supports to hold the cabinets and side panels in place while we screwed them together. Drill holes through the cabinet sides a few inches from each corner. Then carefully line up the panels so the tops and bottoms are flush with the cabinets, and attach them with 1-1/4-in. screws.

26 **Attach the towers to the wall.** Transfer the stud locations to the inside of the cabinet and drive 2-1/2-in. screws into the studs to secure the towers. Use the 12-in.-wide shoe shelves as spacers at the top and bottom to position the second tower.

27 **Finish up by adding the tops, doors, drawers and shelves.** Tilt the top into place and attach it with 1-1/2-in. screws from inside the base cabinet. Then clip the doors onto the hinge plates and slide the drawers into the drawer slides to finish the job.

Materials list (for one tower)

ITEM	QTY.	ITEM	QTY.
4' x 8' x 3/4" maple plywood	3*	Blum 120-degree clip-top hinges	4
4' x 8' x 1/2" shop-grade plywood	1	Blum frameless 0mm screw-on mounting plates	4
4' x 8' x 1/4" shop-grade plywood	1	1/4" shelf pins	12
3/4" x 5-1/2" x 8' maple board	1	Screws, nails, wood glue, drawer and door pulls, finishing supplies	
13/16" maple veneer edge banding	75 ln. ft.	Optional 6" file drawer slide for super-size drawer	1
16" full-extension drawer slides	3 pairs	Optional hamper for super-size drawer	2

* Leftover materials can be used to make a drawer front for the super-size laundry drawer and the shoe shelves.
The Blum hardware and the file drawer slide are available at woodworking stores and online.

Figure E: Plywood cutting diagrams

1/4" PLYWOOD

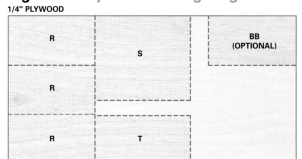

3/4" PLYWOOD

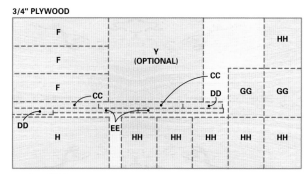

3/4" PLYWOOD

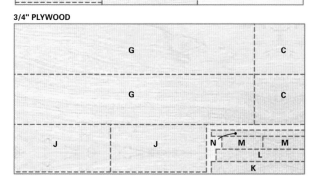

3/4" PLYWOOD

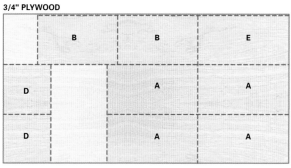

1/2" PLYWOOD

Cutting list

KEY	DIMENSIONS	QTY.	NAME
3/4" maple plywood			
A	15-7/8" x 30-1/2"	4	Cabinet tops and bottoms
B	15-7/8" x 27"	2	Lower cabinet sides
C	15-7/8" x 16"	2	Upper cabinet sides
D	15-3/4" x 15-7/8"	2	Upper cabinet doors
E	15-7/8" x 30-3/8"	1	Upper cabinet shelf
F	8-7/8" x 31-3/4"	3	Lower cabinet drawer fronts
G	16-1/8" x 79-3/4"	2	Side panels
H	16-1/8" x 32"	1	Lower cabinet top
J	15-1/4" x 31-7/8"	2	Shelves
K	4" x 30-1/2"	1	Base front (extend as needed for two towers)
L	4" x 29"	1	Base back
M	4" x 13-1/2"	2	Base sides
N	2" x 30-1/2"	1	Upper cabinet hanging strip
1/2" shop-grade plywood			
P	7-1/2" x 28-1/2"	6*	Drawer fronts and backs (cut backs to fit)
Q	7-1/2" x 15-3/4"	6	Drawer sides
1/4" shop-grade plywood			
R	15-1/2" x 29"	3	Drawer bottoms
S	27" x 32"	1	Lower cabinet back
T	16" x 32"	1	Upper cabinet back
3/4" solid maple			
U	1" x 79-3/4"	2	Side panel edging
V	1" x 32"	1	Lower cabinet top edging
W	1" x 31-7/8"	2	Shelf edging
X	1/4" x 32"	2	Spacers

*Adjust size to compensate for plywood thickness

KEY	DIMENSIONS	QTY.	NAME
OPTIONAL LARGE DRAWER			
3/4" maple plywood			
Y	26-7/8" x 31-3/4"	1	Grooved drawer front
1/2" shop-grade plywood			
Z	15-3/4" x 25"	2	Drawer sides
AA	28-1/2" x 25" *	2	Drawer front and back (cut back to fit)
1/4" shop-grade plywood			
BB	15-1/2" x 29"	1	Drawer bottom
OPTIONAL PANTS RACK			
3/4" maple plywood			
CC	2" x 28-3/8"	2	Front and back
DD	2" x 13-1/8"	2	Sides
EE	1-1/2" x 28-1/2"	2	Cleats
5/8" dowels			
FF	13-7/8"	9	Dowels
OPTIONAL SHOE SHELVES			
GG	16" x 12"	2	Top and bottom shelves
HH	16" x 11-7/8"	7	Middle shelves

Entry organizer

Cure back-door chaos!

BUILD THIS IN A WEEKEND!

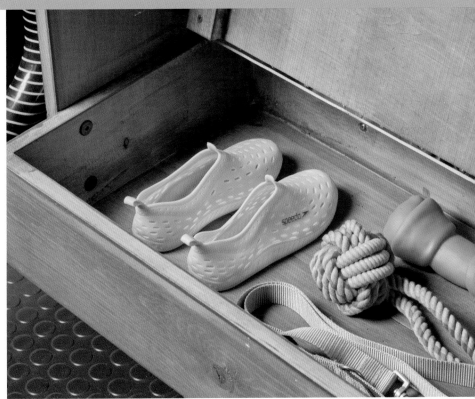

A seat with storage

A hinged lid provides easy access to the compartment under the seat. It's a perfect place to store hats, gloves and all kinds of other small stuff.

If you would love to have a mudroom but just don't have the space, this compact bench and shoe shelf may be exactly what you need. Mount it near the garage service door and you'll have a convenient spot to remove and store your shoes or boots before going inside. There's even a hollow bench with a flip-up lid to store your hats and gloves.

All of the parts for this project are cut from standard pine boards, so you don't need to haul big sheets of plywood home or worry about finishing exposed plywood edges. You do need to choose your lumber carefully, though. The wide pine planks tend to cup and warp, so look for boards that are flat and straight. And plan to build the project soon after buying the lumber. If you leave the lumber sitting around for weeks, it may begin to warp or twist.

Cut out the parts

Start by choosing the four straightest, best-looking 1x12s for the shelf sides. Cut these to 72 in. Then use the Cutting List on p. 61 to cut the remaining parts (Photo 1). If you're lucky enough to own a sliding miter

WHAT IT TAKES

TIME: One weekend

SKILLS: Beginner

TOOLS: Tape measure, large square, level, cordless drill, drill bits, circular saw, hacksaw, clamps.

1 Cut the parts. Cut the boards to length, following the Cutting List on p. 61. Running your circular saw along a large square ensures straight, square cuts. Parts F, G and N also have to be ripped to width. You can do this with your circular saw or on a table saw.

2 Mark the screw locations. On the inside of the shelf sides, mark the middle shelf location. On the outside, make light pencil lines at the center and 3/8 in. from both ends. These light marks will help you position the screws. Drill 1/8-in. pilot holes at the screw locations to avoid splitting the boards.

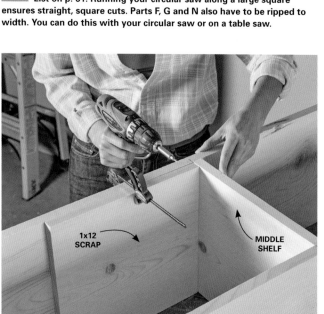

1x12 SCRAP

MIDDLE SHELF

3 Assemble the shelves. Arrange the parts on a flat surface and clamp them together. Clamp a scrap along the centerline to help you position the middle shelf. Then drive trim-head screws through your pilot holes to connect the parts. If you want to fill the screw holes later, recess the screws slightly.

BENCH FRONT

4 Build the bench frame. Drill pilot holes in the sides of the bench frame and clamp the parts together. The wide part (E) is the front of the bench, so face the best-looking side out.

saw, you can use it to cut the parts to length. Otherwise a circular saw will work fine. The boards for three sides of the bench and one of the bench bottoms have to be ripped a little narrower. You can use a circular saw or table saw for this. After cutting the lumber, sand it with 100-grit sandpaper to remove any marks and smooth out any ripples left from the milling process. A random orbital sander works great for this, but you could hand-sand if you don't own a power sander.

Assemble the parts with screws

We joined the parts with 2-in. trim-head screws, recessing them slightly to make room for the wood filler. But you can substitute regular screws if you don't mind the look of screw heads. Even though our screws had self-drilling tips, for extra insurance against splitting the wood we drilled 1/8-in. pilot holes for the screws.

Clamping the parts together before you drive in the screws

Figure A
Entry organizer

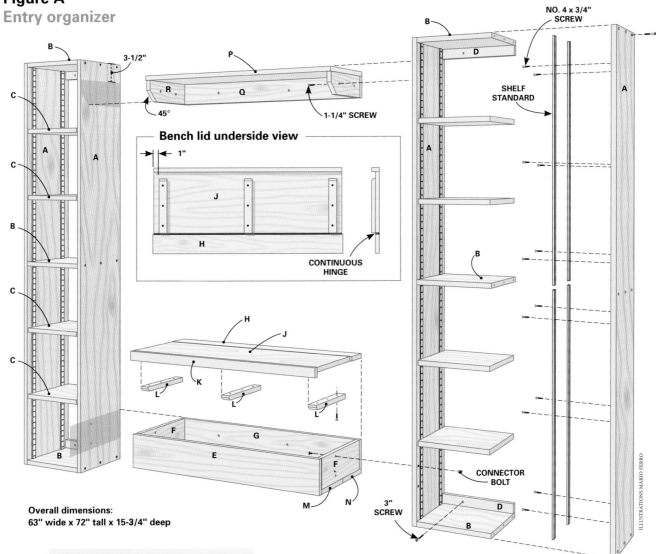

Overall dimensions:
63" wide x 72" tall x 15-3/4" deep

Labels in illustration: B, C, 3-1/2", A, P, R, Q, 45°, 1-1/4" SCREW, Bench lid underside view, 1", J, H, CONTINUOUS HINGE, H, J, K, L, L, L, F, G, E, F, M, N, 3" SCREW, B, NO. 4 x 3/4" SCREW, D, SHELF STANDARD, A, B, CONNECTOR BOLT, D, B

ILLUSTRATIONS MARIO FERRO

Materials list

ITEM	QTY.
1x12 x 8' standard pine boards	6
1x8 x 6' standard pine boards	1
1x6 x 10' standard pine boards	1
1x4 x 8' standard pine boards	1
1x2 x 10' standard pine boards	1

Hardware

2" trim-head screws	100
1-1/4" screws	14
3" cabinet screws	10
No. 4 x 3/4" screws (for shelf standards)	Sm. box
1-1/2" connector bolts	4
1-1/2" x 36" continuous hinge	1
72" shelf standards	8
Shelf clips	32
Coat hooks	
Wood filler and 100-grit sandpaper	

Cutting list

KEY	DIMENSIONS	QTY.	NAME
A	3/4" x 11-1/4" x 72"	4	Sides
B	3/4" x 11-1/4" x 12"	6	Top, bottom, middle shelf
C	3/4" x 11-1/4" x 11-5/8"	8	Shelves
D	3/4" x 1-1/2" x 12"	4	Hanging strips
E	3/4" x 5-1/2" x 36"	1	Bench front
F	3/4" x 4-3/4" x 13-1/4"	2	Bench sides
G	3/4" x 4-3/4" x 36"	1	Bench back
H	3/4" x 3-1/2" x 36"	1	Bench top (back)
J	3/4" x 11-1/4" x 35-5/8"	1	Bench top lid
K	3/4" x 1-1/2" x 35-5/8"	1	Bench lid nosing
L	3/4" x 1-1/2" x 10"	3	Bench seat cleats
M	3/4" x 7-1/4" x 36"	1	Bench bottom
N	3/4" x 6-3/4" x 36"	1	Bench bottom
P	3/4" x 11-1/4" x 36"	1	Top shelf
Q	3/4" x 3-1/2" x 36"	1	Top shelf back rail
R	3/4" x 3-1/2" x 10-1/4"	2	Top shelf side rail

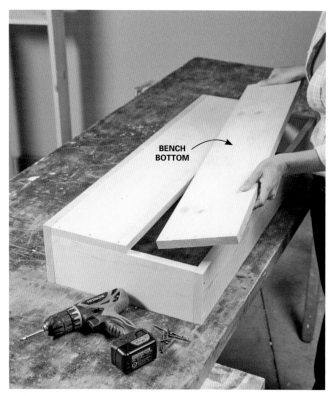

5 **Attach the bench bottom.** To make sure the bench frame is square, measure diagonally from opposite corners. Adjust the frame until the two diagonal measurements are equal. Then screw the bottom boards to the frame.

6 **Mount the seat hinge.** Clamp the lid and the back rail together as shown. Center the hinge on the two lid parts and attach it with four screws, two on each end. Then drill 5/64-in. pilot holes and drive in the remaining screws.

7 **Install the shelf standards.** Cut each of the 72-in. shelf standards into two 34-3/4 in. pieces using a hacksaw. Measure from the ends to the centers to retain factory ends on each piece. We spray-painted the standards to match the finish.

8 **Install temporary support.** Locate the wall studs with a stud finder and mark them with strips of masking tape. Install a 1x2 ledger with the top edge 7-1/2 in. above the floor to support the shelves and seat while you install them.

HANGING STRIP

9 **Install the first shelf unit.** Rest the shelf on the ledger. Drive a screw through the top hanging strip into a stud. Then use a level to make sure the sides of the shelf unit are plumb. If necessary, push the bottom one way or the other to plumb the sides. Drive a screw through the lower hanging strip into a stud to secure the shelf unit.

10 **Install the coat-hook shelf.** Screw the coat-hook shelf to the studs, making sure it's level. Then level the shelf from front to back and attach it to the side of the tall shelf with 1-1/4-in. screws. Attach the opposite side after you've installed the second shelf unit.

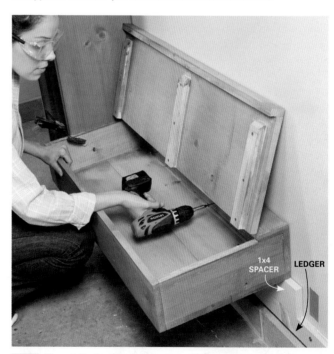

1x4 SPACER   LEDGER

11 **Mount the bench.** Rest a scrap of 1x4 spacer on top of the temporary ledger to elevate the bench to the correct height. Set the bench on the spacer. Then drive screws through the back of the bench into the studs.

makes it easier to keep the parts aligned. And if the wood is a little twisted or cupped, you can flatten it with clamps before driving the screws. We also added three cleats to the bottom of the seat board to hold it flat. Spread wood glue on these cleats and attach them with 1-1/4-in. screws.

We chose a continuous hinge for the lid. Cut the hinge to 35-5/8 in. with a hacksaw. Since you'll also have to cut all the

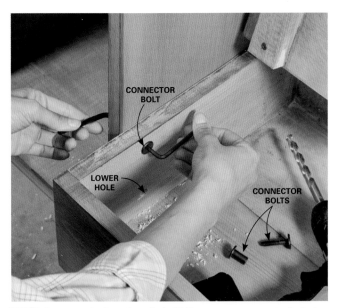

12 **Connect the bench and shelf.** Use two-part connector bolts to connect the front of the bench to the shelves on each side (connect the second side later after the second shelf is mounted). These bolts provide more support than screws to ensure the bench will be safe to sit on. The bolts we used required two Allen wrenches to tighten.

metal shelf standards to fit, buy a sharp, new 32-tooth blade. Photo 6 shows how to attach the hinge. Finish up the assembly by cutting and attaching the metal shelf standards (Photo 7).

Hang the project on the wall

First, locate the wall studs. An electronic stud finder makes it easy. Mark the stud locations with strips of masking tape. Now choose a position for the project that will allow you to attach each of the 12-in.-wide shelf units to at least one stud. Next, screw the temporary 1x2 ledger to the studs, making sure it's level and the top is located 7-1/2 in. from the floor (Photo 8). The ledger supports the shelf units and bench while you attach them to the wall. Photos 9 – 13 show the installation steps. Finish up by choosing the locations for the adjustable shelves and installing them with the shelf clips. We prefinished the project with Behr Semi-Transparent Waterproofing Wood Stain.

13 **Finish up with the second tall shelf.** Rest the second shelf unit on the ledger and tip it up into place. Attach it to the wall by driving 3-in. screws through the top and bottom hanging strips and into the stud. Then connect the bench with the connector bolts and attach the other side of the upper shelf with 1-1/4-in. screws.

MEET THE EXPERT

Jeff Gorton took advantage of his nearly two decades of experience building projects for *The Family Handyman* to design this simple entryway storage project.

Twin closet shelves

Check out your closet shelf some day and you may discover a whole lot of unused real estate up there. Consider this—if one shelf is good, two might be better. And the upper shelf could be 15 in. deep instead of 12 in. because there's no closet rod hanging out below. The deep baskets (bought at a craft store) help with the organization; cabinet knobs make for easier access. We show a two-tier shelf; you can install three if your closets (and you) are tall enough.

WHAT IT TAKES

TIME: 1 hour
SKILL: Beginner
TOOLS: Circular saw, drill

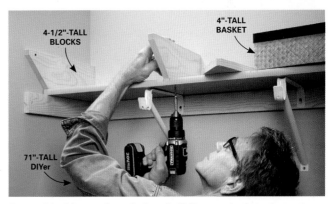

4-1/2"-TALL BLOCKS

4"-TALL BASKET

71"-TALL DIYer

Secure blocking to the existing shelf. Buy your baskets, then cut spacer blocks 1/2 in. wider than the baskets are tall. Cut the ends of the blocks at an angle to accommodate the wider top shelf. Screw blocks to the bottom shelf, spacing them 1/2 in. farther apart than the baskets are wide. Then install and secure the top shelf.

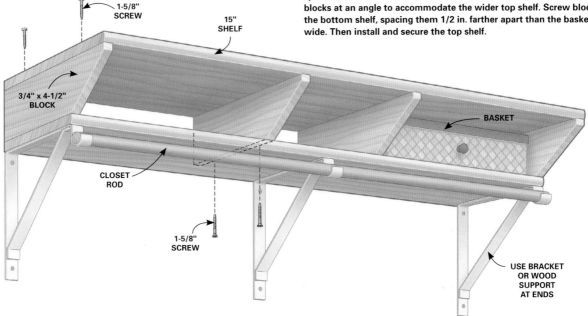

1-5/8" SCREW

15" SHELF

3/4" x 4-1/2" BLOCK

BASKET

CLOSET ROD

1-5/8" SCREW

USE BRACKET OR WOOD SUPPORT AT ENDS

Under-bed rollout drawer

Some of the most useful and underutilized storage space in your home is right under the bed, and you can take advantage of it with this durable rollout drawer, made from a single sheet of plywood. Plastic versions are also available, but wood looks better, lasts longer and lets you custom-size your rollout.

Measure the distance between the floor and the bottom of the bed. Subtract 1/2 in. for clearance under the bed and 1/2 in. (on bare wood) to 1 in. (on thick carpet) for casters. Subtract another 1/2 in. for the hinged top to arrive at the maximum height for the storage box sides.

Figure A
Rollout construction

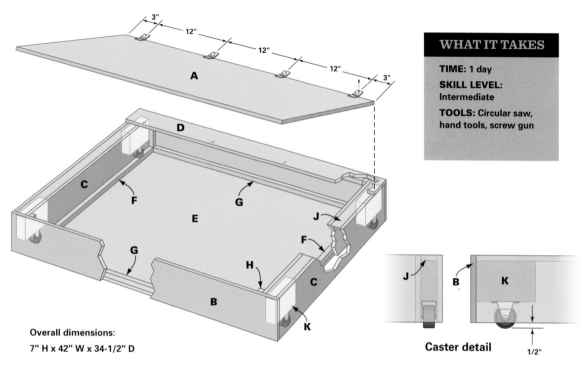

Overall dimensions:
7" H x 42" W x 34-1/2" D

Caster detail

1/2"

Materials list

ITEM	QTY.
AC-grade 4' x 8' x 1/2" plywood	1
3' x 3/4" x 3/4" square dowels	6
2x6 x 2' pine	1
2" fixed caster wheels	4
1-1/2" hinges	4
1" and 1-1/2" brad nails	

Note: All materials and dimensions are
for a 7-1/2-in.-tall under-bed space. If you
have more or less space, adjust these
measurements.

Cutting list

KEY	PCS.	SIZE & DESCRIPTION
A	1	42" x 30-1/2" top
B	2	42" x 6" front and back
C	4	33" x 6" sides
D	1	42" x 4" fixed top
E	1	37" x 33" base
F	2	33" x 3/4" x 3/4" side nailers
G	3	35-1/2" x 3/4" x 3/4" front and back nailers
H	4	4-3/4" x 3/4" x 3/4" corner nailers
J	2	33" x 1-1/2" filler strips
K	4	3-5/8" x 1-1/2" x 5-1/2" caster supports

Note: All 1/2" plywood

Mark all the pieces on a sheet of plywood and cut
them with a table saw or a circular saw. Fasten 3/4-in.
square nailers to the edges of the base with glue and
finish nails or screws (1/2-in. plywood is too thin
to nail into on edge). Attach the sides to the base,
adding square nailers at the corners. Fasten the caster
supports to the sides, then nail the outer side pieces

to the caster supports.

Attach the front and back. Add the filler strips on
top of the caster supports and the last nailer along
the top edge of the back. Finally, nail on the fixed top,
set the hinged top against it and screw on the hinges.
Attach the hinges using 1/2-in. screws so the screws
don't stick through the top.

Hide-the-mess lockers

Build simple boxes and add store-bought doors

In many houses, there's a big coat closet by the front door, but the garage is in the back, so everyone uses the back door.

We designed and built these hide-the-mess lockers with those houses in mind. Each locker is big enough to stash a coat, backpack, boots, hats, and odds and ends that normally wind up on the floor. Since they're modular and space efficient, you can build one for each member of the family—including the dog (leashes, toys, food, you name it). Now everyone has a personal place for stashing stuff— and the responsibility for keeping it organized.

The louvered door is made from one of a pair of closet bifold doors, which you can buy at almost any home center. Since the doors come in pairs and you can get two locker "boxes" from each sheet of plywood, you'll make the best use of materials by building them in twos. Here's how to do it.

Money, materials and tools

The total materials cost was only around $100 per locker. Since we were planning to paint the lockers, we used inexpensive "AC" plywood. If you plan to stain your lockers, and use hardwood plywood such as oak or birch and hardwood doors, you'll spend more. On a row of lockers, only the outer sides of the end lockers show, so you can use inexpensive plywood for the inner parts and more expensive material for the outer parts. Expect to spend at least a day buying materials, rounding up tools and building a pair of lockers. Set aside another day for finishing.

A table saw is handy for cutting up plywood, but a circular saw with a guide will provide the same results. You'll also need a miter saw to cut the screen molding. A finish nailer will help you work faster, but hand-nailing will work too as long as you drill holes to prevent splitting.

Buy the doors first

There are a variety of bifold doors available. If you need more ventilation, use full louvered doors; if ventilation isn't an issue, use solid doors. The doors you buy may not be exactly the same size as ours, so you may have to alter the dimensions of the boxes you build. Here are two key points to keep in mind as you plan your project:

■ You want a 1/8-in. gap surrounding the door. So to determine the size of the box opening, add 1/4 in. to the height and width of the door. Since our bifold doors measured 14-3/4 x 78-3/4 in., we made the opening 15 x 79 in.

■ To determine the depth of the shelves, subtract the door thickness from the width of the sides (including the 1/4-in. screen molding). Our doors were 1-1/8 in. thick, so we made the shelves 10-7/8 in. deep (12 minus 1-1/8 equals 10-7/8 in.). When the doors are closed, they'll rest against the shelves inside and flush with the screen molding outside.

WHAT IT TAKES

TIME: One weekend

SKILL LEVEL: Intermediate

TOOLS: Hand tools, screw gun, 18-gauge nailer, table or circular saw

---

1 **Build a simple box.** Cut the plywood parts and assemble them with trim-head screws. Make sure the box opening is 1/4 in. taller and wider than the door itself.

2 **Square it up.** Take diagonal corner-to-corner measurements, then adjust the box until the measurements are equal and the box is square. Install the back, using one edge of the back to straighten the box side as you fasten it. Check once again for squareness, then secure the other edges of the back.

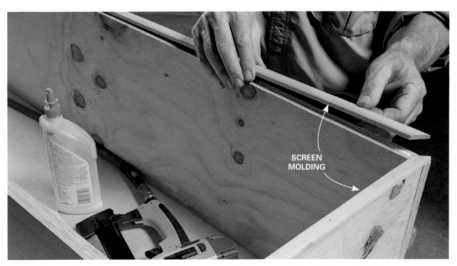

3 **Cover the plywood edges.** Install screen molding over the front edges of the box. Apply wood glue lightly and use just enough nails to "clamp" the molding in place while the glue dries.

Get building!

Use a table saw or straight-cutting guide to cut the plywood sides (A) and top and bottom (B). The Cutting List on p. 71 gives the parts dimensions for the lockers. If you plan to paint or stain the lockers, it's a good idea to prefinish the insides of parts. Once the lockers are assembled, brushing a finish onto the insides is slow and difficult.

Assemble the boxes with 2-in. trim-head screws (Photo 1). Trim-head screws have smaller heads than standard screws and are easier to hide with filler. Cut the 1/4-in. plywood back (C) to size. Make certain the box is square by taking diagonal measurements (they should be equal; see Photo 2), and then secure the back using 1-in. nails. Use the edges of the back as a guide to straighten the edges of the box as you nail the back into place.

Cut 1/4 x 3/4-in. screen molding and use glue and 1-in. finish nails or brads to secure it to the exposed front edges of the plywood (Photo 3). Cut the shelf front and back (D), sides (E) and slats (F) to length, then assemble the three slatted shelf units (Photo 4). With the locker box standing upright, position the shelves and hold them temporarily in place with clamps or a couple of screws. Adjust the shelf spacing based on the height of the locker's user and the stuff that will go inside. Once you have a suitable arrangement, lay the locker on its back and screw the shelves into place (Photo 5). The shelves are easy to reposition in the future as needs change.

Add the hardware and finish, and then install

Remove the hinges that hold the bifold doors to each other. Determine which way you want the door to swing, then mount the hinges onto the door accordingly. (Note: You'll need to buy another set of hinges if you're building two lockers.) Remember, you want the louvers to point downward on the outside! With the locker on its back, position the door and secure

Figure A
Locker construction

Overall dimensions:
16-1/2" wide x 81" tall x 12-1/4" deep

Materials list (for two lockers)

Because bifold doors are sold in pairs, and one sheet of 3/4-in. plywood yields two lockers, you can make the best use of materials by building an even number of lockers.

ITEM	QTY.
30" bifold door pack (2 doors)	1
3/4" x 4' x 8' plywood	1
1/4" x 4' x 8' plywood	1
1/4" x 3/4" x 8' screen molding	5
3/4" x 1-1/2" x 8' solid wood	9

2" trim-head screws, 1-1/4" screws, 1" nails, 1-1/2" nails, wood glue, no-mortise hinges, door handles and magnetic catches.

Cutting list (for two lockers)

These locker parts suit a door measuring 14-3/4 x 78-3/4 in. Verify the exact size of your doors before building.

KEY	QTY.	SIZE & DESCRIPTION
A	2	11-3/4" x 80-7/8" sides (3/4" plywood)
B	2	11-3/4" x 15" top/bottom (3/4" plywood)
C	1	16-1/2" x 80-1/2" back (1/4" plywood)
D	2	3/4" x 1-1/2" x 15" shelf front/back (solid wood)
E	2	3/4" x 1-1/2" x 9-3/8" shelf sides (solid wood)
F	6	3/4" x 1-1/2" x 15" shelf slats (solid wood)

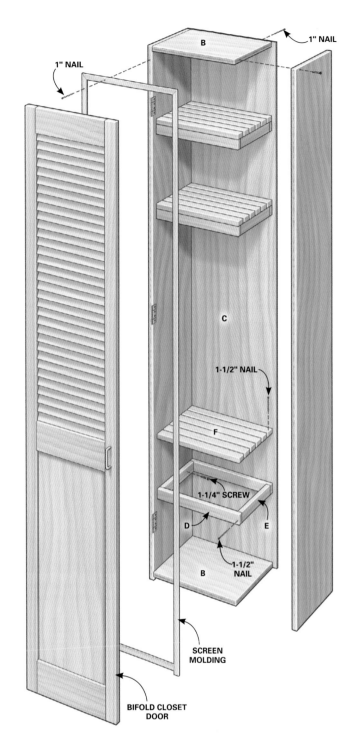

1" NAIL
B
1" NAIL
C
1-1/2" NAIL
F
1-1/4" SCREW
D
E
B
1-1/2" NAIL
SCREEN MOLDING
BIFOLD CLOSET DOOR

Figure B
Cutting diagrams

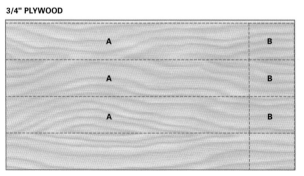

3/4" PLYWOOD

A B
A B
A B

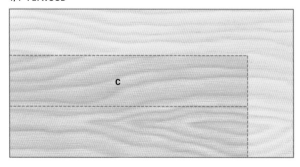

1/4" PLYWOOD

C

4 **Build slatted shelves.** Plywood shelves would work fine, but slatted shelves allow better ventilation so wet clothes and shoes can dry. Space the slats with a pair of wood scraps.

5/16" SPACER

THICKNESS OF DOOR

5 **Install the shelves.** Stand your locker up and position the shelves to suit the stuff that will go in it. Mark the shelf locations, lay the locker on its back and screw the shelves into place. Make sure the shelves are inset far enough to allow for the door.

"NO-MORTISE" HINGE

6 **Mount the hinges.** Remove the hinges from the doors (they'll be pointed the wrong way) and reinstall them on the door based on the direction you want it to swing. Prop up the door alongside the box and align the door so there will be a 1/8-in. gap at the top and bottom of the box. Then screw the hinges to the box.

the hinges to the plywood side (Photo 6). Install door handles and magnetic catches to hold them closed.

Remove the doors (but don't finish them yet!) and install the locker boxes. Your lockers can stand against baseboard, leaving a small gap between the backs of the lockers and the wall. Or—if you remove the baseboard—they can stand tight against the wall. Either way, installing them is a lot like installing cabinets: Fasten all the boxes together by driving 1-1/4-in. screws through the side of one locker into the next. Then screw the entire assembly to wall studs.

Install the unfinished doors to make sure they all fit properly, then remove them again. This may seem like a waste of time, but there's a good reason for it: Your locker boxes may have shifted a little during installation, and the doors may not fit properly. If a door or two need some edge sanding, you want to do that before finishing.

When you've checked the fit of all the doors, remove them one last time for finishing. Whether you're using paint or a natural finish, louvered doors are a real pain. If your plans include a clear coat, consider polyurethane or lacquer in spray cans: You'll get better results in far less time, though you'll spend a bit extra. After finishing, install the doors and load up those lockers!

Throw & go bins

Storage for a family on the move

Shelves and cabinets are great places to store kid stuff, but when you're in a hurry (and kids always are), it's nice to just throw and go. That's why we built these bins. They're great for sports gear but handle all kinds of miscellaneous entryway clutter.

We wanted something with a little character, so we loosely based the design on a row of bins at an old-fashioned country store. It was worth the little bit of extra effort to

WHAT IT TAKES

TIME: One day to build, plus painting

SKILL: Beginner to intermediate

TOOLS: Table saw or circular saw, drill, jigsaw or handsaw

1 **Lay out the side profiles.** After measuring and marking the location of the bin fronts, use a square to mark the recessed portion of the front.

SIDE BOARD

RAFTER SQUARE

2 **Connect the dots.** Use a straightedge to connect the dots. You only need to lay out one side board. Once it's cut, that board will act as a pattern for the rest.

3 **Cut two at a time.** Clamp two sides down and cut them both at the same time. That way, if you make any small cutting errors, the pair of sides will still match up. Make most of the cut with a circular saw, and then finish it off with a jigsaw.

build something that brings back good memories yet serves a practical purpose in the present.

Cut the parts

Cut the sides, top and bottom from 3/4-in. plywood using a table saw or circular saw. We used "BC" plywood, which is good enough for paint, but you may want to buy birch veneer plywood if you plan to use stain.

This project requires a full sheet of plywood plus a 2 x 4-ft. section. Many home centers carry 4 x 4-ft., and some even stock 2 x 4-ft., so you don't have to buy two full sheets. However, they charge a premium for smaller sheets, and you won't save more than a few bucks, so buy two full sheets and use the leftover on other projects. The same goes for the 1/4-in. plywood—you only need a 4 x 4-ft. sheet, but a 4 x 8-ft. is a better value.

The fronts of the bins get the most abuse, so build them from a solid 1x6 pine board. Solid wood holds up better than a plywood edge. You can rip down the two center boards when you're cutting up the other parts, but hold off on cutting them to length until the top and bottom boards are in place. That way you can cut them exactly to size.

Mark the side profile

This part of the process seems a little tricky, but it's really quite simple if you follow these directions. Hook a tape measure on the bottom front of one of the side boards. Measure up and mark the edge of the board at: 0, 4 in., 15-1/2 in., 19-1/2 in., 31 in. and 35 in. Now go back and measure over 4 in. at the following locations: the bottom, 15-1/2 in., 31 in. and the top (Photo 1). These marks represent the indented portion of the side. Start at the end of the board, and connect the dots (Photo 2). It's just that easy.

Cut and sand the sides

Clamp two side boards down to your work surface. Arrange them so the best sides of the plywood will be on the outside of the bins. Use a circular saw to make most of each cut. (Sometimes it's necessary to hold the blade guard up when you start a cut at an angle.) Finish the cuts with a jigsaw

Figure A
Bin overview

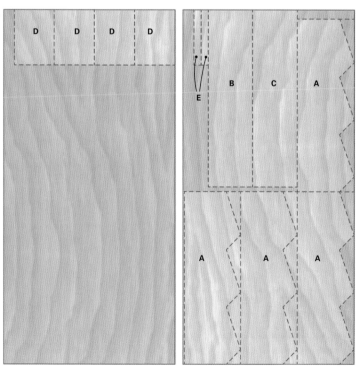

2" SCREW

B

2" SCREW

A

D F

E

D F

E

C F

Overall dimensions: 16-1/8" wide x 48" tall x 48" long

Figure B
Side layout

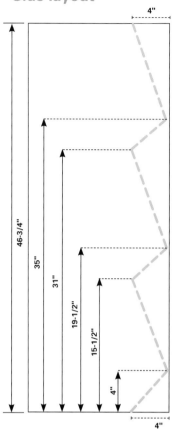

4"

46-3/4"

35"

31"

19-1/2"

15-1/2"

4"

4"

Figure C
Cutting diagram for 3/4" plywood

D D D D

E

B C A

A A A

Materials list

ITEM	QTY.
4' x 8' x 3/4" BC sanded plywood	2
1x6 x 8' pine	1
4' x 8' x 1/4" underlayment plywood	1
2" trim-head screws	
1-1/2" 18-gauge brads	
Gallon of paint/primer	

Cutting list

KEY	QTY.	SIZE & DESCRIPTION
A	4	15-7/8" x 46-1/2" x 3/4" BC sanded plywood (sides)
B	1	12-1/2" x 48" x 3/4" BC sanded plywood (top)
C	1	12-1/2" x 48" x 3/4" BC sanded plywood (bottom)
D	4	15" x 11-1/4" x 3/4" BC sanded plywood (bin bottom)
E	2	2" x approx. 15" BC sanded plywood (center board)
F	6	15" x 5-1/2" pine 1x6 (bin front)

(Photo 3). A handsaw will work fine if you don't own a jigsaw.

Sand the edges with 80-grit sandpaper while the sides are still clamped together (Photo 4). Use one of the two cut side boards to mark one of the other uncut side boards, and repeat the process.

If you've already chosen a color for your project, now would be a good time to sand and finish all the parts. That way, you'll only have to touch up the fastener holes after assembly. Some of the plywood edges may have voids, which can be filled with wood putty or patching compound.

4 **Sand two at a time.** Smooth out the cuts before you unclamp the sides. Make sure to keep each pair together when you assemble the bins.

Assemble the bins

Lay out two of the sides back to back with the good side of the plywood facing down. Using a straightedge, mark lines between the notches to serve as a reference line for the bottoms of the bins. The bottom of the whole unit will serve as the bottom of the lowest bins, so fasten the bottom on the second lowest bin first. Align the board above the reference line.

Fasten the bottoms and the fronts with three 1-1/2-in. brads. Once it's all put together, go back and reinforce it all with two 2-in. trim-head screws in each side of every board.

Once the bottoms are in place, come back and install the 1x6 fronts (Photo 5). Align them flush with the outside edge of the plywood. You'll notice a small gap between the bin bottom and the front. This makes assembly easier, especially if your side cuts weren't perfect. It won't be noticeable when it's up against the wall. Once the first bank of bins is done, assemble the second one.

Finish it up

Fasten the top and bottom flush with the outside edges of the bins. Again, drive three brads into each side board and go back and secure them with a couple of trim-head screws.

Use the 1/4-in. plywood back to square up the project. Start with the two factory-cut sides of the plywood, and start fastening it to either the top or bottom, making sure it's perfectly flush with the edge. Then fasten one side, working away from the previously fastened top or bottom, straightening and nailing as you go. Install one screw through the back into each bin bottom for a little extra support. Before you finish the other two sides, set up the project and check that things are square.

Measure between the two banks of bins, and cut your center boards to that size. Pin them in with brads and secure them with a screw. The center boards can be located anywhere you want depending on the type of items you're going to store.

If your project is going to be sitting on the concrete, you may want to install a couple of strips of treated lumber on the bottom. Rip 5/8-in. strips of treated lumber and tack them onto the perimeter of the bottom.

You can screw the project to the wall if you know your kids will be using it as a ladder, but it's pretty stable as it is. All that's left is to go tell the family that there are no more excuses for throwing stuff on the floor.

18-GAUGE BRAD NAILER

5 **Assemble the bins.** Build the bin sections before you install the top and bottom. If you have a brad nailer, make assembly easier by tacking all the parts together before you drive in the screws.

Closet & entryway tips

Shoe solution

You can hang coats at the entry door, so why not shoes? Keep your house clean and your front door uncluttered with coat-hanger hooks for shoes.

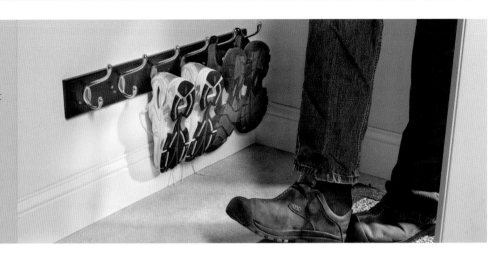

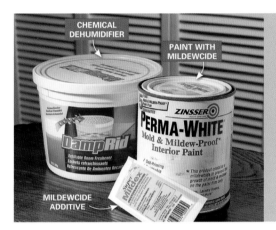

Fight closet mildew

Because they're dark and lack air circulation, closet walls are especially prone to mildew. Here are a few proven solutions:

- Add mildewcide to paint or use paint that already contains mildewcide (check the label).
- Run a dehumidifier in damp rooms.
- Cut closet humidity. Chemical dehumidifiers are nontoxic products that absorb moisture from the air.
- Leave closet doors open or replace solid doors with louvered doors to increase airflow.

High and dry

Wet boots left by the front door tend to sit in water all day and never really dry. To solve the problem, elevate them over a tray using old cooling racks. The boots will be dry when you put them on, and the water will evaporate from the tray quickly.

S-hook hang-up

Turn any closet into a useful hang-up storage space by adding S-hooks to wire shelving. This provides tidy storage for mops, brooms and other cleaning tools.

S-HOOK

Temporary valet rod

When you need temporary clothes-hanging space around the house, keep an extra shower tension bar handy. Put it between the jambs in the laundry room door on heavy laundry days. Or, use it in the bedroom closet to pack for trips or stick it in the closet opening in the guest room/den so overnight guests can hang up their clothes. It's a quick and easy way to gain an extra closet!

SHOWER TENSION BAR

Sliding tie and belt rack

If you need a handy place to hang ties and belts, build a simple rack from plywood, dowels and a full-extension 12-in. drawer slide. Drill holes in the wood and pound in the dowels (use a dab of glue if they're loose). Attach the drawer slide to the side of your closet shelves and to the rack. If you need even more hanging room, add a block of wood to the side of your shelves to offset the slide, and attach dowels to both sides of the rack. The drawer slides come in pairs, so you might as well make another one while you're at it!

Simple bathroom cabinet (made from store-bought closet doors)

Modern console (made from customized IKEA cabinet)

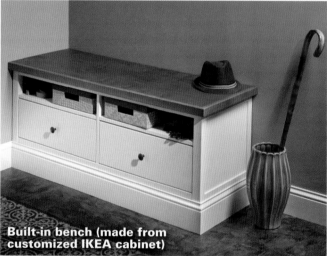

Built-in bench (made from customized IKEA cabinet)

Craft center (made from customized IKEA cabinet)

Fold-up workbench (made from prehung door)

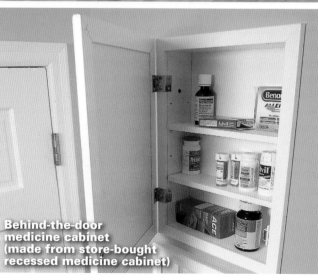

Behind-the-door medicine cabinet (made from store-bought recessed medicine cabinet)

Simple bathroom cabinet

In most bathrooms, a picture or small shelf hangs above the toilet. But you can make better use of that space with an attractive cabinet that offers about three times as much storage as a typical medicine cabinet.

This article will show you how to build it. The simple joinery and store-bought doors make this a great project for the woodworking novice. Assembling the crown and base is a bit trickier, but this article shows that process, too.

You'll need a miter saw to cut the trim. A table saw and a brad nailer will save time, but you can make all the cuts with a circular saw and drive the nails by hand if you prefer.

The height and width of your cabinet may differ slightly from this one, depending on the bifold doors available at your home center. So choose your doors first and then alter the lengths of the sides, top, bottom and middle shelves if necessary. Bifold closet doors are sold as a pair, usually joined by hinges. Each of the doors shown here measured 11-15/16 in. wide, and were cut to length as shown in the photo in the sidebar on p. 82.

The easy-to-install inset, ball tip hinges used here are available online. All the other tools and materials, including the cabinet doors, are available at home centers. You may not find the exact same crown and base moldings used here, but most home centers carry a similar profile. Any 2-1/4-in. crown molding is appropriate for this project. For a more contemporary look, you can skip the crown and base altogether since they're purely decorative.

Build a basic box

Cut the plywood parts to size. The dimensions used here are given in the Cutting List (p. 81). To make the short end cuts, use the homemade guide shown in Photo 3 and described below.

Assemble the cabinet box with glue and screws, followed by wood dowels for extra strength (Photo 1). You can buy long dowels and cut them into short pieces, but dowels precut and fluted for woodworking are easier to work with. This assembly method is quick, easy and strong. But because it requires lots of wood filler to hide the fasteners, it's for painted work only. If you want to use stain and a clear finish, biscuits or pocket screws are a better choice.

Drill 1/8-in. pilot and countersink holes for the screws using a drill bit that does both at once. Attach the top, bottom and cleats to one side, then add the other side. Mark the middle shelf position on the sides, slip it into place and fasten it (there's no need for glue).

Before you drill the dowel holes, make sure the box is square by taking diagonal measurements; equal measurements mean the box is square. If necessary, screw a strip of plywood diagonally across the back of the box to hold it square. For clean, splinter-free holes, drill the dowel holes with a 3/8-in. brad-point bit, making the holes 1/8 in. deeper than the length of the dowels. That way, you can sink the dowels below the surface of the plywood and fill the holes with wood filler. With the box completed, drill holes for the adjustable shelf supports (Photo 2) using a brad-point drill bit. Most shelf supports require a 1/4-in. hole.

Cut and hang the doors

Cut the doors using a saw guide (Photo 3). To make a guide, screw a straight 1x3 to a 14 x 18-in. scrap of 3/4-in. plywood. Then run your saw along the 1x3 to cut off the excess plywood and create a guide that steers your saw perfectly straight and indicates the exact path of the cut. Simply mark the doors, align the guide with the marks, clamp it in place and cut.

Screw the hinges to the doors 3 in. from the ends (Photo 4). The fronts and backs of louvered doors look similar, so check twice before you drill. Stand the doors against the cabinet, setting them on spacers to create a 1/8-in. gap at the bottom. The gap between the doors should also be about 1/8 in. Clamp each door in position and screw the hinges in place (Photo 5). If the doors don't align perfectly because the box is slightly out-of-square, don't worry. You can square the box when you hang it. The hinges also adjust up or down 1/16 in.

Figure A: Bathroom cabinet

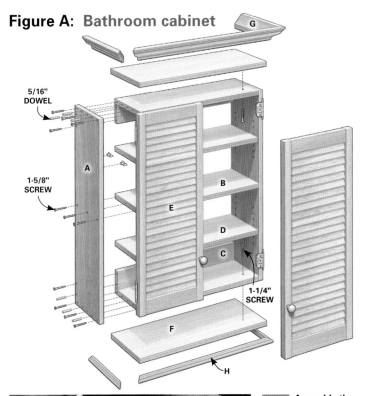

5/16" DOWEL

1-5/8" SCREW

A

B

E

D

C

F

G

H

1-1/4" SCREW

Materials list

ITEM	QTY.
4' x 8' x 3/4" birch plywood	1
2-1/4"-wide crown molding	5'
3/4"-tall base cap molding	5'
1-1/4" screws	1 box
1-5/8" screws	1 box
5/16" or 3/8" dowels	16
1-1/2" finish nails	1 box
Inset ball tip hinges	4
Shelf supports	8
Spray primer	1 can
Spray paint	2 cans
Wood glue	
Wood filler	

Cutting list

KEY	QTY.	SIZE & DESCRIPTION
A	2	8" x 32-5/8" sides
B	3	8" x 22-1/2" top, bottom and middle shelf
C	2	3" x 22-1/2" top and bottom cleats
D	2	8" x 22-1/4" adjustable shelves
E	2	11-15/16" x 32-3/8" doors
F	2	9" x 24" crown and base frames
G	3	2-1/4"-wide crown molding (cut to fit)
H	3	3/4"-tall base molding (cut to fit)

Except for moldings, all parts are 3/4" plywood.

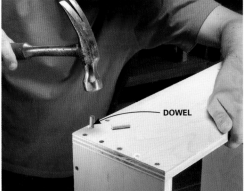

1 Assemble the cabinet box quickly with glue and wood screws. Then add glued dowels for rock-solid joints. Drill splinter-free dowel holes with a brad-point bit.

DOWEL

BRAD-POINT BIT

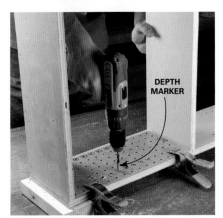

DEPTH MARKER

2 Drill shelf support holes using a scrap of pegboard to position the holes. Wrap masking tape around the drill bit so you don't drill all the way through.

SAW GUIDE

CLOSET DOOR

3 Cut the doors using a homemade saw guide to ensure a straight cut. Lay the door face down so any splintering takes place on the back of the door.

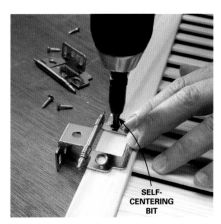

SELF-CENTERING BIT

4 Mount the hinges on the doors. A self-centering drill bit positions the screw holes for perfectly placed hinges.

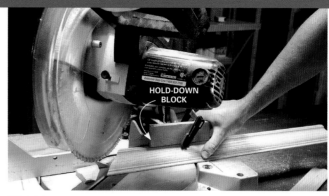

5 Position the doors carefully and clamp them to the cabinet. Then screw the hinges to the cabinet from inside for a foolproof, exact fit.

6 Cut the crown molding upside down and leaning against the fence. Clamp a block to the saw's fence so you can hold the molding firmly against the fence.

7 Nail the crown to the frame. Nail the mitered corners only if necessary. If they fit tight and are perfectly aligned, let the glue alone hold them together.

8 Center the crown on the cabinet and fasten it with screws driven from inside. Then center the cabinet on the base and attach it the same way.

Add the crown and base

Measure the top of the cabinet (including the doors) and cut the plywood crown and base frames to that size. Set your miter saw to 45 degrees and cut the crown molding upside down, leaning against the fence (Photo 6). Also miter a "tester" section of molding to help you position the sidepieces when you nail them in place. To avoid splitting, be sure to predrill nail holes. With the sides in place, add the front piece of crown molding. Cut it slightly long and then "shave" one end with your miter saw until it fits perfectly. Add the molding to the base frame the same way. Screw both the crown and base to the cabinet (Photo 8).

A quick finish

Brushing paint onto louvered doors is slow, fussy work, but you can avoid that hassle by using aerosol-can primer and paint. First, remove the doors and hinges. Cover the dowels, nails and screw heads with wood filler and sand the filler smooth. Also fill any voids in the plywood's edges. Sand the cabinet box, crown, base and doors with 120-grit paper. Spray all the parts with a white stain-blocking primer (such as BIN, Cover Stain or KILZ). When the primer dries, sand it lightly with a fine sanding sponge. Finally, spray on at least two coats of spray paint. High-gloss paint will accentuate every tiny surface flaw, so consider using satin or matte.

To hang the cabinet, locate studs and drive two 3-in. screws through the top cleat. Then rehang the doors. Close the doors to check their fit. Nudge the bottom of the cabinet left or right to square it and align the doors. Then drive screws through the bottom cleat.

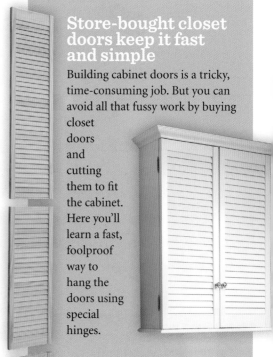

Store-bought closet doors keep it fast and simple

Building cabinet doors is a tricky, time-consuming job. But you can avoid all that fussy work by buying closet doors and cutting them to fit the cabinet. Here you'll learn a fast, foolproof way to hang the doors using special hinges.

Customized IKEA furniture

Modern console

Built-in bench

Craft center

Spend a little, get a lot. That's the idea behind ready-to-assemble (RTA) furniture. But RTA furniture isn't just inexpensive. It's also super adaptable. Because you assemble it yourself, RTA furniture invites tinkering. In fact, customizing RTA pieces is so common that it has its own name: "hacking."

We used furniture pieces from IKEA. You can also find RTA furniture at discount stores and home centers.

Modern console

Mimic a mid-century modern classic by turning a simple shelving unit on its side, wrapping it with plywood inside and out, and attaching legs.

Build it

Notice that the end panels of the original assembled Kallax shelving unit protrude beyond the sides. Remove both panels (Step 1) and trim off the protruding edges (Step 2). Then reattach both panels flush with the sides (Step 3). Cut hardwood plywood panels to wrap around the unit (Step 4). Make the top and bottom panels long enough to cover the side panels, and cut the side panels to fit tightly between the top and bottom pieces. Cut all the panels wide enough to create a 3/16-in. lip around the front of the shelving unit. Adhere iron-on edge banding to these pieces.

Fasten the panels with flat-head sheet metal screws after drilling countersink pilot holes through the unit. The unit's frames are hollow, so be careful not to punch through their thin faces when drilling the countersinks. Make sure the screw heads seat flush.

Cut plywood to cover the bottom and sides inside the unit (Step 5). Don't fasten these pieces with screws; instead, go for a friction fit. Apply iron-on edge banding to the exposed edges.

Remove all the plywood parts to apply finish. Finish the legs too. Reinstall the panels and inserts—tack the inserts with small nails or brads. Then attach the legs (Step 6).

Basic unit

Step 1
Remove end panels

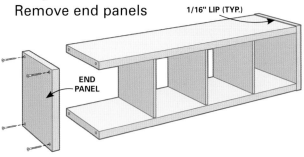

1/16" LIP (TYP.)

END PANEL

Step 2
Trim end panels

REMOVE 1/16"

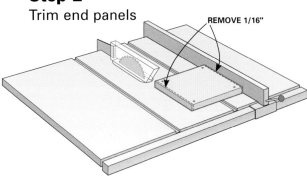

Step 3
Attach end panels

FLUSH

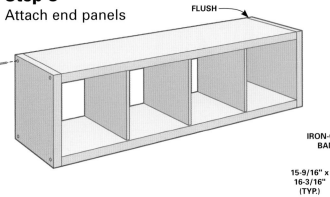

Step 4
Attach plywood panels

15-9/16" x 59-3/16" (TYP.)

IRON-ON EDGE BANDING

15-9/16" x 16-3/16" (TYP.)

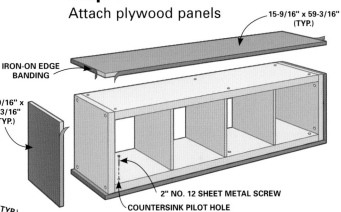

2" NO. 12 SHEET METAL SCREW

COUNTERSINK PILOT HOLE

Step 5
Install plywood inserts

15-1/16" (TYP.)

Step 6
Attach legs

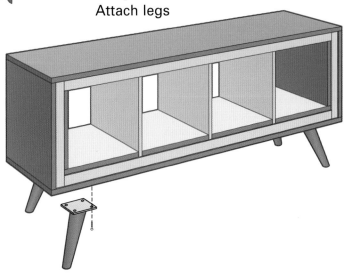

Materials list

ITEM	QTY.
IKEA Kallax Shelving Unit, Birch, No. 902.758.44	1
8" McCobb legs, soft maple (tablelegs.com)	4
Angle top plate for legs (tablelegs.com)	4
4' x 8' x 3/4" birch plywood	1
Birch iron-on edge banding	25'
No. 12 x 2" flat-head sheet metal screws	24
Wood stain and polyurethane	

Craft center

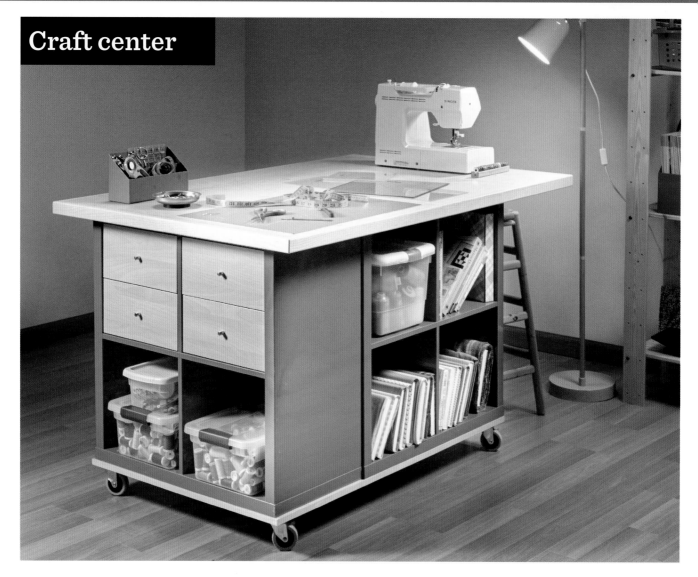

Build a worktable with a huge surface, convenient storage and easy mobility by sandwiching three small storage units between a base with casters and a plywood top with hardwood edging.

Build it

Cut hardwood plywood for the top and base and install hardwood edging and iron-on edge banding as shown in Step 1. Position two Kallax shelving units back to back and fasten them to the base with flat-head sheet metal screws after drilling countersink pilot holes through the Kallax frames (Step 2). The frames are hollow panels, so be careful not to punch through their thin faces when drilling the countersinks. Make sure the screw heads seat flush.

Install the third Kallax unit across the front of the base, using the same method. Then tip the assembly over onto the top and fasten it as before (Step 3). Install locking swivel casters (Step 4). Then tip the assembly right-side up and round over all the top's sharp edges with a router and a round-over bit. Complete the job by installing Kallax drawer inserts and applying your favorite finish to the top (Step 5).

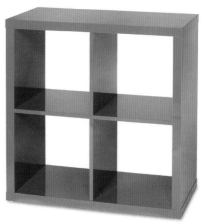

Basic unit

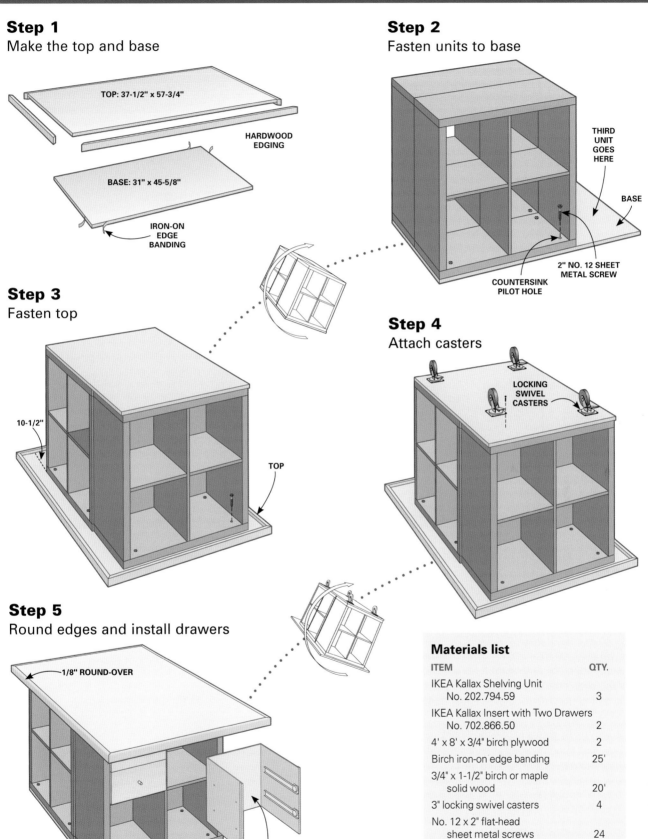

Step 1
Make the top and base

TOP: 37-1/2" x 57-3/4"

HARDWOOD EDGING

BASE: 31" x 45-5/8"

IRON-ON EDGE BANDING

Step 2
Fasten units to base

THIRD UNIT GOES HERE

BASE

2" NO. 12 SHEET METAL SCREW

COUNTERSINK PILOT HOLE

Step 3
Fasten top

10-1/2"

TOP

Step 4
Attach casters

LOCKING SWIVEL CASTERS

Step 5
Round edges and install drawers

1/8" ROUND-OVER

DRAWER INSERT

Materials list

ITEM	QTY.
IKEA Kallax Shelving Unit No. 202.794.59	3
IKEA Kallax Insert with Two Drawers No. 702.866.50	2
4' x 8' x 3/4" birch plywood	2
Birch iron-on edge banding	25'
3/4" x 1-1/2" birch or maple solid wood	20'
3" locking swivel casters	4
No. 12 x 2" flat-head sheet metal screws	24
Polyurethane, wood glue	

Built-in bench

Create a classic mudroom bench by fastening base molding and a new top to a cabinet designed to display a flat-screen TV.

Build it

Assemble the Hemnes TV unit through Step 27 of the manufacturer's instructions. Move it into position and shim the legs as necessary to level it. Then install a support block under the rails beneath the center divider (Step 1). This allows the unit to be used as a bench. Fasten the unit to the wall through its upper back rail (Step 2).

Build a new top by gluing hardwood edging to 3/4-in.-thick hardwood plywood and then rounding over all the sharp edges (Step 3). Sand the top, stain it and apply your favorite finish. Use corner brackets to fasten the top to the bench (Step 4). Then fasten base molding around the bench to build it in (Step 5). Install the drawers to complete the project.

Basic unit

Step 1
Install support block

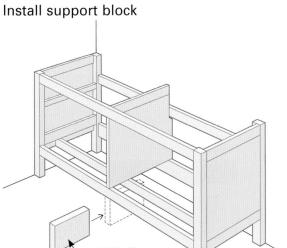

4-1/2" x 7"
SUPPORT
BLOCK

Step 2
Fasten bench to wall

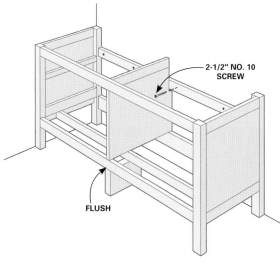

2-1/2" NO. 10
SCREW

FLUSH

Step 3
Build plywood top

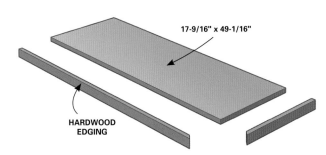

17-9/16" x 49-1/16"

HARDWOOD
EDGING

Step 4
Install top

1/8" ROUND-OVER

1" CORNER
BRACKET

Step 5
Fasten molding

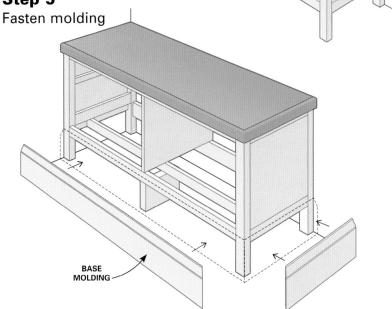

BASE
MOLDING

Materials list

ITEM	QTY.
IKEA Hemnes TV Unit No. 002.509.61	1
4' x 8' x 3/4" birch plywood	1
3/4" x 1-1/2" birch or maple solid wood	8'
1" corner brackets	10
5-1/2" base molding	6' min.
Wood stain, polyurethane, wood glue	

ILLUSTRATION FRANK ROHRBACH III

Fold-up workbench

If you thought you didn't have enough room for a workbench, check out this one made from an old door. Any old door with a jamb will do, but flush (smooth face veneer) doors work best because they give you a flat work surface. If you want to do heavier work, choose a solid-core door. You'll be able to pound on big stuff and even mount a vise. For lighter work, a hollow-core door will work fine, but you'll need to mount the leg hinges close to the bottom and top of the door to get the screws into the solid part of the door frame.

3" SCREWS INTO STUDS

DOOR JAMB

FLUSH INTERIOR DOOR

1 Fasten the hinge-side jamb of the door to a wall by screwing five or six 3-in. drywall screws into the studs at a comfortable working height. Ours is at 3 ft., standard countertop height.

TIP

You can also find cheap damaged or returned doors at lumberyards and home centers.

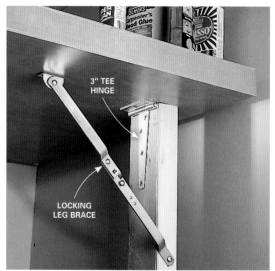

3" TEE HINGE

LOCKING LEG BRACE

2 Cut two 2x4s to the height you've chosen and screw them to the door with 3-in. strap or tee hinges. Position the hinges about 6 in. in from the strike-side edge of the door. For added safety and stability, fasten some locking knees onto the door and legs to prevent the table legs from accidentally being kicked in and causing your workbench to collapse.

Behind-the-door medicine cabinet

A recessed medicine cabinet for added storage space

Almost every bathroom needs more storage space. And most bathrooms have a spot—usually next to the door—that's perfect for an extra medicine cabinet. If you install a recessed cabinet that fits inside the wall between the studs, you won't lose an inch of space in the bathroom. If wall space allows, you can even install two cabinets this way, side-by-side or over-under. Recessed medicine cabinets are available at home centers and kitchen and bath showrooms.

How to install a behind-the-door medicine cabinet

The biggest challenge in installing a recessed cabinet is finding unobstructed stud cavities in an open wall. The wall behind the door is usually open, but make sure that pipes, ducts and wiring don't get in the way. To choose the location for the cabinet, begin by finding the studs with a stud finder. Hold the cabinet to the wall at the best height and mark the cabinet near one side of a stud. Find the exact location of that stud by sawing through

TIP

Before you cut a full-size hole in the wall, cut a 6 x 6-in. hole and shine a flashlight inside to check for obstructions.

the drywall until the blade is stopped (Photo 1). Use the cuts to define one cabinet side, and draw the cabinet outline.

Cut out the drywall and then cut off the exposed stud (Photo 2). Add the framing, then screw the cabinet to the framing (Photo 5). Add trim around the edges if necessary to conceal the rough drywall edges.

1 Outline the inset medicine chest to fall against a stud on one side and cut out the opening with a drywall saw.

2 Cut the intermediate stud flush with the drywall on the back side. Push it sideways to release the drywall screws on the back side and remove the stud.

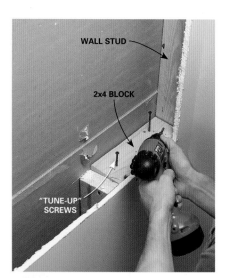

3 Screw blocking to adjacent studs at the top and bottom of the opening. Drive temporary "tune-up" screws into the block to help position it.

4 Cut and tap in vertical backing flush with the drywall edge, then toe-screw it to the blocking.

5 Slip the cabinet into the opening and anchor it with pairs of 2-in. screws. Add trim if needed.

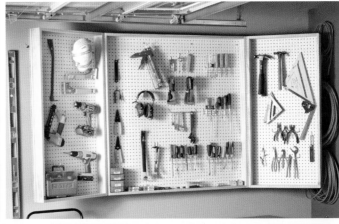

Chapter 3

WORKSHOP

Ultimate tool corral 94
Rolling shop cart............................. 101
Compact tool cabinet 103
Hardware organizer....................................... 107
Space-saver workstation 110
Classic workbench...116
Workshop tips 121

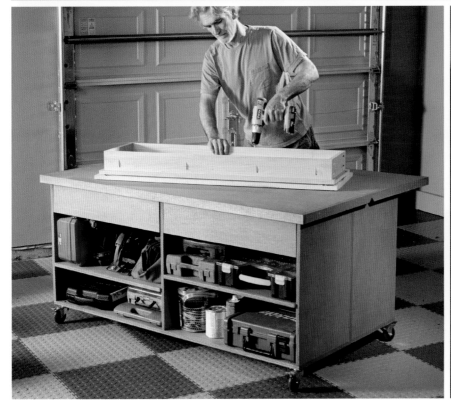

Ultimate tool corral

A cabinet designed with tools in mind

OPEN SHELVES FOR
INSTANT ACCESS

A WORK SURFACE FOR
CHANGING BITS AND BLADES

DRAWERS FOR SUPPLIES
AND ACCESSORIES

WHAT IT TAKES

TIME: Two weekends
SKILL: Intermediate
TOOLS: Table saw,
router, drill, brad nailer or
23-gauge pin nailer

This cabinet provides a home for all your tools. Park often-used power tools on the shelves and occasional-use tools in the deep drawers. The shallower drawers are perfect for hand tools, blades, bits and accessories. And the countertop is just large enough for tool setup or adjustments. We built a double-wide cabinet out of hardwoods. You could cut costs by using pine lumber.

Edge the plywood

Most home centers carry "screen molding," which works great for edging plywood. But we couldn't find it in birch, so we cut our own edging from birch boards. Start by ripping approximately 100 ft. of solid wood into 3/16-in. strips (LL). We used a simple (and safe!) setup to cut multiple thin strips: Just round the end of a 1x4 slightly and clamp it to the saw table (Photo 1). Position this block slightly in front of the blade, not directly next to it.

Next, cut the plywood parts (B–G, N) but cut them 1/4 to 1/2 in. extra long. The extra length allows you to trim the parts to final size after the edging is on.

Cut the edging strips to approximately the same length as the oversized plywood and attach with glue and nails (Photo 2). Make sure the edging overhangs the plywood as you tack it down. Also clamp the edging (Photo 3).

After the glue dries, the protruding edging needs to be flushed up to the plywood. You could use a sander, but you run the risk of sanding through the thin veneer and ruining the part. Instead use a trim router retrofitted with an offset base. Set the router on the plywood and lower the bit until it just touches and trim the edging flush to the plywood (Photo 4). All that's left is a little hand sanding and you've got perfect edging.

Materials list

ITEM	QTY.
4' x 8' x 3/4" birch plywood	4
4' x 8' x 1/2" birch plywood	2
4' x 8' x 1/4" birch plywood	4
1" x 6" x 3/4" birch or maple	60 lin. ft.
48" shelf standards	15
Shelf clips	32
Connector bolts	6

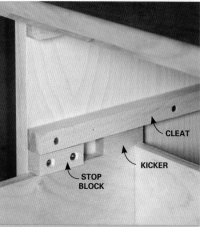

CLEAT

KICKER

STOP BLOCK

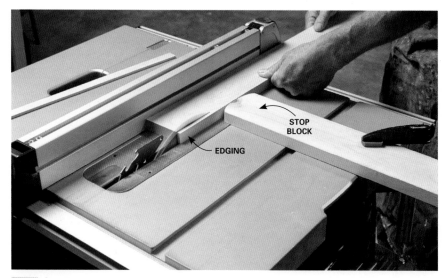

STOP BLOCK

EDGING

1 **Cut the edging safely.** Don't simply set the fence 3/16 in. from the blade to cut the edging strips. That can lead to kickbacks when the thin strips get pinched between the fence and the blade. Instead, clamp a stop block 3/16 in. from the blade. Set the stock against the stop block, position the fence against the stock and you're ready to rip. You'll need to reset the fence after each cut.

Simpler slides for the drawers

Manufactured drawer slides are either expensive or too wimpy for heavy tools—or both. So these drawers are set on simple cleats. Rub a candle on them and the drawers glide very smoothly. To keep the drawers from pulling all the way out, glue kickers to the drawers and screw stop blocks to the cabinets.

2 **Tack on the edging.** Spread a little glue and tack the edging onto the plywood parts with a pinner or brad nailer. Center the edging by "feel," allowing it to overhang slightly on both sides. The edging can also overhang the plywood at one end. But the other end should be flush with the plywood.

3 **Clamp the edging.** Clamps alone won't force the flimsy edging tight against the plywood. So use a thicker board or "caul" to distribute the pressure evenly.

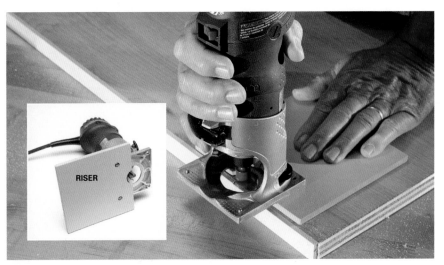

4 **Trim the edging flush.** A straight router bit set at just the right depth will trim off the protruding edging without cutting into the plywood. Remove the plastic base plate from your router and mount the router on a "riser" scrap of MDF, plywood or melamine.

Trim the cabinet parts to their final length on the table saw. Set the fence a little long and use a miter gauge to cut one end. Then, set the fence to the final length and cut the opposite edge. This leaves your edging perfectly flush and square to the plywood on both ends.

Build the cabinets

Set the cleats (GG, HH) on the lower cabinet sides with screws. Use MDF spacers to ensure correct spacing (Photo 5). Align the cleats flush with the front edge of the cabinet sides. Leave a 1/4-in. gap at the back to prevent dust accumulation that would interfere with the drawer closing.

Assemble the lower cabinets, using trim-head screws for the top shelf. The bottom shelf is fastened with regular wood screws through the bottom cleat (Photo 6). Cut the backs and attach them with just a few screws for now.

Assemble the upper cabinets with regular screws. They'll be covered with trim later. The adjustable shelves are notched to prevent the shelves from accidentally pulling out when you drag your circular saw off the shelf. We notched the shelves four at a time. Attach a wood sub-fence to your miter gauge. Clamp the shelves together then clamp the set to your sub-fence to gang-cut the notches (Photo 7). Shift the stack for each cut until the notch is cut full width. Lay out the notch locations on one shelf according to shelf standard spacing. We put ours 2 in. in from the front and back. Make the notches 1/4 in. deep and 3/4 in. wide.

Attach the two base cabinets to each other with screws. Measure and cut the plywood top (A). Apply the edging (CC, DD) to the top with nails and glue, then clamp with cauls. Attach the top and set the upper cabinets. Join the upper cabinets with connector bolts.

Build the drawers

Cut the drawer parts (P–Y and BB). To start, build just one drawer box and check for fit. We used No. 6 x 1-5/8-in. trim-head screws to build the drawer boxes. Make sure the drawer is square, then secure the bottom with No. 6 x 1-in. screws. Test the drawer fit in its opening on both cabinets. If the drawer slides smoothly, go ahead and assemble the other drawers. If it's tight, trim the fronts and backs down a bit for a good fit. Countersink all the screw heads into the plywood bottom so they don't interfere with the sliding of the drawer on the cleats.

Remove the backs on the lower cabinets and set the drawers in their openings. Add a couple of short shims on the cabinet sides at the back of the cabinet to center the drawer when it's shut. Glue the shims to the sides with the tapered edge facing forward. The shims ensure the drawer shuts in the same position each time. This will help maintain an even margin on the drawer fronts when the drawers are closed.

Cut your drawer fronts (H–M), leaving them a little oversize. Add edging to the bottom of each drawer front. Flush-trim the edging. Cut the drawer fronts to final length on the table saw. Add the trim to the sides, flush-trim and

5 Mount the drawer cleats. Position the drawer-support cleats with scrap wood spacers. Use the same set of spacers on all four cabinet sides to ensure identical spacing.

6 Assemble the cabinets. No need for glue—just use screws. The bottom shelf is attached to the bottom cleat. Use trim-head screws for the top shelf. The small holes are easy to fill and will be virtually invisible below the top edging.

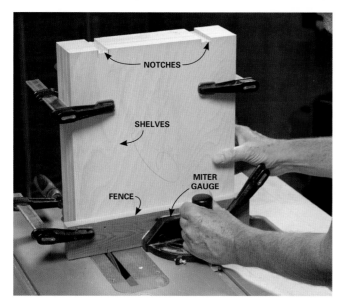

7 Notch the shelves. Notches fit over the shelf supports and prevent the shelves from slipping out of the cabinet. To cut notches, mount a fence on your miter gauge and clamp the shelves to it. Make several passes to complete each notch.

8 Bevel the handle stock. Set the table saw blade to 45 degrees and mount featherboards on the table to hold the stock tight against the fence. As you reach the end of the cut, drive the stock with a push stick to keep your fingers away from the blade.

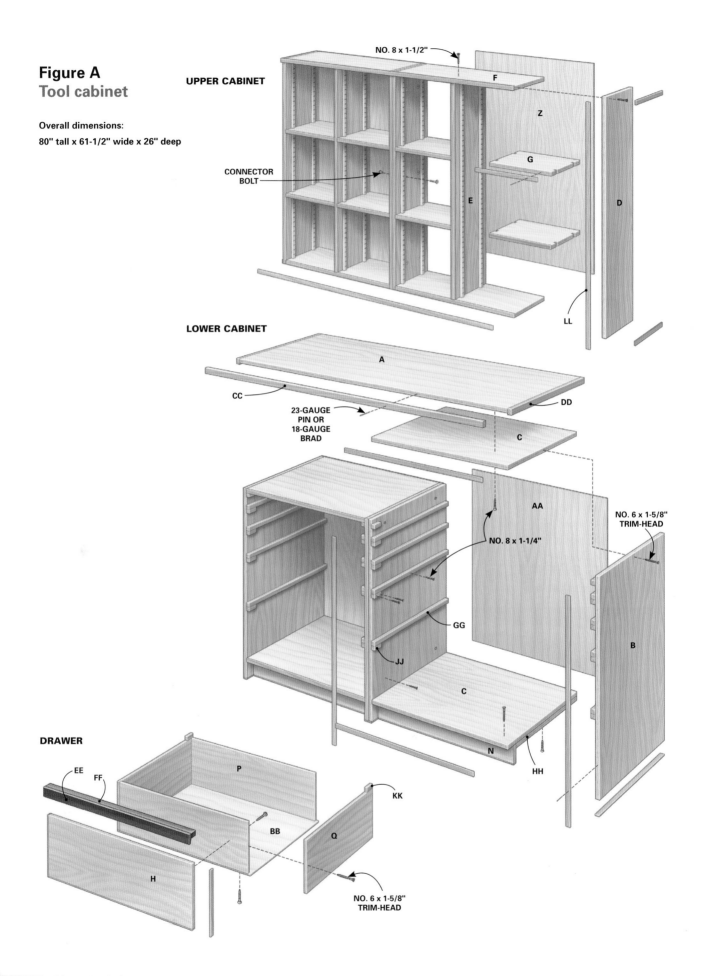

Figure A
Tool cabinet

Overall dimensions:
80" tall x 61-1/2" wide x 26" deep

NO. 8 x 1-1/2"

UPPER CABINET

F

Z

CONNECTOR BOLT

G

E

D

LL

LOWER CABINET

A

CC

DD

23-GAUGE PIN OR 18-GAUGE BRAD

C

AA

NO. 6 x 1-5/8" TRIM-HEAD

NO. 8 x 1-1/4"

GG

JJ

C

N

HH

B

DRAWER

EE FF

P

KK

BB

Q

H

NO. 6 x 1-5/8" TRIM-HEAD

rip the drawer front to the final width.

Now it's time to build the handles. Cut the drawer handle parts (EE, FF). Cut a 45-degree bevel on part EE (Photo 8). Glue and clamp the parts to form the handle. When the glue has set, sand the handles smooth and attach to the drawer fronts. We used glue and nails, but you could use trim-head screws to attach the handles as well.

With the drawers in their openings, hold the top drawer front in place so the bottom of the drawer front is flush with the bottom of the drawer box and even with the outside edge of the cabinet. Pin the drawer front in place with a brad nailer or a 23-gauge pin nailer. Carefully open the drawer by pushing on it from behind. Clamp the drawer front in place and secure with No. 10 x 1-in. washer head screws. Use a 3/32-in.-thick strip of wood to space the other drawer fronts as you work your way down.

We finished our cabinets with a penetrating oil finish, then added the drawer stops. You can add dividers or line the bottoms with nonslip mats so your hand tools don't rattle around. Best of all, you'll know right where to find your tools— that is, if you remember to put them away. But that's not something we can help you with.

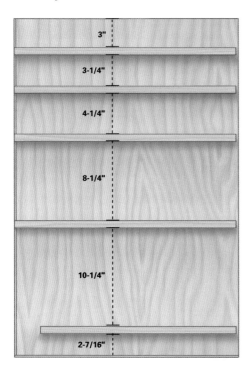

9 Attach stop blocks with screws. Stop blocks add a measure of safety so the drawer can't be pulled all the way out and crash to the floor.

Figure B
Cleat positions

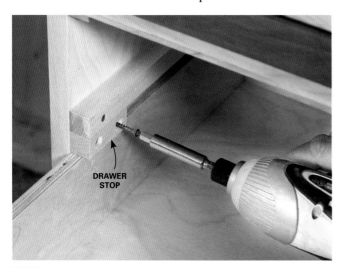

3"

3-1/4"

4-1/4"

8-1/4"

10-1/4"

2-7/16"

Cutting list

KEY	QTY.	DIMENSIONS	NAME
3/4" plywood			
A	1	25-1/4" x 60"	Top
B	4	23-13/16" x 35"	Lower cabinet sides
C	4	23-13/16" x 28-1/2"	Lower cabinet top and bottom
D	4	11-13/16" x 44"	Upper cabinet sides
E	2	11-13/16" x 42-1/2"	Upper cabinet dividers
F	4	11-13/16" x 28-1/2"	Upper cabinet top and bottom
G	8	11-1/2" x 13-7/8"	Upper cabinet adjustable shelves
H	2	10" x 29-5/8"	Drawer front
J	2	8" x 29-5/8"	Drawer front
K	2	4" x 29-5/8"	Drawer front
L	2	3" x 29-5/8"	Drawer front
M	2	1-1/2" x 29-5/8"	Drawer front
N	2	3-1/8" x 28"	Toe-kick
1/2" plywood			
P	4	8-1/2" x 27-3/8"	Drawer box front and back
Q	4	8-1/2" x 24"	Drawer box side
R	4	7-1/4" x 27-3/8"	Drawer box front and back
S	4	7-1/4" x 24"	Drawer box side
T	4	3-1/4" x 27-3/8"	Drawer box front and back
U	4	3-1/4" x 24"	Drawer box side
V	4	2-1/4" x 27-3/8"	Drawer box front and back
W	4	2-1/4" x 24"	Drawer box side
X	4	1-9/16" x 27-3/8"	Drawer box front and back
Y	4	1-9/16" x 24"	Drawer box side
1/4" plywood			
Z	2	30" x 44"	Upper back
AA	2	30" x 35-1/4"	Lower back
BB	10	24" x 28-3/8"	Drawer bottom
Solid wood			
CC	1	3/4" x 1" x 61-1/2"	Top edging
DD	2	3/4" x 1" x 25-1/4"	Top edging
EE	10	1/2" x 1-1/4" x 30"	Drawer pull
FF	10	3/4" x 1-1/4" x 30"	Drawer pull
GG	16	3/4" x 3/4" x 23-3/4"	Drawer cleat
HH	4	3/4" x 3/4" x 21-1/4"	Bottom shelf cleat
JJ	20	3/4" x 3/4" x 2"	Drawer stop
KK	20	1/2" x 1/4"– 3/4" x 2"	Drawer kicker
LL	1	3/4" x 3/16" x 100'	Edging

Figure C: Cutting diagrams

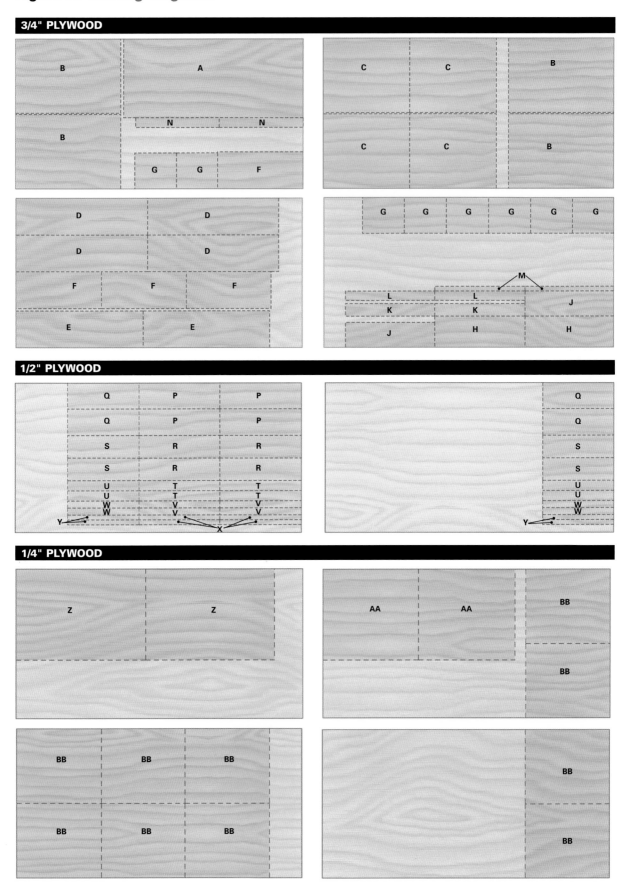

Rolling shop cart

Whether your shop is big or small, it's sure handy to have a cart or two for moving stacks of parts from one machine to another. Our carts make an endless journey around the shop, from planer to table saw to drill press to sander, and on and on. They're never empty!

Constructing this cart is simple—all the parts are just glued and screwed or nailed together. You'll need one full sheet of 3/4-in. plywood and a box of 1-1/4-in. screws.

If you want to use a cart to support table saw work, build it the same height as your saw and buy the casters for your cart before cutting any parts to size. (We recommend using casters that are at least 2-1/2 in. in diameter.) Then measure the total height of one caster and alter the lengths of the cart's legs as needed.

We've laid out the parts so you can crosscut your plywood into three 32-in. pieces before having to cut anything to exact size. It's OK if these crosscuts are rough; a jigsaw or circular saw would work fine. After this, it's best to use a table saw for ripping the parts and a miter saw or table saw for cutting them to length.

After breaking down the plywood into manageable sizes, cut all the leg pieces (A and B). Glue them together, using nails or screws to hold them together while the glue dries. Make sure their ends are even.

Cut the parts for the upper and lower boxes (C, D, E and F) and glue and screw them together. Next, cut the shelf and bottom (G) to fit the boxes and glue and screw these pieces into place. (Adding a bottom to the upper box makes it easier to clamp things to the top of the cart. Without a bottom, you'd only have a narrow 3/4-in. edge to clamp to.) Make sure the shelf and bottom don't overhang each box or the legs won't fit correctly. To avoid any overhang, you could cut the shelf and bottom 1/16 in. smaller all around.

Fasten the legs to the boxes, using three screws at each corner. Finally, cut the caster supports (H) and top (J) to size and add them to the cart. Fasten the casters using 3/4-in. No. 14 sheet metal screws.

Figure A
Rolling shop cart

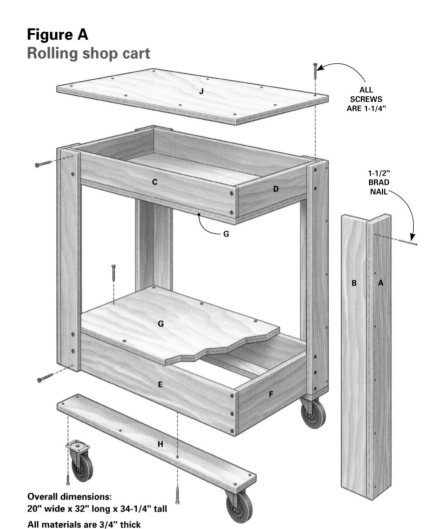

ALL SCREWS ARE 1-1/4"

1-1/2" BRAD NAIL

Overall dimensions:
20" wide x 32" long x 34-1/4" tall

All materials are 3/4" thick

Cutting list

KEY	QTY.	DIMENSIONS	NAME
A	4	3/4" x 4" x 29"	Wide leg pieces
B	4	3/4" x 3-1/4" x 29"	Narrow leg pieces
C	2	3/4" x 3-1/2" x 30-1/2"	Upper box, long sides
D	2	3/4" x 3-1/2" x 17"	Upper box, short sides
E	2	3/4" x 5" x 30-1/2"	Lower box, long sides
F	2	3/4" x 5" x 17"	Lower box, short sides
G	2	3/4" x 18-1/2" x 30-1/2"	Shelf and bottom
H	2	3/4" x 4" x 32"	Caster supports
J	1	3/4" x 20" x 32"	Top

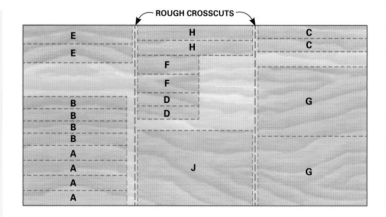

ROUGH CROSSCUTS

Compact tool cabinet

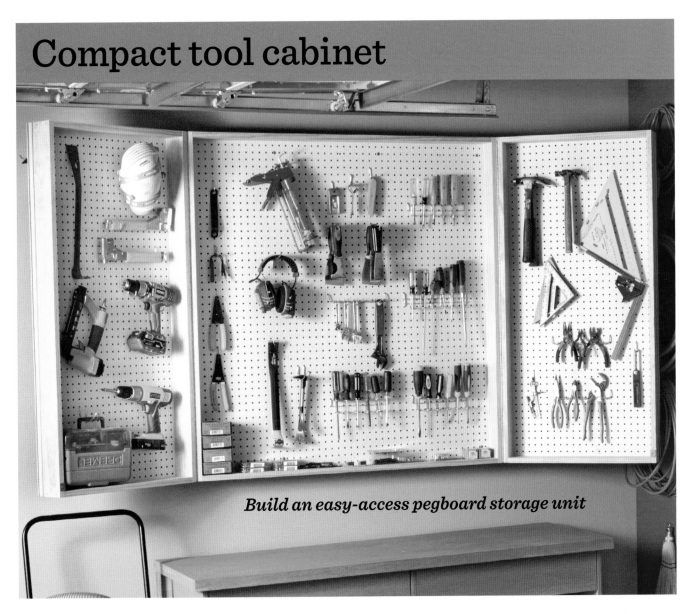

Build an easy-access pegboard storage unit

This pegboard cabinet delivers the best of both worlds: It provides almost 48 sq. ft. of pegboard storage while taking up only 16 sq. ft. of wall space.

Build the base frame

Cut your 1x4 frame boards to size. We used a higher-grade pine because it was worth the extra money to be able to work with straight, knot-free wood. Sand all the boards with 100-grit sandpaper before assembling the frames. Glue the joints and nail them with 1-1/2-in. brads, just to hold them together. When the base is fully assembled, go back and drive in two 2-in. trim-head screws. If you don't have a brad nailer, no problem; the screws are plenty strong on their own.

Attach the pegboard to the base frame

We wanted solid material along all the edges, which meant we couldn't just measure 47-3/4 in. from the end of the sheet and assume the holes wouldn't be exposed. Not all sheets of pegboard are the same size, and sometimes the holes aren't perfectly centered on the sheet. Square up the frame and hold it in place with a couple of temporary cross braces and brads. Lay a half sheet of pegboard on top of the frame so all the rows of holes are inset at least 1/4 in. before fastening it down. Fasten the sheet with 1-in. brads every 8 in. or so (Photo 1), and use glue on all the unfinished sides of the pegboard.

Once the pegboard is secure, trim off the excess material with a router equipped with a flush-trim bit (Photo 2). If you don't own a flush-trim bit, this is an excellent opportunity to buy a tool you'll definitely use again. Trimming down pegboard creates clouds of very fine dust, which seems to get into everything, so move the operation outdoors if possible. Don't even think about doing this without wearing a dust mask. If you don't have a router to trim off the

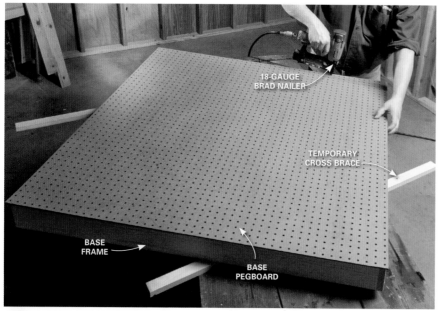

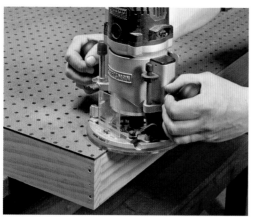

1 Fasten pegboard to the base frame. Attach temporary braces to hold the base frame perfectly square. Lay a 4 x 4-ft. sheet of pegboard over the frame. The oversize sheet lets you position the holes so they won't be along the outer edge of the cabinet. Note: If you don't have a router to trim off the excess pegboard (see Photo 2), position the pegboard, mark it with a pencil and cut it to size before nailing it in place.

2 Trim the pegboard flush. Install a flush-trim bit in your router and trim off the overhanging pegboard. Routing pegboard whips up a dust storm, so wear a mask.

3 Complete the doors. A 3/4-in. spacer between the two layers of pegboard creates space for the hooks.

excess, just mark the outline of the base frame onto the half sheet of pegboard and trim it with a saw.

Build the doors

Use the same process to build the door frames and install the pegboard as you did on the base. Again, pay special attention to the spacing of the holes before you attach the pegboard and rout it flush. The only difference this time is that the first layer of pegboard should be facing down.

Once the first layer of pegboard is in place, rip down 3/4-in. strips of wood to act as a spacer between the first and the second layers (Photo 3). This will allow clearance for the peg hardware on both sides of the door. Align the spacers the same way you did with the frame, so the end grain cannot be seen from the sides. Tack them in place with 1-1/2-in. brads.

Tack on the outer layer of pegboard or dry-erase board (white/gloss hardboard panel board) with 1-in. brads, and then drive in 2-in. trim-head screws about every 8 in. or so. Pegboard and other hardboard materials tend to pucker when you screw into them, so predrill the holes with a small countersink drill bit. Don't attach the screen mold on the outside of the doors until the doors are hung onto the base.

Finish the back side of the base

There needs to be space for the peg hardware on the back of the base, so install 3/4-in. strips of pine on the back two sides of the base. Fasten them with glue and 1-1/2-in. brads. Next, install a full pine 1x4 on the top and bottom of the back side of the base. These are the boards you'll screw through when you hang the cabinet on the wall. Glue and tack these boards into place, and then drive 2-in. trim-head screws through the boards into the base frame.

Use another 3/4-in. strip of pine to brace up the center of the pegboard. Install this center brace between the holes. Secure it with glue and a few 1-in. brads from the front side of the base. This will prevent the 4 x 4-ft. sheet of pegboard from getting too floppy.

The doors will be thicker than the base

Figure A
Pegboard cabinet

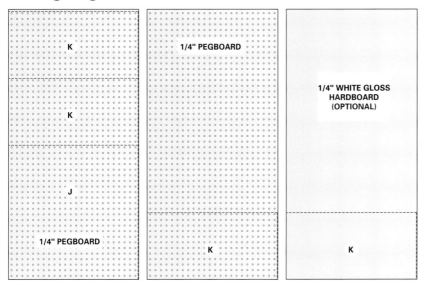

Overall dimensions:
47-3/4" wide x
47-3/4" tall x
9-1/2" deep

2" SCREW

Figure B
Cutting diagram

1/4" PEGBOARD

1/4" PEGBOARD

1/4" WHITE GLOSS HARDBOARD (OPTIONAL)

Materials list

ITEM	QTY.
1x4 x 8' pine	7
4' x 8' x 1/4" pegboard	2
4' x 8' x 1/4" white/gloss hardboard panel board	1
1/4" x 3/4" x 8' screen mold	3
Wood glue	
4' piano hinges	
Magnet catches	
2" trim screws	
1-1/2" 18-gauge brads	
1" 18-gauge brads	
1 qt. of polyurethane	

4 **Add filler strips.** Installing filler strips on the back of the base will allow the doors to open a little wider.

5 **Install the doors.** Clamp the doors to the cabinet and install the piano hinges. A self-centering screw hole punch helps you center the screws in the hinge holes.

Materials list

KEY	QTY.	SIZE & DIMENSIONS
A	2	3-1/2" x 46-1/4" x 3/4" pine (base top/bottom)
B	6	3-1/2" x 47-3/4" x 3/4" pine (base/door sides)
C	4	3-1/2" x 22-1/4" x 3/4" pine (door tops/bottoms)
D	2	3/4" x 40-3/4" x 3/4" pine (base side spacers)
E	2	3-1/2" x 47-3/4" x 3/4" pine (base top/bottom spacer)
F	1	3/4" x 40-3/4" x 3/4" pine (base center brace)
G	4	3/4" x 22-1/4" x 3/4" pine (door top/bottom spacer)
H	4	3/4" x 47-3/4" x 3/4" pine (door side spacer)
J	1	48" x 48" x 1/4" pegboard (base pegboard); trim after attaching to frame
K	4	48" x 24" x 1/4" pegboard* (door pegboards); trim after attaching to frame
L	2	1" x 47-3/4" x 1/4" pegboard filler strips for base sides
M	2	3-1/2" x 45-3/4" x 1/4" pegboard filler strips for base top and bottom
N		24' of screen mold; cut to fit

*Or white gloss hardboard panel

once you add the screen molding. This means they'll make contact with the walls before they fully open. If you add filler strips of pegboard on the back side of the pine boards you just installed, the doors will open farther, and you'll get another cool-looking dark strip resembling a walnut inlay (Photo 4). Even with the filler strips, the cabinet doors will make contact with the wall about 4 in. before they fully open. If you really, really want the doors to open all the way, you can add another 1/4 in. of filler to the back. But if you hang tools on the front of the cabinet or on the walls on either side, it shouldn't matter at all.

Attach the doors

The cabinet is a little shorter than the hinges; use a hacksaw to trim them down. Install the hinges to the base first. Fold it over the front edge of the base at a 90-degree angle and install the screws. Clamp the doors into place before you screw the other half of the hinge. Use a self-centering screw hole punch or a Vix bit to make sure the screws were perfectly aligned (Photo 5). Make sure the doors stay shut by installing a magnet catch on the top and bottom.

If the gap between the doors isn't perfectly even, adjust the screen mold on the front of the doors as you install them until it is. Fasten the screen mold with 1-in. brads.

Finish it up

After filling the holes with putty, cover the wood with clear polyurethane. It kept the wood color light and really darkened up the edges of the pegboard. Don't use an aggressively sticky tape when you tape off the hardboard/dry-erase board or you may pull the finish right off them. Screw the cabinet to the wall with screws that penetrate the studs at least 1-1/4 in., and try to hit at least three studs on the top and three on the bottom. You can install handles on the bottom if you like.

Now that you're done, it's time to shop for the hardware you'll need to hang all your tools. Here's a suggestion for you: Avoid 1/8-in. hooks. They fit in the 1/4-in. holes but tend to pull out when you remove a tool.

Hardware organizer

Flexible, portable—and possibly free!

French cleats make it neat

This simple hanging system—made from a 1x4 cut at a 45-degree bevel—lets you grab a bin and take it to the job, or rearrange bins instantly as your needs change.

DIY isn't just about building and fixing things. It's also about inventory management: maintaining a supply of the stuff you need and knowing where to find it. This simple bin system is the perfect project to get you organized. It's modeled on the systems used in cabinet shops, plumbers' vans and mechanics' garages.

These homemade bins offer two big advantages over a store-bought light-duty system. They're far tougher than plastic bins, and you can customize them to suit your stuff. Plus, they make the perfect scrap-wood project because all the parts are small. We built these bins from leftovers and didn't spend a dime.

Mass-produce parts

Begin by measuring the items you want to store. We found that the basic bin (see Figure A on p. 109) was just right for most stuff: nuts and bolts, construction screws, plumbing and electrical parts. For larger items, we made a few bins wider, but didn't change the bin sides (A). That approach is the most efficient because the sides are the most complex parts and changing them requires more fuss.

Once you've determined the sizes you

Materials list

To build an organizer similar to the one shown here, you'll need:

ITEM	QTY.
4' x 8' x 1/2" plywood	1
2' x 4' x 1/8" hardboard	1
1x4 x 8' pine	3

1" brads, 2-1/2" screws, wood glue and penetrating oil finish

1 **Cut the parts.** Rip strips of plywood to width on a table saw, then cut them to length with a miter saw. Clamp a scrap of plywood to the saw's fence to act as a stop block. That lets you cut identical lengths from several strips with one chop.

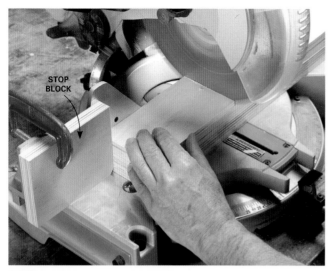

2 **Cut divider slots.** Mount a fence on your saw's miter gauge and position a stop block on the fence. Run the bin side across the blade. Then rotate the side 180 degrees and make a second pass to widen the slot. Caution: You have to remove the guard for this step. Be extra careful!

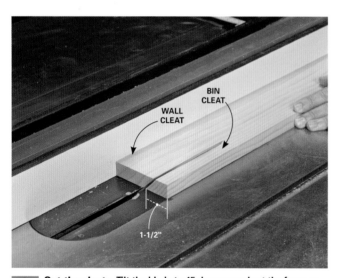

3 **Cut the cleats.** Tilt the blade to 45 degrees and set the fence so that the bin cleat is 1-1/2 in. wide. Getting the fence positioned may take some trial and error, so cut a test scrap first. Our guard was removed for photo clarity. Use yours!

4 **Assemble the bins.** Join the parts with glue and brads. The glue will provide plenty of strength, so drive only as many brads as needed to hold the parts together while the glue sets.

want, fire up your table saw and rip plywood into strips. If you're following our plan, you'll need strips 1-3/4, 3-1/2 and 6 in. wide. Then cut the strips to length, making parts for one box only. Test-assemble the box to check the fit of the parts. **Note:** "Half-inch" plywood is slightly less than 1/2 in. thick, so the bin bottom (B) needs to be slightly longer than 6 in. Start at 6-1/8 in., then trim as needed. When you've confirmed that all the parts are the right size, mass-produce them by chopping the strips to length (Photo 1).

If you want dividers (E) in any of the bins, your next step is to cut the divider slots. Set your table saw blade to a height of 3/16 in. Screw a long fence to your miter gauge and run the fence across the blade to cut a notch on the fence. Position a stop block 3-1/4 in. from the center of the notch. Place a side (A) against

the block, run it across the blade, rotate it and cut again (Photo 2). Check the fit of a divider in the slot and reposition the block slightly to adjust the width of the slot. It may take two or three tries before you get the width right.

When you're done cutting slots, it's time to clip off one corner of each side. Set your miter saw 45 degrees to the right. Clamp on a stop block and "gang-cut" sides just as you did when cutting parts to length (similar to Photo 1). Remember this: Slotted sides require left/right pairs. For every side that you cut with the slot facing up, cut another with the slot down.

Next, cut the cleats (Photo 3). The 45-degree bevel cuts will leave sharp, splintery edges, so crank the table saw blade back to zero degrees and shave 1/8 in. off each cleat before cutting them to length.

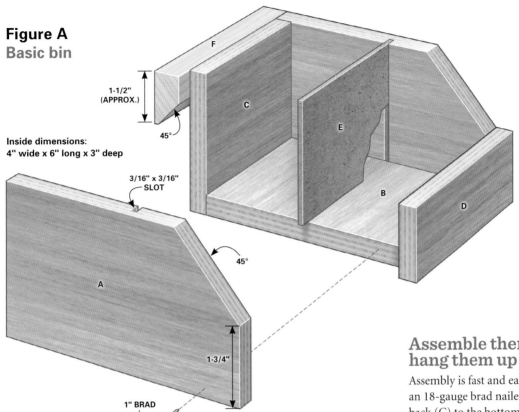

Figure A
Basic bin

1-1/2"
(APPROX.)

45°

Inside dimensions:
4" wide x 6" long x 3" deep

3/16" x 3/16"
SLOT

45°

F

C

E

B

D

A

1-3/4"

1" BRAD

Assemble them and hang them up

Assembly is fast and easy with glue and an 18-gauge brad nailer. First, tack the back (C) to the bottom (B), then add the sides (A), the front (D) and finally the cleat (F). After assembly, we wiped on two coats of penetrating oil finish to keep the wood from absorbing greasy fingerprints and oils from hardware.

When mounting the wall cleats, start at the bottom. Make sure the bottom cleat is level and straight. Then cut spacers at least 1-3/4 in. tall and use them to position the remaining wall cleats (Photo 5). Larger cleats will create more space between rows of bins, making it easier to reach in and grab stuff. Bins filled with hardware put a heavy load on the cleats, so drive a screw into every wall stud.

Cutting list

KEY	QTY.	SIZE & DESCRIPTION
A	2	3-1/2" x 6-1/2" (sides)
B	1	4" x 6" (bottom)
C	1	3-1/2" x 4" (back)
D	1	1-3/4" x 5" (front)
E	1	3" x 4-5/16" (divider)
F	1	3/4" x 1-1/2" x 5" (cleat)

Dividers are hardboard. Cleats are pine. All other parts are plywood.

SPACER

5 **Mount the wall cleats.** Mark the stud locations with tape and screw on the lowest cleat. Then work your way up the wall, using spacers to position each cleat.

Space-saver workstation

EASY-ACCESS DRAWERS WITH FULL-EXTENSION SLIDES

FLIP-UP TOP DOUBLES THE WORK SURFACE IN SECONDS

SHELVES FOR ADDITIONAL STORAGE

SMOOTH-ROLLING LOCKING CASTERS

A big work surface when you need it—compact storage when you don't

Most of us don't have space to keep a large worktable set up in the middle of the garage or basement. But this cleverly designed cabinet solves that problem. Smooth-rolling locking casters allow you to roll the cabinet out when you need it. And it only takes seconds to flip up the top and swing out the support wings to double the work surface.

We built this project from shop-grade plywood purchased at a home center. It wasn't the least expensive choice, but we liked the smooth surface and almost void-free veneer core. We ordered 3-in.

WHAT IT TAKES

TIME: One weekend

SKILL: Intermediate

TOOLS: Standard hand tools, saw, drill, self-centering hole punch. A table saw, miter saw and brad nail gun will give you better results and speed up the job.

This rolling workstation is designed to set up quickly and pack up small to get out of the way. Just load your stuff into the drawers or onto the shelves, fold in the wings and drop the top, and you're ready to roll it up against the wall. And when it comes time to work again, it's just as quick to roll it out and set it up.

polyurethane-wheeled casters online, and we used full-extension ball-bearing slides for the drawers. You'll find a full Materials List on p. 112.

Construction-wise, this is closer to a cabinet than to a workbench, and it requires accurate cuts for the best results. You could use a circular saw with a straightedge guide to make the cuts, but a table saw is a better choice. If you don't already have one, now is a good time to make a crosscutting sled for your table saw. It's the perfect tool to cut the wide strips of plywood to length.

Follow Figure D and the Cutting List to cut out the parts. Since 3/4-in. plywood is usually a little undersize, and your plywood may not be the same thickness as the plywood we used, we've indicated on the Cutting List which dimensions will need to be adjusted for plywood thickness.

Build the cabinet box

It's easier to drill the shelf pin holes in the sides and divider before you assemble the cabinet box. In Photo 1 we show using a shelf pin jig to drill the shelf-pin holes, but you can use a

scrap of pegboard for a jig or simply mark and drill the holes.

Since there is no caster in the center to support the weight, it's important to glue and screw all the parts. The combination of the screws and the strong 3/4-in. plywood back creates a box-beam effect for a rigid box. It's easier to tack the parts together first with a nail gun and 1-1/2-in. brads (Photo 2). Then drill pilot holes and drive the 1-1/2-in. screws. We like GRK or Spax brand screws with a torx-drive head. They reduce splitting and are easy to drive in.

When the cabinet box is done, attach the two front casters (Photo 3). To avoid splitting the plywood, move the casters back about 1/2 in. from the front. Use 1/4 x 1-in. lag screws on the outside edges and 1/4 x 1-in. carriage bolts through the cabinet bottom on the inside edges. Drill 5/32-in. pilot holes for the lag screws and 1/4-in. holes for the carriage bolts. Insert the carriage bolts from inside the cabinet and tap the head to seat them in the plywood before tightening the nuts.

Assemble and mount the wings

Follow Figure A to assemble the wings. Glue and nail all the parts. The wings are 1/4 in. shorter than the cabinet box so they can swing open without hitting the hinges. Nail a 1/4-in.-thick plastic furniture glide to the top side of each wing, opposite the hinge side. The plastic glides make up for the 1/4-in. height difference and slide easily across the flipped-up top.

Mount the casters to the wing bottoms with 1/4 x 1-in. lag screws. Hold them back from the front edge about 1/2 in. Photo 4 shows how to mount the wings with piano hinges. Lining up and driving all those little screws is much easier if you make starter holes with either a self-centering punch or a self-centering drill bit. Line up the hinge and anchor both ends with a screw. Then make the starter holes and drive in the remaining screws.

1 Drill shelf-support holes. Drill holes in the cabinet sides and divider for shelf pins. It's easier to do before the cabinet is assembled.

SHELF PIN JIG

CABINET SIDE

2 Assemble the cabinet. Glue and nail the cabinet parts together. With brad nails holding the parts in place, drilling pilot holes and driving screws are a lot easier.

BRAD NAILER

Build the drawers

Ball-bearing slides like the ones we're using require a close tolerance to operate smoothly. The drawer must be between 1 in. and 1-1/16 in. smaller than the space between the cabinet side and the divider. Photo 5 shows an accurate method to measure for the front and back parts of the drawer that compensates for the thickness of the plywood you're using. Subtract exactly 1-1/16 in. from this measurement and cut the drawer fronts and backs to this length. Nail and glue the sides to the front and back. Then measure for the bottom and cut it to the correct length. Finish the drawer boxes by nailing on the bottom (Photo 6).

The full-extension slides we're using have two parts. One part mounts to the drawer (Photo 7). The other part mounts to the cabinet (Photo 8). There is a release catch on the slides that allows you to separate the parts.

Draw a line parallel to the top edge and 2-3/8 in. down on each side of both drawers. Align the center of the slide mounting holes with this line and screw them on (Photo 7). On the cabinet, draw horizontal lines 3 in. down from the top. Center the slides on these lines when you mount them (Photo 8). To install the drawers, line up the slide parts and push the drawers in.

Finish the drawers by installing the fronts. Measure the distance between the cabinet side and the divider and subtract 1/4 in. to determine the length of the drawer fronts. Cut the fronts to this length. Photo 9 shows how to line up the fronts perfectly before attaching them with 1-1/4-in. screws (Photo 10).

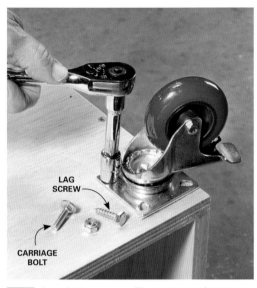

3 **Attach the casters.** The casters need super-strong connections to the cabinet. Fasten the inside edge of the caster plate with two carriage bolts. At the outside edge, drive two lag screws through the bottom and into the cabinet sides.

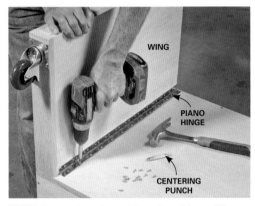

4 **Mount the wing with a piano hinge.** Align the wing with the cabinet side, making sure the top is 1/4 in. below the cabinet top. A center punch creates divots at the center of each screw hole and makes positioning all those screws a lot easier.

5 **Measure for the drawer.** Hold two scraps of the plywood against the cabinet side to represent the thickness of the drawer sides. Measure the exact distance to the center divider. Subtract exactly 1-1/16 in. from this measurement to determine the lengths of the fronts and backs of the drawers.

6 **Build the drawer box.** Glue and nail the drawer sides to the front and back. Then square the drawer and glue and nail the bottom to the sides, front and back.

Materials list

ITEM	QTY.
4' x 8' x 3/4" plywood	3
3" double lock casters	4
24" x 1" piano hinges	5
14" full-extension drawer slides	2 pair
1/4" x 1" lag screws	12
1/4" x 1" carriage bolts	4
1/4" locking nuts	4
1-1/2" screws	60
1-1/4" screws	20
1-1/2" brad nails	1 lb.
Bottle of wood glue	1
1/4" shelf pins	8
1/4"-thick plastic furniture glides	2

Figure A
Workstation

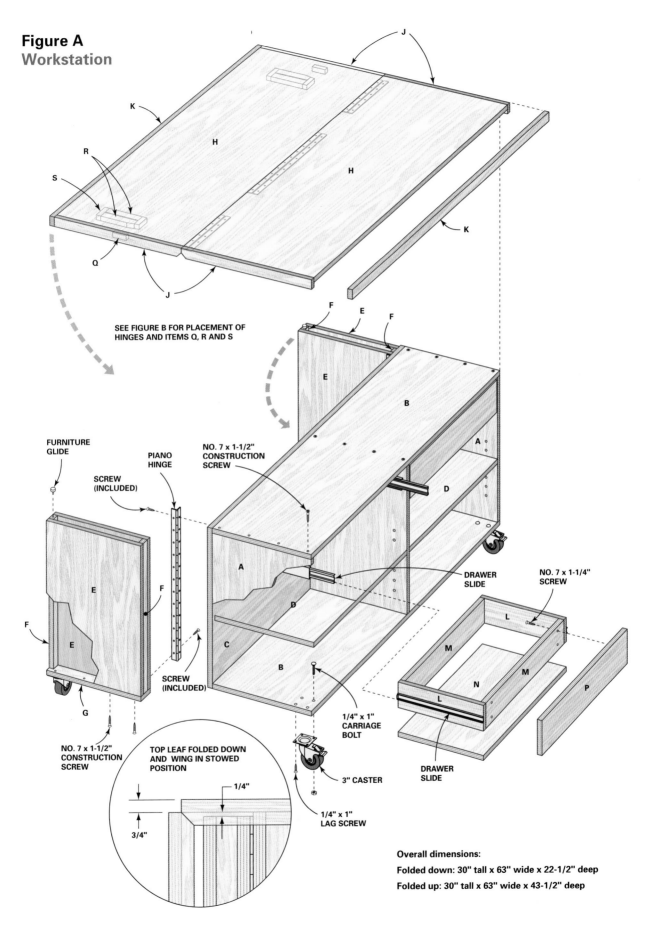

J

K

R

S

H

H

Q

J

K

SEE FIGURE B FOR PLACEMENT OF
HINGES AND ITEMS Q, R AND S

F   E   F

E

B

A

FURNITURE
GLIDE

PIANO
HINGE

NO. 7 x 1-1/2"
CONSTRUCTION
SCREW

SCREW
(INCLUDED)

D

DRAWER
SLIDE

NO. 7 x 1-1/4"
SCREW

E

F

E

F

A

D

C

B

L

M

M

N

P

SCREW
(INCLUDED)

L

G

NO. 7 x 1-1/2"
CONSTRUCTION
SCREW

TOP LEAF FOLDED DOWN
AND WING IN STOWED
POSITION

1/4"

3/4"

1/4" x 1"
CARRIAGE
BOLT

3" CASTER

1/4" x 1"
LAG SCREW

DRAWER
SLIDE

Overall dimensions:

Folded down: 30" tall x 63" wide x 22-1/2" deep

Folded up: 30" tall x 63" wide x 43-1/2" deep

Figure B
Latch and wing details

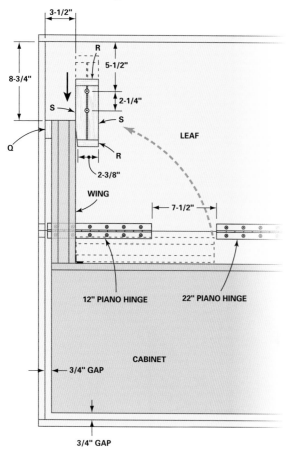

3-1/2"

8-3/4"

R

5-1/2"

2-1/4"

S

S

Q

R

LEAF

2-3/8"

WING

7-1/2"

12" PIANO HINGE

22" PIANO HINGE

CABINET

3/4" GAP

3/4" GAP

Figure C
Drawer slide placement

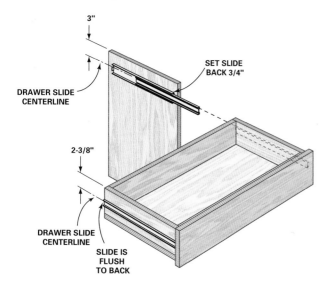

3"

SET SLIDE
BACK 3/4"

DRAWER SLIDE
CENTERLINE

2-3/8"

DRAWER SLIDE
CENTERLINE

SLIDE IS
FLUSH
TO BACK

Assemble and mount the top

The top consists of two equal-size pieces of plywood joined by piano hinges and edged with 1-1/2-in. plywood strips. Photo 11 shows how to attach the piano hinges. The gaps between hinges allow the plastic furniture glides on the top of the wings to pass unobstructed. After you connect the top with hinges, flip it over onto the cabinet. Measure to align the top so that it overhangs 3/4 in. on the sides and front. Then drive 1-1/4-in. screws up through the cabinet top to secure the top. Finish the top by gluing and nailing on the plywood edging (Photo 12).

With the cabinet built and top mounted, there's just one final detail to take care of. To prevent the wings from moving around when the top is folded up, mount stop blocks and wing latches to the underside of the flip-up side of the top (Photo 13). Build the latches by gluing and nailing strips of plywood, leaving a 3/16-in. space between them. Trim a slight bevel on the wing side of each latch to allow it to slide by without catching. Figure B shows details.

Finish the project by filling any voids in the plywood with wood filler and sanding all the plywood edges. Then apply your choice of paint, stain or a clear finish.

7 **Mount the drawer slides.** Draw a line on the drawer side to indicate the center of the slide. Take the slide apart and screw the drawer part of the slide to the drawer side, making sure to align the screws with the centerline.

DRAWER
SLIDE

8 **Mount the drawer slides in the cabinet.** Draw a centerline for the cabinet part of the drawer slides. Hold the slide 3/4 in. back from the cabinet front. Line up the holes in the slides with the centerline and screw the slides to the cabinet sides.

Figure D
Plywood cutting diagrams

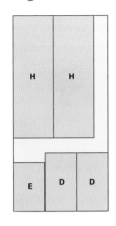
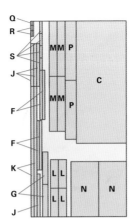

Cutting list
(3/4" plywood)

KEY	QTY.	SIZE & DESCRIPTION
A	3	15-7/8" x 23-3/4" (sides and divider)
B	2	15-7/8" x 60" (cabinet top and bottom)
C	1	25-1/4" x 60" (cabinet back)*
D	2	15-7/8" x 28-7/8" (shelves)*
E	4	15-7/8" x 24-1/4" (wing sides)
F	4	1-1/4" x 24-1/4" (wing spacers)
G	2	2-3/4" x 15-7/8" (wing bottoms)
H	2	21" x 61-1/2" (tops)
J	4	1-1/2" x 21" (side trim; bevel one end)
K	2	1-1/2" x 64" (front and back trim; cut length to fit)
L	4	4" x 14" (drawer box sides)
M	4	4" x 27" (drawer box fronts; and backs cut length to fit)
N	2	14" x 28" (drawer bottom; cut length to fit)
P	2	5-1/2" x 29" (drawer fronts; cut length to fit)
Q	2	3/4" x 2" (wing stops)
R	4	3/4" x 2-11/16" (latch fronts and backs)
S	4	1-1/4" x 6" (latch sides)

* Adjust for plywood thickness.

9 **Position the drawer fronts.** From inside the drawer box, drive four screws until the tips protrude slightly. Then position the drawer front and tap it against the screws with a soft mallet. The screws will bite into the drawer front and hold it in place.

10 **Screw on the drawer fronts.** Finish driving the screws through the drawer box and into the drawer front.

11 **Hinge the tops.** Lay the two halves tightly together on a flat surface with the best-looking sides facing down. Cut one 2-ft. piano hinge in half and the other one to 22 in. long. Install the piano hinges and then mount the top on the cabinet.

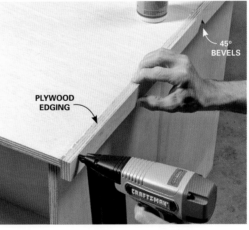

12 **Trim the top.** Glue and nail on the end trim. Cut the 45-degree bevels that allow the top to fold down without binding. Then mark and cut the front and back trim and nail it on.

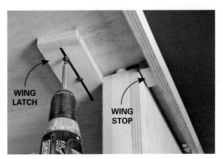

13 **Mount the wing stops and latches.** Glue and nail the stop blocks against the top trim. Then mount the sliding wing latches. Together these parts lock the wings in place when the tabletop is up.

Classic workbench

A timeless design that's simple and strong

WHAT IT TAKES

TIME: One day

SKILL LEVEL: Beginner

TOOLS: Circular saw, drill, No. 6 countersink bit

If this workbench looks familiar, it's probably because you've seen one a lot like it in your father's or grandfather's shop. Variations of this design have been around for decades, and for good reason: The bench is strong, practical and super easy to build. You can run to the lumberyard in the morning, grab a few boards, and by noon you'll have a perfectly functional workbench.

The workbench isn't fancy—it's built from standard construction lumber. But you can easily customize it with drawers or other features now or later. To see some of the improvements you can make, go to familyhandyman.com and search for "workbench upgrade."

If you can cut a board, you can build this bench. And you don't need any fancy tools either. In addition to a small square and a tape measure, you'll need a circular saw to cut the parts and a drill to drive the screws.

Getting started

You'll find all the materials at a lumber-yard or home center (see Materials List on p. 119). Choose lumber that's straight and flat, and that doesn't have too many gouges, slivers or cracks. We used Torx-head screws with self-drilling tips. But you can substitute any construction screw. If you're not using screws with self-drilling tips, drill pilot holes to avoid splitting the wood.

Cut the parts according to the Cutting List on p. 119. We used a miter saw, but a circular saw will work fine. Mark the 2x4s with a Speed square or combination square. Then carefully cut the boards to length. If you plan to stain or paint the bench, now is the time to sand the parts. And to really simplify your job, you could also stain or paint the parts before you assemble the bench.

Start by building the top and shelf frames

We used an old door propped up on sawhorses as a work surface, but the floor will work too. Lay the 2x4s for the front and back of the top and shelf on the work surface and mark the centers. Remember, if you're not using self-drilling screws, drill pilot holes for the screws. Photo 1 shows how to assemble the frames. Set the top frame aside and screw the shelf boards to the shelf frame (Photo 2).

Build and attach the leg assemblies

Photo 3 shows how to build the leg assemblies. You'll notice that the leg assemblies are 1/8 in. narrower than the

> **TIP**
>
> Tip: If your car is too small for the long boards, you can ask to have the boards cut to length. Just remember to take the Cutting List with you to the store.

1 **Build the frames.** Use 3-in. screws to assemble the frames that support the top and the shelf. To avoid splitting the 2x4s, either drill pilot holes or use self-drilling screws. Build both frames and set the top frame aside.

2 **Attach the shelf boards.** Attach the outside boards first. Then position the two remaining boards to create equal spaces between them and screw them to the frame. Before driving screws, drill pilot holes with a countersink bit.

3 **Assemble the legs.** Drill five holes about 2 in. from the edge of the pegboard with the countersinking bit. Spread a bead of construction adhesive on the legs and attach the pegboard with 1-1/4-in. screws. If glue oozes through the holes, wait for it to dry. Then shave it off with a sharp chisel.

4 **Screw the legs to the top frame.** Apply construction adhesive where the legs contact the top frame. Then attach the legs with screws.

TOP FRAME

SHELF

BOTTOM OF PEGBOARD

5 **Add the shelf.** Rest the bench on one end. Slide the shelf between the legs and line it up with the bottom of the pegboard. Screw through the shelf into the legs.

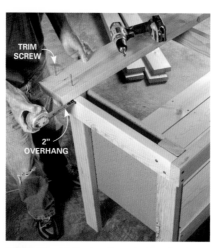

TRIM SCREW

2" OVERHANG

6 **Mount the top boards.** Starting at the back, align the first 2x6 flush to the back and measure for the 2-in. overhang on the side. Attach the 2x6 with trim screws. Attach the rest of the boards the same way. The front 2x6 will overhang the frame about 2 in.

7 **Install the backboard.** Attach the 1x4 shelf to the 1x10 backboard. Then add a 2x4 block at each end. Rest the backboard assembly on the workbench and drive screws through the back to hold it in place.

inside dimension of the top. That's so you can install the legs without binding, which would cause the pegboard to bow. Also, if the only pegboard you can find is thinner than the 1/4-in. pegboard specified, add the difference to the front and back of the shelf frame (C). For example, if you buy 1/8-in. pegboard, add 1/4 in. to parts C.

The pegboard is useful for hanging tools, but its real function is to stabilize the workbench as a brace. We added the construction adhesive to make sure the assemblies stayed strong and rigid. Be aware, though, that some of the adhesive will be visible through the holes.

The pegboard holes are a little too big to use as screw holes, so use a No. 6 countersink bit to drill pilot holes and make countersinks for the screws. Secure five evenly spaced 1-1/4-in. screws into each leg.

The next step is to attach the legs to the top frame. Apply construction adhesive to the top 3 in. of the legs. Then attach the leg assemblies with 3-in. screws (Photo 4).

Add the shelf and top

Stand the workbench on one end. Then it's simple to slide the shelf into place and line it up with the pegboard (Photo 5). Drive 3-in. screws through the shelf frame into the legs to support the shelf.

The top of this bench is 2x6s, placed tight together. The boards overhang the frame 2 in. on the sides and front. The overhang makes it easier to use clamps on the edges of the workbench. Photo 6 shows how to get started. We attached the 2x6s with trim screws, but you could substitute 16d casing nails.

Attach the back brace and backboard

The 1x10 back brace keeps things from falling off the back of the shelf, but it also stiffens the bench to prevent side-to-side rocking. Apply construction adhesive before attaching the brace with 2-in. screws.

The backboard is a 1x10 with a 1x4 shelf attached. On the side of the 1x10 you want facing out, draw a line the length of the board, 1-3/4 in. down from

Figure A
Classic workbench

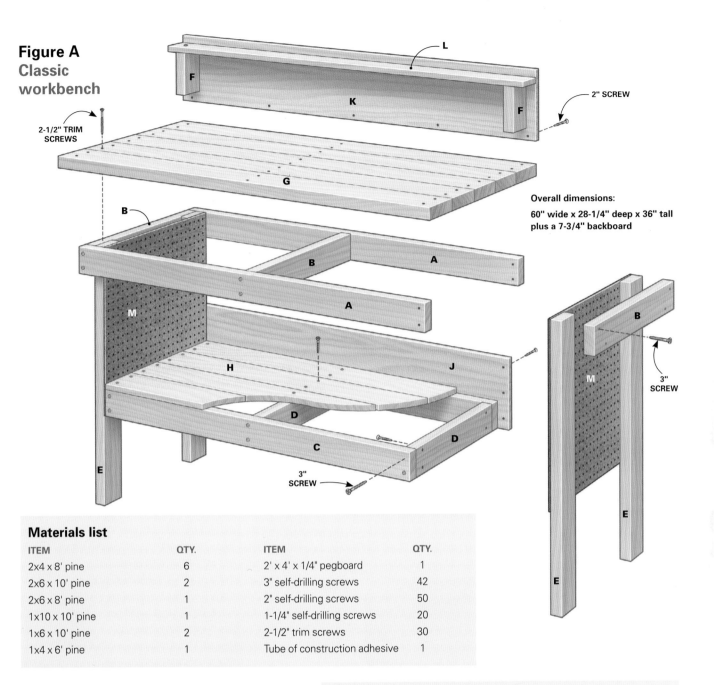

2-1/2" TRIM SCREWS

2" SCREW

3" SCREW

3" SCREW

Overall dimensions:
60" wide x 28-1/4" deep x 36" tall
plus a 7-3/4" backboard

Materials list

ITEM	QTY.	ITEM	QTY.
2x4 x 8' pine	6	2' x 4' x 1/4" pegboard	1
2x6 x 10' pine	2	3" self-drilling screws	42
2x6 x 8' pine	1	2" self-drilling screws	50
1x10 x 10' pine	1	1-1/4" self-drilling screws	20
1x6 x 10' pine	2	2-1/2" trim screws	30
1x4 x 6' pine	1	Tube of construction adhesive	1

the top. This is where you'll align the bottom of the 1x4. Draw a second line 1-3/8 in. from the top. Drill pilot holes with the countersink bit every 8 in. along this line. Now ask a helper to hold the 1x4 on the line while you drive 2-in. screws into the shelf through the pilot holes. After the shelf and 2x4 blocks at each end are attached, screw the backboard to the workbench (Photo 7).

You can modify your bench to fit your space and work style. We mounted an inexpensive woodworking vise on the front of the workbench and drilled holes in the 1x4 shelf to hold screwdrivers. If you've got a pint-size carpenter in the family, check out the mini version of the bench on p. 120. It would make a great project to build with your kids or grandkids.

Cutting list

KEY	QTY.	SIZE & DESCRIPTION
A	2	1-1/2" x 3-1/2" x 56" top frame front and back
B	3	1-1/2" x 3-1/2" x 22-1/2" top frame crosspieces
C	2	1-1/2" x 3-1/2" x 49-1/2" shelf frame front and back
D	3	1-1/2" x 3-1/2" x 19-1/2" shelf crosspieces
E	4	1-1/2" x 3-1/2" x 34-1/2" legs
F	2	1-1/2" x 3-1/2" x 6" back shelf supports
G	5	1-1/2" x 5-1/2" x 60" top boards
H	4	3/4" x 5-1/2" x 49-1/2" shelf boards
J	1	3/4" x 9-1/4" x 53" back brace
K	1	3/4" x 9-1/4" x 60" backboard
L	1	3/4" x 3-1/2" x 60" backboard shelf
M	2	22-3/8" x 22-3/8" x 1/4" pegboard leg braces

Mini-classic for mini DIYers

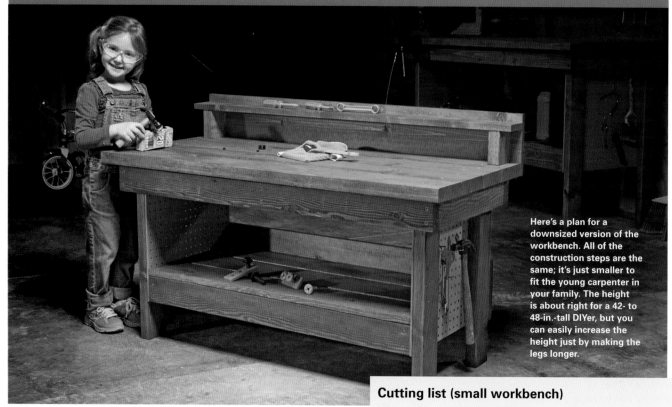

Here's a plan for a downsized version of the workbench. All of the construction steps are the same; it's just smaller to fit the young carpenter in your family. The height is about right for a 42- to 48-in.-tall DIYer, but you can easily increase the height just by making the legs longer.

Figure B: Small bench

Overall dimensions: 48" wide x 22-3/4" deep x 24" tall plus a 5-3/4" backboard

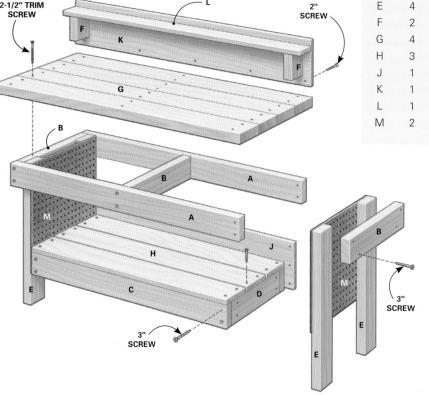

Cutting list (small workbench)

KEY	QTY.	SIZE & DESCRIPTION
A	2	1-1/2" x 3-1/2" x 45" top frame front and back
B	3	1-1/2" x 3-1/2" x 17-1/2" top frame crosspieces
C	2	1-1/2" x 3-1/2" x 38-1/2" shelf frame front and back
D	3	1-1/2" x 3-1/2" x 14-1/2" shelf crosspieces
E	4	1-1/2" x 3-1/2" x 22-1/2" legs
F	2	1-1/2" x 3-1/2" x 4" back shelf supports
G	4	1-1/2" x 5-1/2" x 48" top boards
H	3	3/4" x 5-1/2" x 38-1/2" shelf boards
J	1	3/4" x 7-1/4" x 42" back brace
K	1	3/4" x 7-1/4" x 48" backboard
L	1	3/4" x 3-1/2" x 48" backboard shelf
M	2	17-3/8" x 17-3/8" x 1/4" pegboard leg braces

Materials list (small workbench)

ITEM	QTY.
2x4 x 8' pine	4
2x6 x 8' pine	2
1x8 x 8' pine	1
1x6 x 10' pine	1
1x4 x 4' pine	1
2' x 4' x 1/4" pegboard	1
3" self-drilling screws	42
2" self-drilling screws	40
1-1/4" self-drilling screws	16
2-1/2" trim screws	24
Tube of construction adhesive	1

Workshop tips

Bucket-lid blade holder

I got tired of my extra saw blades banging around in the drawer every time I opened it, so I attached them to a 5-gallon bucket lid with a bolt and a thumbscrew. Now they stay put, and the lid protects my hands when I'm digging around for other stuff.

5-GALLON BUCKET LID

1/4" CARRIAGE BOLT

MAGNET

A safe chuck key holder

I used to hang the chuck key for my drill press on a string taped to the press. That worked well until the day I bumped it and the string caught the moving chuck and sent it flying. Luckily, it left an indentation in the wall instead of in me. Now I use a magnet to keep the chuck key handy—lesson learned.

Tape measures always within reach

I have a dozen tape measures, but there was never one around when I needed it. So I bought a bunch of electrical junction boxes and nailed them up in strategic locations—next to the miter saw, the table saw, on my workbench, in the garden shed—and put a tape measure and pencil in each one. No more searching for a tape in the middle of a project.

In-line workshop

Place your planer, router table and radial arm saw all in a line and at the same height with roller stands on each end. This allows you to take a long piece of stock and cut, rout or plane it all on one worktable.

READER PHOTO

Build shallow drawers

I have a pretty organized shop with lots of drawers, and here's my tip. If you're going to build drawers, build lots of shallow ones and very few deep ones. Here's why. Just about everything you store for a shop is fairly thin—hand tools, blades, fasteners, sandpaper, etc. If you have a ton of shallow drawers, you can dedicate each one by category. Plus, it's easier to find what you need when it's not buried under 8 inches of other junk in the same drawer.

–Travis Larson, *TFH* **Senior Editor**

Wire dispenser

A plastic crate is a great place to store anything on a spool. Just slip the spools onto a piece of metal conduit and secure the conduit with washers and bolts. There's even space below the spools for tools or scraps of wire.

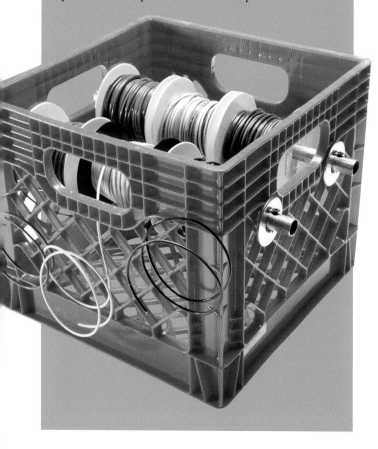

Keep track of screw bits

It's common now for a box of screws to include a bit—for star or Torx heads, for example. But small bits always seem to disappear just when you need them. So next time you buy a box of screws, store them in a glass jar and glue a magnet to the inside of the lid. The magnet holds the bit, and you don't have to dump out all the screws to find it.

Extension cord smarts

To prevent tangled extension cords, use hook-and-loop tape to keep long cords organized. Wind the cord in 10-ft. loops and wrap each coil with hook-and-loop tape. That way you can easily unwrap only what you need for a given job. It keeps the work site safer and you don't have to unwind and rewind 50 ft. of cord when you only need 11.

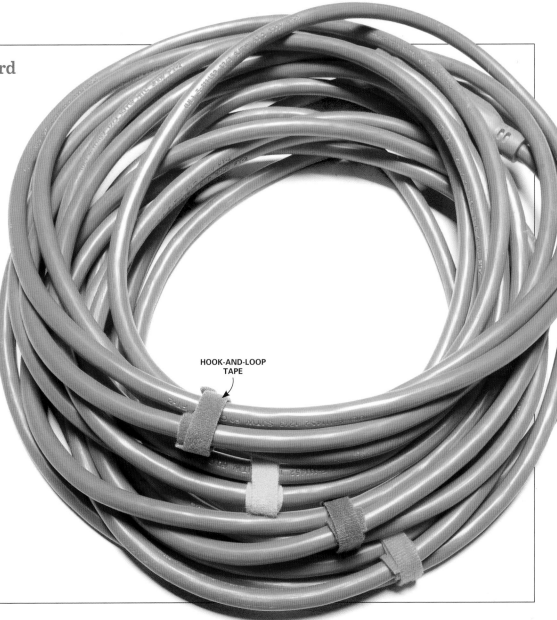

HOOK-AND-LOOP TAPE

Sheet metal drawer liners

If you're one of those people who uses old kitchen cabinets in your workshop, here's a tip for you. It's a bad idea to throw oily, greasy tools into those drawers, where the wood soaks up everything. Instead, take some careful measurements of the width, depth and height to any HVAC shop. The interiors will look like new, and you'll be able to clean them as needed.

Drywall knife protector

Here's a nifty way to keep the fine edges of your drywall knives from getting dinged up. Buy 3/8-in. clear tubing at the hardware store and cut lengths to fit the blades. Then take a sharp utility knife and slit the tubing lengthwise and slip it over the blade. The tubing is somewhat clingy, so it stays put even in a toolbox tote.

Handy razor blade storage

It's convenient to keep extra utility and straight box cutter blades near your workbench and in the garage. But the question is how to store them when they're not in use. One solution is to glue a magnetic business card (a refrigerator magnet) to the inside of a cupboard door and to your workbench with the magnetic side out. The magnet is strong enough to hold the blades in place even if you slam the cupboard door.

Saving hardwood scraps

Short scraps of hardwood are too good to throw away but hard to store neatly. So buy a 4-ft. tube form made for concrete footings, cut it in half (the cardboard-like material cuts easily) and set the tubes on end. Tack the tubes to a wall or a bench leg so they don't fall over. With the wood scraps stored upright, it's easy to find a piece just the right length. Tube forms are available in various diameters at home centers.

Blade storage tubes

If you use your reciprocating saw a lot, the tool case can become a mess. To keep the blades in order, make storage tubes from 1-1/4-in. PVC waste pipe and end caps. Just cut the pipe to length, glue one end and then label and store the blades. The open end gets friction-fitted with the cap. Now you can find the right blade at a glance!

Parts sorter

If you've stopped playing with your old Frisbee disc you can use it for sorting through small screws and parts in the shop. Just cut a notch in the rim to make it easy to pour the contents back into the original container.

Cake-pan hardware sorter

Here's another way to sort through your fasteners—make this timesaving device from an old baking pan. Using a bimetal hole saw, drill a hole slightly smaller than your jar opening. Carefully file and then sand the sharp edges around the cut edge. Now you can pour the contents into the pan, find what you need and then rake the contents through the hole back into the jar!

Shop-made parts boxes

Have you priced those plastic parts bins? Too expensive! Instead make your own out of scrap. The trick is to keep them modular. Make the front, back and bottom from 3/4- or 1/2-in. material, and the sides from 1/4-in. plywood. Nailed and glued together, they're plenty tough. These are 12 in. front to back (perfect for old kitchen upper cabinets), 3 in. tall, and either 3-1/2 in. or 7 in. wide. Save up some scrap and you can make a couple dozen in an hour or so.

Color-coded toolboxes

Are your tools constantly migrating from toolbox to toolbox? Solve the problem, by marking the handles of the tools and the corresponding toolbox with a band of colored electrical tape. Now all the tools will stay in the box where they belong.

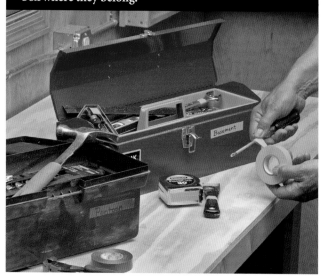

Plastic laminate labels

For quick, cheap drawer labels try scraps of plastic laminate. Round the corners, smooth the edges and attach them with hot-melt glue. You can write on the labels with pencil or marker, and erase them with a little solvent.

Caulk tube organizer

Tired of having your caulk tubes lying all over the workbench or your shelves? Make this organizer from a scrap of 2x8 and a piece of 1/4-in. plywood. Just lay out a pattern for your 2-in. hole saw to follow and drill holes through the 2x8. Then glue the plywood to the bottom. Now you can set it on a shelf and easily identify the tube you're looking for.

Easy-to-access cordless tool chargers

Mount charger stands for your cordless tools on scrap pieces of pegboard and hang them on a pegboard wall. Just pull one out for charging, or plug it into a power strip under the pegboard and charge batteries right on the pegboard. Most chargers have mounting holes or keyhole slots on the bottom. For those that don't, use a large hose clamp to mount them.

HOSE CLAMP

Circular saw luggage

An old bowling ball bag makes a great portable home for your circular saw. The saw easily slides in and out of the zippered opening, so there's no more coaxing it into that molded plastic case and fumbling with those stubborn plastic snaps. And there's plenty of room for spare blades, a rip guide and the blade-changing wrench. So, if you're spending more time building frames than bowling them, nab a secondhand bag for a couple of bucks at a yard sale or secondhand store.

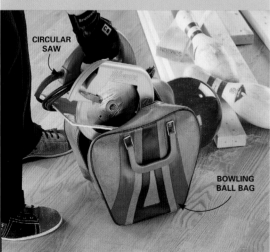

CIRCULAR SAW

BOWLING BALL BAG

Cordless drill holster

Make a nifty cordless drill holster by screwing a 45-degree 4-in. PVC elbow to the side of your workbench. Quick-draw the drill out of the holster when you're ready for action.

45° 4" PVC ELBOW

Floating shelves

*Customize them
to suit your room!*

You can buy inexpensive floating shelves in stores or online. But before you do that, consider building your own. For about the same cost, you can get the exact size, thickness and look you want. You can even finish them to match your trim or furniture. And your homemade shelves will be sturdier than most store-bought shelves— ours can support about 50 lbs. each. Plus, you'll earn serious bragging rights when you're done.

WHAT IT TAKES

TIME: Two to three hours per shelf

SKILLS: Beginner

TOOLS: Circular saw, belt sander (optional), brad nailer, edge-band trimmer, random orbit sander, drill/ driver, stud finder, 4-ft. level.

Money, time and tools

A pair of shelves cost us about $150 to build. We were able to make two shelves from a single 4 x 8-ft. sheet of 1/2-in.-thick red oak plywood. It can be tough to find locally, so call around before you shop, or choose different plywood.

Our shelves are 2-1/2 in. thick and 72 in. long, so finding veneer long enough on store shelves is also a challenge. You can special-order it at some home centers, however. We bought ours online from Rockler Woodworking and Hardware (rockler.com). You can find less expensive veneer, but we love this stuff because you don't have to heat it or apply any glue—it's just peel and stick! Expect to spend about $20 on stain and other assorted materials.

It took us a couple of hours to build each shelf, including sanding, staining and mounting on the wall. We made ours using a circular saw and cutting guide, but you can make them much faster with a table saw. And you can certainly hand-drive small nails, but it's much faster and easier to use a pneumatic brad nailer. You'll need a small compressor to power it. It also helps to have a random orbit sander, especially for sanding the sides flush before applying the veneer (see p. 130). Bonus points if you own a belt sander for scribing!

MEET THE EXPERT

Jason White has 15 years of woodworking experience and is an associate editor at *The Family Handyman.*

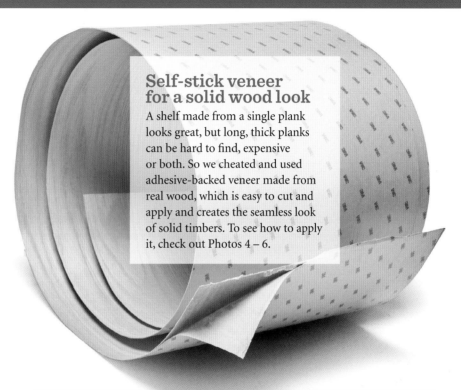

Self-stick veneer for a solid wood look

A shelf made from a single plank looks great, but long, thick planks can be hard to find, expensive or both. So we cheated and used adhesive-backed veneer made from real wood, which is easy to cut and apply and creates the seamless look of solid timbers. To see how to apply it, check out Photos 4 – 6.

CUTTING GUIDE

Build cutting guides for perfect cuts

It's hard to get nice, straight cuts without something to help guide your circular saw. That's where a cutting guide comes in. We used a self-squaring crosscut guide for short cuts and a longer guide for "rip" cuts. The guide shown here is just a narrow piece of 3/4-in. plywood attached on top of a wider piece of 1/4-in. plywood, with a squaring fence on the bottom. The base of the saw rides against the guide's "fence." To see how to make one, go to familyhandyman.com and search for "saw cutting guide."

1 **Cut the parts.** Using a 60-tooth blade in your circular saw and a cutting guide, cut all the parts to size (see "Build Cutting Guides for Perfect Cuts," p. 129.) A 4 x 8-ft. sheet of plywood will yield enough parts for two shelves.

CUTTING GUIDE

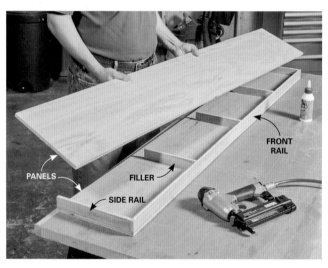

2 **Glue and nail the frame together.** Apply carpenter's glue to the edges of the rails and fillers and nail on the first panel with 1-in. brads. Then flip the shelf over and nail on the other panel.

PANELS

FILLER

SIDE RAIL

FRONT RAIL

3 **Sand the front and sides flush.** Using a random orbit sander and 100-grit sandpaper, sand the front and sides of the shelf so that the rails and panels are flush with each other. This will give you a flat, smooth surface on which to apply the veneer.

Cut and assemble the parts

Set a full sheet of 1/2-in. plywood on three or four 2x4s laid across sawhorses (Photo 1). Measure and mark the plywood for each of the shelf parts and use a circular saw and cutting guide (see "Build Cutting Guides for Perfect Cuts" on p. 129) to make your cuts. The cutting guide will help keep your cuts perfectly straight and minimize chip-out.

Next, glue and nail all the parts together (Photo 2). It helps to draw pencil lines on the top and bottom panels first so you'll know where to drive the nails for the fillers after you cover them with the top and bottom panels. With all eight parts cut to size, it's fairly easy to assemble the shelf with glue and nails. Start by laying the front rail (C) on end on top of your worktable (an old hollow-core door or plywood scrap on sawhorses works great), plus a couple of short support blocks cut from a 2x4. These blocks will support the top panel (A) while you glue and nail it onto the front rail. Carefully align the top and front pieces and use an 18-gauge pneumatic brad nailer to drive 1-in. brads.

Now stand the side rails (D) on end and glue and nail them to the top panel. Flip the whole thing over and install the fillers (E) with glue and brads. The fillers should be evenly spaced, but don't be too fussy because they'll be hidden once you install the bottom panel (B). Nail through the front rail into each of the fillers.

Then flip the whole thing over again and nail through the top panel into each of the fillers. Now flip the whole works over one more time and nail through the bottom panel into the fillers.

Apply the wood veneer

The top and bottom panels have exposed plywood edges that get covered with veneer. If those edges aren't perfectly smooth and flush with the faces of the front and side rails, the veneer won't stick properly. Sand everything flush with a random orbit sander and 100-grit sandpaper (Photo 3). Lay out the roll, veneer side down, and draw a straight line using a marker and straightedge at 3 in. wide along the entire length of the roll. This will give you 1/4 in. of overhang when you apply the veneer to the front and sides of the shelf.

Cut along the line with a pair of scissors and then cut the strip of veneer into three pieces for the front and two sides, leaving them long enough so there's 1/4 in. of overhang on each end (Photo 4). Apply the veneer to the sides first, being careful to keep the veneer aligned with the shelf (Photo 5). Don't peel and stick more than a few inches at a time, and rub a block of wood over the veneer to press it on. Cutting the pieces slightly oversize helps in case you don't get it on perfectly straight.

Pull an edge-banding trimmer apart and use one of the two sides to trim the veneer flush with the shelf (Photo 6). This method works well going with the grain of the veneer, but not when trimming across it. For the short cuts across the grain, back the veneer up with a block of wood and trim the veneer flush (on the sticky side) with a sharp utility knife. A handheld router with a flush-trimming bit also works well. Install the front veneer piece after the sides. Then drill several countersink holes in the back of the shelf for some No. 8 wood screws (Photo 7). Space the holes about 12 in. apart and 3/4 in. from the back edge.

Make a wall cleat

Cut a wall cleat (H) out of a straight 2x4 and make it 1-1/2 in. x 1-3/8 in. x 70-3/4 in. (Photo 8). Use your circular saw and the same cutting guide you used to cut the plywood pieces to width (set another 2x4 under the guide to keep it from tipping). Rip the cleat to width and then crosscut it to length. The narrow part of the cleat should slip into the hollow opening in the shelf with just a bit of wiggle room.

Using an electronic stud finder and painter's tape, find and mark the stud locations on the wall. Transfer the stud locations to the wall cleat and predrill holes in the cleat slightly smaller than the diameter of the shanks of the lag screws.

4 Cut the veneer to size. Using scissors, cut three pieces of oak veneer big enough to cover the front and sides of the shelf. Make them 3 in. wide so you'll have 1/4 in. of overhang on each side.

5 Stick on the veneer. Peel off the back and stick on the veneer, leaving a little bit of overhang on all four edges. Press the veneer on firmly with a block of wood.

VENEER

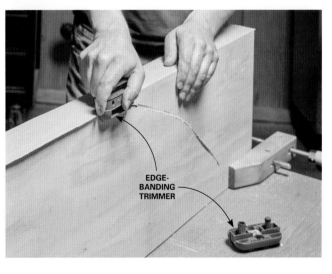

6 Trim the veneer flush. Using half of a handheld edge-banding trimmer, trim the veneer flush with the edges of the shelf. You can also use a router with a flush-trimming bit.

EDGE-BANDING TRIMMER

COUNTERSINKING DRILL BIT

7 **Drill holes for screws.** Drill countersink pilot holes in the top of the shelf for some No. 8 wood screws. Drill them 3/4 in. from the "wall" edge and space them about 12 in. apart.

8 **Cut the cleat to size.** Using a circular saw and a cutting guide, rip a wall cleat out of a 2x4. Make sure the 2x4 you're cutting from is dead straight.

STUD LOCATIONS

LAG SCREW

9 **Screw the cleat to the wall.** Drill pilot holes in the cleat and wall and secure the cleat with 4-in. lag screws. There's no need for fender washers if you use washer-head type screws like the ones shown.

10 **Scribe for a tight fit.** Hold the shelf over the cleat and firmly against the wall and drag a pencil along the wall to trace a scribe line onto the shelf. Scribing and sanding (next photo) allow shelves to fit perfectly against wall contours, but you can skip these steps if you don't mind a few gaps.

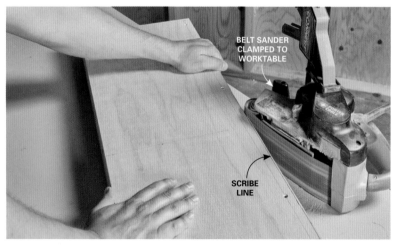

BELT SANDER CLAMPED TO WORKTABLE

SCRIBE LINE

11 **Sand to the scribe line.** Using a belt sander clamped to a sacrificial worktable, sand up to the scribe line on the shelf.

WOOD FILLER

12 **Fill nail holes.** Push "stainable" wood filler into the nail holes, leaving it slightly proud of the plywood in case of shrinkage.

Figure A
Exploded view

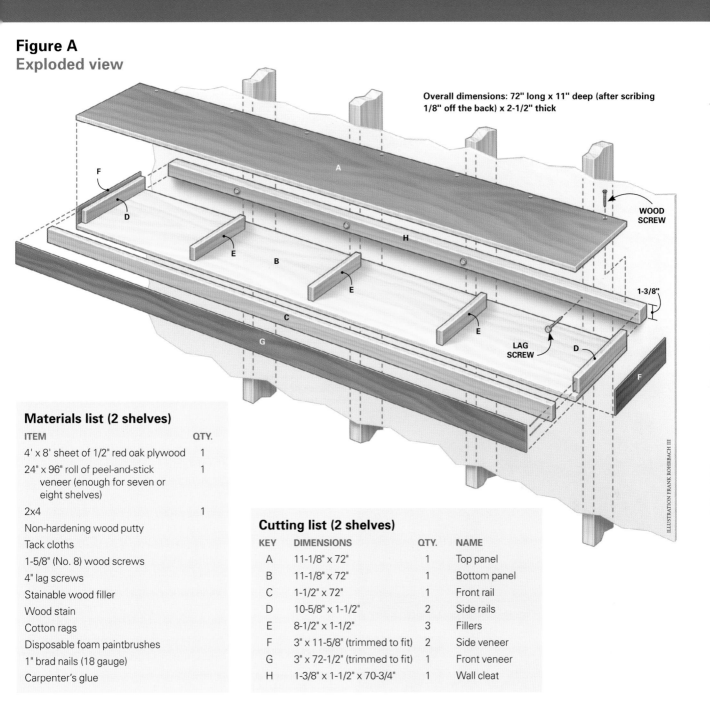

Overall dimensions: 72" long x 11" deep (after scribing 1/8" off the back) x 2-1/2" thick

WOOD SCREW

1-3/8"

LAG SCREW

ILLUSTRATION FRANK ROHRBACH III

Materials list (2 shelves)

ITEM	QTY.
4' x 8' sheet of 1/2" red oak plywood	1
24" x 96" roll of peel-and-stick veneer (enough for seven or eight shelves)	1
2x4	1
Non-hardening wood putty	
Tack cloths	
1-5/8" (No. 8) wood screws	
4" lag screws	
Stainable wood filler	
Wood stain	
Cotton rags	
Disposable foam paintbrushes	
1" brad nails (18 gauge)	
Carpenter's glue	

Cutting list (2 shelves)

KEY	DIMENSIONS	QTY.	NAME
A	11-1/8" x 72"	1	Top panel
B	11-1/8" x 72"	1	Bottom panel
C	1-1/2" x 72"	1	Front rail
D	10-5/8" x 1-1/2"	2	Side rails
E	8-1/2" x 1-1/2"	3	Fillers
F	3" x 11-5/8" (trimmed to fit)	2	Side veneer
G	3" x 72-1/2" (trimmed to fit)	1	Front veneer
H	1-3/8" x 1-1/2" x 70-3/4"	1	Wall cleat

Hold the cleat to the wall and drill pilot holes in the wall using the cleat as a drilling guide.

Drive 4-in. lag screws through the cleat and into the wall (Photo 9). Start by driving a lag screw on one end of the cleat, check for level, then screw down the other end before driving the middle screws.

Fit the shelf to the wall

Slip the shelf onto the cleat and tight to the wall. If your wall isn't perfectly flat, you'll see some small gaps between the shelf and the wall. You can eliminate those gaps by "scribing" the shelf to fit the contours of the wall (Photo 10), but this step is optional—skip it if you don't mind the gaps. To scribe, drag a pencil against the wall and trace a line onto the top of the shelf. The line follows the contours of the wall.

Now use a belt sander to sand up to the pencil line (Photo 11). Trying to sand freehand with the belt sander is tricky because if you don't hold the sander perfectly perpendicular to the shelf, the scribe on the top and bottom panels won't match and the shelf won't fit tight to the wall. Instead, turn the belt sander on its side and clamp it on top of a temporary worktable like an old door or scrap of plywood. Turn it on and adjust the belt tracking

13 **Sand and stain the shelf.** Sand all the sides of the shelf using 100- and 150-grit sandpaper. Remove all dust after sanding with the 100-grit to prevent loose granules from scratching the plywood's surface.

14 **Attach the shelf to the cleat.** Hold the shelf against the wall and drive 1-5/8-in. wood screws through the shelf's pilot holes and into the wall cleat.

WOOD SCREW

15 **Hide the screw heads.** Hide the screw heads with wood putty that matches the color of your stain. Use "non-hardening" putty so you can dig it out if you decide to remove the shelf someday.

NON-HARDENING WOOD PUTTY

so that the belt just barely disappears below the surface of the worktable (not all belt sanders let you do this). Run the shelf flat against your worktable and slowly sand up to the pencil line.

Sand, stain and install!

Using a fingertip or putty knife, push some "stainable" wood filler into each of the nail holes (Photo 12). The filler might shrink when it dries, so leave a bit extra in each hole–enough that it sits proud of the plywood. Once it dries, sand all sides of the shelf using a random orbit sander and 100- and then 150-grit sandpaper. After sanding with the 100-grit, vacuum or wipe off the sawdust so loose granules don't scratch up the shelf when you sand with the 150-grit. Vacuum up the dust or wipe it off with a tack cloth and apply stain following the directions on the can (Photo 13). If you want the shelf to look darker, wait a few hours and apply a second coat. Wait a day or two after staining and then brush on three coats of polyurethane for protection.

Holding the shelf over the cleat and tight to the wall, drive 1-5/8-in. wood screws through the pilot holes that you drilled earlier and into the wall cleat (Photo 14). Drive one of the middle screws first to help hold the shelf in place while you drive the others.

With the shelf secured, cover the exposed screw heads with a "non-hardening" type of wood filler colored to match your stain (Photo 15). This type of putty stays soft, allowing you to dig it out should you decide to remove the shelf someday.

Above-door display shelf

Your house has a couple dozen windows and doors. Which means you have a couple dozen places for installing display shelves.

As a bonus, if you increase the height and depth of the "box" that forms the core of each shelf, these shelves can double as valances for window curtains or blinds.

Your materials will vary based on the size of your window or door. There are a few key measurements to keep in mind as you customize this design to fit:

■ Make the inside of the box 1/8 in. longer than the door or window trim. That way, the box will easily fit over the trim.

■ The height of the box should be about the same as the width of the window or door trim (or you risk having the door hit the shelf when it opens). If this is

doubling as a valance, the box can hang below the trim.

■ The top shelf should overhang the three edges (the front and the two sides) of the box equally so the crown molding fits symmetrically.

Crown molding comes in a variety of styles and widths (from 2-1/4 in. to 6 in. and larger.) Mock up a small section of shelf to determine the best size and proportion of molding for your project.

Mount the completed shelf to the wall above the window or door. In most cases you'll be able to secure the shelf to the trim and framing along the sides and top of the opening. If not, use L-brackets mounted to the top of the shelf. **Note:** Use extra care if you mount this over an entry door (or one that your teenager slams a lot). Be sure all the displayed items are arranged securely behind the "lip" created by the cove molding.

1 **Build the core of the shelf.** Build the three-sided 1x3 box so it fits over your door trim. The 1x6 shelf should overhang the ends the same amount as it does the front.

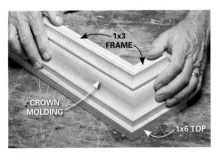

2 **Install the crown molding.** Cut and install the crown molding. Install the 3/4-in. cove molding along the edge of the top shelf, letting it protrude 1/4 in. upward to create a lip.

Figure A
Display shelf

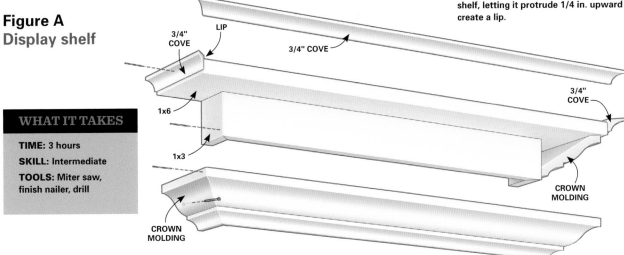

WHAT IT TAKES

TIME: 3 hours

SKILL: Intermediate

TOOLS: Miter saw, finish nailer, drill

Showcase shelving
Stunning looks—and more space!

Nightstands are just not big enough for everything: lamp, alarm clock, phone, photos of your kids ... so books, magazines, your tablet or your cup of tea ends up on the floor.

This shelf unit gives you about 10 times more space for decorative and essential stuff. And its dazzling design will transform your room. Best of all, it's easy to build with basic tools.

1 Cut plywood sheets into strips. Mark the width of the cut on both ends of the sheet. Align the ends of the straightedge guide with the marks and clamp the ends. Make sure to place the guide on the "keeper" side of the marks. Run the saw along the guide to complete the cut.

STRAIGHTEDGE SAW GUIDE

CROSSCUT SAW GUIDE

2 Cut the strips to length. A crosscut guide allows you to make perfectly square cuts exactly where you want them. Mark the cut location and line up the guide. Clamp the guide and make the cut. Make sure to keep the saw bed tight to the guide fence as you make the cut.

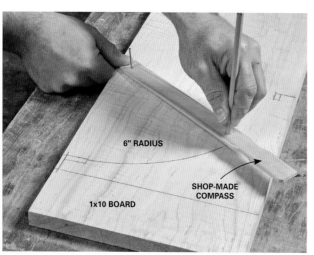

6" RADIUS

SHOP-MADE COMPASS

1x10 BOARD

3 Mark the curved brackets. Use the dimensions in Figure A to mark the shape of the bracket on the 1x10 board. Drill a nail hole and pencil hole in a scrap of wood to use as a compass. Cut out the shape with a jigsaw. Sand the curve until it's smooth. Then use this bracket as a template to mark the three remaining brackets.

Getting started

The first step is to round up the tools and materials you'll need to build this project. We used birch plywood because it provided the closest grain match to our bedroom furniture. If you're planning to stain the shelves to match your furniture, try to find plywood that has a similar grain pattern. For less common plywood like cherry or walnut, check with a local hardwood supplier, cabinet shop or full-service lumberyard.

If you plan to paint, you can build the shelves out of any plywood with tight grain (birch is a good choice). We used a 2-in. cove molding along the top. You probably won't find this molding at a home center, but you can special-order it or choose a similar profile.

We've kept the construction simple to allow you to build this project even if you don't have a shop full of tools. All of the plywood is joined with trim-head screws and there are a few spots where the screw head holes are visible. If you own a biscuit joiner or doweling jig, you could eliminate visible fasteners by joining the plywood with biscuits or dowels.

Cut out the parts

Photos 1 and 2 show how to cut the plywood parts using saw guides and a circular saw. Use the Cutting List (p. 139) and Figure A as a guide. This plan is sized for a queen-size bed. If your bed is wider than 64 in., you'll have to build the center shelf unit wider. We've added 1/16 in. to the length of part H to compensate for plywood that's only 23/32 in. thick. If your plywood is a full 3/4 in. thick, cut these parts to 24-3/4 in. long instead.

WHAT IT TAKES

TIME: One weekend, plus finishing.

SKILL LEVEL: Intermediate to advanced.

TOOLS: Circular saw, jigsaw, miter saw, drill, edge-band trimmer, standard carpentry tools, level.

OPTIONAL TOOLS: Finish nailer, table saw.

Figure A: Showcase shelving

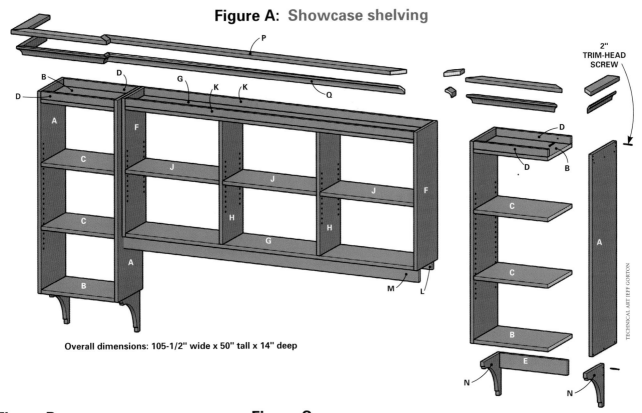

Overall dimensions: 105-1/2" wide x 50" tall x 14" deep

2" TRIM-HEAD SCREW

TECHNICAL ART JEFF GORTON

Figure B
Molding detail

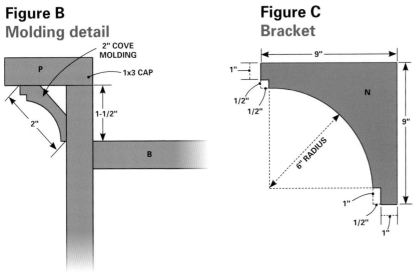

2" COVE MOLDING

1x3 CAP

1-1/2"

2"

P

B

Figure C
Bracket

9"

1"

1/2"

1/2"

N

9"

6" RADIUS

1"

1/2"

1"

Materials list

ITEM	QTY.
4' x 8' x 3/4" plywood	2
1x10 board	4 lin. ft.
1x3 board	14 lin. ft.
2" cove molding	14 lin. ft.
Edge-banding veneer	70 lin. ft.
2-3/4" cabinet screws	10
2" trim-head screws	60
1-1/4" trim-head screws	8
1-1/2" finish nails	
1" finish nails	
1/4" shelf pins	28

Figure D
Pegboard jig

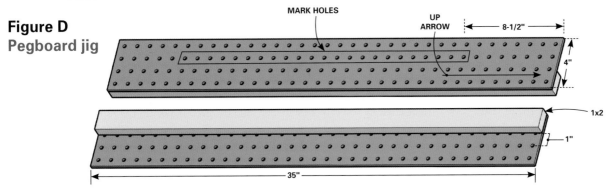

MARK HOLES

UP ARROW

8-1/2"

4"

1x2

1"

35"

For help with building the saw guides, go to familyhandyman.com and search for "circular saw long cuts." Make sure to use a top-quality, 40-tooth carbide blade in your circular saw to reduce chipping and tear-out. A table saw, along with a crosscutting sled, would be a good alternative to a circular saw for cutting the plywood.

Cut the brackets (N) from a solid 1x10 board. Using Figure C as a guide, mark the shape on the 1x10 board. Photo 3 shows how to draw the curve. Cut out the brackets with a jigsaw. Then sand the curves to get rid of saw marks and smooth them out. Use the first bracket as a pattern to mark the rest.

Hide the plywood edges

Using iron-on edge-banding veneer is an easy way to finish the plywood edges. You'll find birch and oak edge-banding veneer at home centers, but if you need cherry or some other species, check online or go to a local woodworking supplier.

Photos 4 and 5 show how to apply the edge banding. You only need to apply edge banding to the edges that show. Parts A, F, L, M and E require edge banding on one end as well as the long side. Buy a cheap iron or find one at a garage sale, but don't use your clothes iron. Set the iron to a high setting like "cotton." Practice on a scrap of plywood to get the hang of how fast to move the iron. You want to melt the glue without burning the veneer. Immediately after you iron on the edge banding, slide a small block of wood from end to end while pressing down firmly. This will ensure good adhesion. Trim off the overhanging ends with a sharp utility knife. Then trim off the overhanging veneer from the edges (Photo 5).

We show a FastCap edge-band trimmer that trims both sides at once, but you can also use a single-edge trimmer. You'll find edge-band trimmers at woodworking stores and online. For more information on edge banding, go to p. 261 or visit familyhandyman.com and search for "edge banding." Finish up by carefully sanding the edges with 120-grit sandpaper to create a perfectly flush, smooth edge.

IRON-ON VENEER EDGE BAND

4 **Apply edge banding with an iron.** Cut iron-on edge banding about an inch longer than you need. Center the strip on the edge of the plywood and iron it on. Keep the iron moving. As soon as you're done applying heat, rub over the entire surface with a small chunk of wood to ensure good adhesion. Trim off the overhanging ends with a sharp utility knife.

EDGE-BAND TRIMMER

5 **Trim edge banding.** Starting at one end, slide the special edge-band trimming tool along the edge banding to slice off any overhanging veneer. Carefully sand the edge to remove any trace of overhanging veneer.

Build the shelf units

With the parts cut and edge-banded, it's time to start building. Photo 6 shows a simple right-angle jig you can build to help hold the parts in position as you screw them together.

Make light pencil lines across parts A and F to indicate the centerline of parts B and G to help you place the screws accurately. Drill 1/8-in. pilot holes 2 in. from each end and in the center to guide the screws. Then drive the 2-in. trim-head screws until they're

RIGHT-ANGLE ASSEMBLY JIG

6 **Hold the box parts square.** It's a lot easier to assemble the pieces if you have a right-angle jig to hold them steady while you drill pilot holes and drive screws. Make the jig out of scraps of plywood. Then line up the parts and clamp them to the jig.

TRIM-HEAD SCREW

7 **Assemble shelves with screws.** For easy assembly, join the sides to the tops and bottoms with trim-head screws. Drill 1/8-in. pilot holes first. Then drive the screws until the heads are slightly recessed. After the first coat of finish, fill the screw head recesses with soft wood putty to match the stain and cover with a final coat of finish.

slightly recessed (Photo 7). Don't worry if the shelves are still a little wobbly. They'll be held firmly in position when you mount them to the wall. While you're at it, screw the pairs of brackets (N) to the cleats (E).

Drill shelf pin holes

For adjustable-height shelves, we drilled a series of 1/4-in. holes to accept shelf pins. If you don't think you'll adjust the height of the shelves, just drill four holes at each shelf

location. It's easier to make sure the holes are aligned if you drill them after you've assembled the shelves. We positioned the shelf pin holes so that a shelf can be centered in the middle unit, and approximately evenly spaced in the two outside units. We also offset the holes in the two center dividers (H) so the pins don't run into each other. Most of the holes are 1 in. from the front and back edges. The holes in the center of the middle unit are 1-1/2 in. from the front and back edges.

Photo 8 shows how to use a 1/4-in. pegboard jig as a guide for drilling the shelf pin holes. To avoid confusion, we made mirror-image jigs to use on the right and left sides of each upright. Make an arrow pointing up to keep the guide properly oriented and mark the holes you intend to drill. Cut a 3/4-in. square scrap of wood or dowel and drill a hole in it to use as a drill stop (Photo 8). Practice on a scrap to get the correct hole depth. Drill all the holes in the taller outside units first. Then cut off the pegboard guides and use them for the middle shelves. Reposition the stop to drill the offset holes for the center shelves.

Mount the shelves

We stained and varnished the shelf units and the moldings that go on top before installing them. If you need help with this part of the project, there's a ton of good information on staining and painting at familyhandyman.com. Whether you're staining or painting the shelves, plan to apply a final coat of finish after they're installed and the moldings are put on. That will allow you to fill the nail and screw head holes and cover them with a coat of paint or varnish.

To get ready for the installation, mark the center of the bed with a piece of masking tape. If you have a headboard, mark the height. Then move the bed out of the way. Use a stud finder or some other method to locate the studs and mark them with tape. Then determine how high you want the center shelves to be. We chose to position the shelves a few inches above the headboard, which in our case was 60 in. above the floor. This

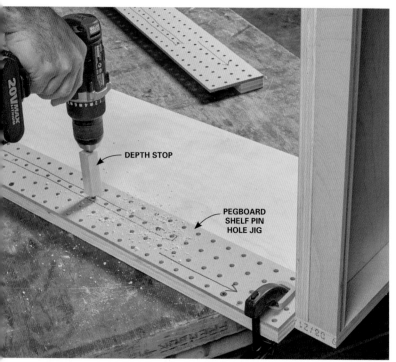

8 Drill holes for shelf pins. To avoid mix-ups, drill the shelf pin holes after assembling the shelves. Build mirror-image drill guides from 1/4-in. pegboard with 1x2 stops. Drill a hole in a block of wood to use as a drill-bit depth stop.

DEPTH STOP

PEGBOARD SHELF PIN HOLE JIG

9 Mount the center shelf. Level the ledger (L) and attach it to the wall studs with trim screws. Rest the center shelf unit on the ledger, aligning the sides with the ends of the ledger. Make sure the sides are plumb. Then drive screws through the hanging cleat into the studs to hold the shelf in place. Drive trim-head screws down through the bottom shelf into the ledger.

LEDGER

STUD MARK

is a good height to allow headroom for sitting up in most beds. Draw a level pencil line at your chosen height. Align the plywood ledger (L) with the mark, center it on the bed location and fasten it to the studs with trim-head screws. Now it's easy to install the center shelf unit by resting it on the cleat. Before you screw the center shelf unit to the studs (Photo 9), make sure the ends are lined up with the plywood ledger and the sides are perfectly plumb.

Next install the two outside shelf units by lining up the tops and screwing through the hanging strip (D) into the studs (Photo 10). Connect the shelf units with 1-1/4-in. trim-head screws.

Snug the brackets (N) up to the bottom of the outside shelves and screw through the hanging cleat (E) into the studs.

Finish up by installing the molding

The final step is to cut and nail on the 1x3 cap and 2-in. cove molding that fits under it (Photo 11). Start by cutting the cap pieces and nailing them onto the top of the shelves. We used a finish nailer. If you're hand-nailing the cap and moldings, drill pilot holes for the finish nails to avoid splitting the cap or moldings. Hold the back edge of the 1x3 cap flush to the back of the plywood and cut 45-degree miters at the corners.

Install the cove molding (Q) after the cap is done. Miter the outside corners. Since the inside corners will be perfectly square, you should be able to miter them rather than cope them. But you can use whichever method you prefer. Take your time and expect to spend several hours on this part of the project. There are a lot of little pieces to cut. Keep your fingers a safe distance from the blade by cutting the small pieces of cove molding from long lengths.

When you're done mounting the shelves and installing the moldings,

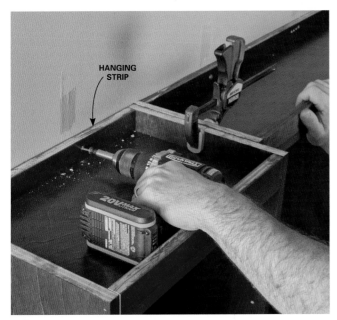

HANGING STRIP

10 Add the end units. Align the top of the outside shelf unit with the top of the center shelf unit. Make sure the top is level. Then drive screws through the hanging cleat into wall studs to support it. Center the decorative brackets under the shelf and attach them to the wall studs with screws.

CAP

COVE

11 Install the cove molding. Finish up by installing the cap and cove molding to the tops of the cabinets. Miter the inside and outside corners. We used a finish nail gun, but you can also drill pilot holes and attach the moldings with trim nails. Fill the nail holes with soft putty to match the stain.

Cutting list

KEY	QTY.	DIMENSIONS	NAME
3/4" plywood			
A	4	11-7/8" x 40"	Outside sides
B	4	11-7/8" x 16-1/2"	Outside tops and bottoms
C	4	11-7/8" x 16-3/8"	Outside shelves
D	4	1-1/2" x 16-1/2"	Outside hanging and filler strips
E	2	3" x 15"	Bracket hanging cleat
F	2	9-7/8" x 27-3/4"	Center sides
G	2	9-7/8" x 64-1/2"	Center top and bottom
H	2	9-7/8" x 24-13/16"	Center dividers
J	3	9-7/8" x 20-7/8"	Center shelves
K	2	1-1/2" x 64-1/2"	Center hanging and filler strips
L	1	1-1/2" x 66"	Center ledger strip
M	1	2-1/2" x 66"	Center light valance
Boards and molding			
N	4	Cut to pattern	Brackets
P	7	3/4" x 2-1/2" (cut to fit)	Cap
Q	7	Cut to fit	Cove molding

Figure E
Cutting diagrams

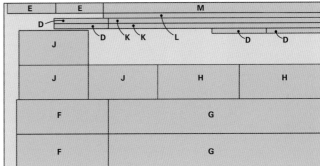

nail and screw head holes will be showing. If your shelves are stained, fill the holes with soft wood putty to match. You can even blend colors to get a closer match. For painted shelves, fill the holes with lightweight spackle, let it dry and sand it. Then apply the final coat of finish.

Lighted display wall

Turn a bland wall into a showstopper!

There aren't many DIY projects that will give you as much bang for the buck as this dramatic drywall showcase. Granted, you'll have a chunk of time invested before you're done, but the materials are readily available and inexpensive. As you'll see, it's just 2x6 framing covered with drywall. And the beauty of this type of construction is that the design is limited only by your imagination. You can build shelves just like ours, or you can design any other size and shape you like. Here we'll show you how to build the frame, hang the drywall, and finish the project with corner bead and drywall tape. We'll also show you how to add an outlet for the TV and wire the switch and lights. For more information on how to hang and tape drywall and install outlets, switches and rough-in wiring, go to familyhandyman.com.

Our wall is 12 ft. wide with a 9-ft. ceiling. We designed the 18-in.-deep shelves to accommodate home theater gear and the center rectangle to fit around a 60-in. TV screen. This arrangement also looks great even if your ceilings are only 8 ft. high. And keep in mind that you don't have to build your shelves wall to wall. You can leave one or both ends exposed and simply finish them with drywall.

We used a computer drawing program called Sketchup to design these shelves. But you can use graph paper or just map it out on the wall. We first added about 5 in. to the width and height of the TV, and then centered this rectangle on the wall. When we were satisfied with the design, we marked the wall at the vertical and horizontal framing locations and chalked lines to get a better sense of how it would look (Photo 1). We left a 1/2-in. space between the 2x6 framing and the floor, walls and ceiling. The 1/2-in. space serves two purposes. First, it allows you to prebuild the framing and slip it in without trying to fit it exactly to the room. And second, the 1/2-in. space creates a perimeter that's the same width (6-1/2 in.) as the rest of the vertical and horizontal dividers after they're covered with drywall.

Getting started

If your room is carpeted, you can either build right over the carpet, or peel it back and hire a carpet layer to reattach it after you're done. You can cut the baseboard molding in place, or remove it like we did and reinstall it when the shelves are done. Make sure the framing isn't going to cover an electrical outlet. If it is, you'll have to relocate the outlet or change your design. We've included a Shelf Materials List on p. 149, but you'll have to adjust the quantities for your design.

Measure the distance from the floor to the ceiling at both ends of your proposed shelves. Then measure the distance between the walls at both the top and the bottom. Subtract 1 in. from the smallest measurement of both the width and the height. Use these dimensions to build the frames.

Build the frames

The 2x6 framing consists of a full-length base and top, four vertical columns and shelves. You can build all of the parts in your garage or backyard (Photo 3) and move them into your room to assemble. Cut the 2x6s for the top and bottom to

Dramatic results with cheap materials

Stunning projects usually carry a stunning price tag. Not this one. It requires only common 2x6 framing lumber, drywall, corner beads and joint compound. And you can get everything off-the-shelf at your local home center or hardware store.

1 **Mark it out on the wall.** Mark the location of the framing and snap chalk lines on the wall. Make sure there's at least 1/2 in. between the outside lines and the walls, floor and ceiling, and that the lines are level and plumb.

COLUMNS

SHELF

3 **Build the frames.** Pick the straightest lumber for the long lengths and cut the parts. Mark the front and the back of the base and top for the column locations. Mark the column sides for the shelves. Then build the U-shape and box-shape backers and nail the parts together.

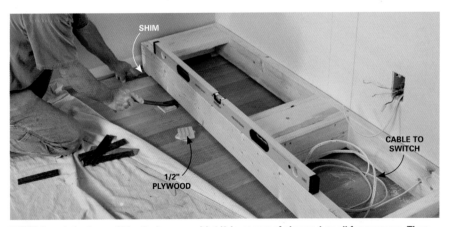

SHIM

1/2" PLYWOOD

CABLE TO SWITCH

4 **Level the base.** Shim the base up with 1/2-in. scraps of plywood on all four corners. Then use a level and add shims as needed to level the frame across the front and from front to back. Add shims under each column. Screw the frame to the wall studs.

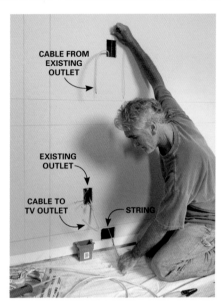

CABLE FROM EXISTING OUTLET

EXISTING OUTLET

CABLE TO TV OUTLET

STRING

2 **Add a switch and outlet.** If your project includes a TV and lights, you'll need another outlet and a switch. Start by turning off the power to the existing outlet. Cut a hole for the new TV outlet and another hole directly below, near the floor. Extend NM (nonmetallic) electrical cable from the existing outlet to the new TV outlet. Run another cable from the new outlet through the hole near the floor. Leave enough cable to reach your switch location plus at least 12 in. of extra cable (Figure B).

length and mark the column locations. If you have a miter saw, set up a stop and cut all the short crosspieces you'll need.

You can see from Figure A that you'll need three crosspieces, assembled into a U-shape at each column location. Use L-shape crosspieces at the ends. Nail the top and bottom frames together. Then build the columns. The center columns have 2x6 boxes at each shelf location to provide backing for the drywall on both sides. We added flatwise 2x6s to provide backing for our glass-shelf supports. Finally, build the shelves.

Prepare for wiring

If you're going to add lights and another outlet, add the new outlet box and the cable that runs to the switch before you install the framing (Photo 2). The first step is to turn off the power to the outlet, and double-check that the power is off by testing the wires with a noncontact voltage detector. Then remove the outlet and twist wire connectors onto the black wires as an extra precaution. Determine whether the wires are 12 or 14 gauge. Then count the wires in the box and calculate the box size required, including the extra hot, neutral and ground wire you'll be adding. Go to familyhandyman.com and search for "dimmer switch" for information on calculating box sizes. If the box is too small, cut it out and add a larger one.

Remove a knockout from the top of the box for the new cable. If the box is metal and doesn't include built-in cable connectors, add a cable connector to the new cable. Next, cut the hole for the TV outlet. To make running new cable much easier, try to choose a location that's in the same stud space as the existing outlet. If this isn't possible, you'll have to cut out some drywall to drill through studs. Mark around the remodel box and cut the hole. Also cut a hole near the floor, directly under the TV outlet hole.

Match the gauge of the new cable—12 or 14 gauge—to the gauge of the wire in the existing box. Run the NM (nonmetallic) cable with ground from the existing outlet to the new outlet, and from the new outlet to the hole near the floor. Leave 12 in. of extra cable at the new outlet. Then run enough cable from the new outlet through the hole near the floor to reach your new switch location. Be generous with the cable to the switch to be certain you'll have at least an extra foot at the switch location. That's all the wiring you need to do for now.

Install the framing

Tack small squares of 1/2-in. plywood to the four corners of the bottom frame. Drill a 3/4-in. hole in the back 2x6 to feed the cable through. Set the frame in place and level it by adding shims if necessary (Photo 4). When the frame is level, add scraps of 1/2-in. plywood and shims under the two column locations. Make sure the frame is centered, with a 1/2-in. space on each end, and screw it to the wall. Next, install the columns

5 **Set the columns.** Screw the outside columns to the base. Plumb them and attach them to the wall with screws or drywall anchors. Position the center columns, plumb them and attach them the same way.

(Photo 5). Use a level to make sure the end column is plumb and screw it to the bottom frame and to the wall. If there is no stud to drive screws into, use toggle-type drywall anchors to hold the column against the wall. Then use the shelves as spacers to make sure the columns are in the correct locations before you screw them to the base. There should be a 1/2-in. space between the wall and the end columns.

Next, set the top frame in place on the columns. Screw the top frame to the wall, and screw the top of the columns to the top frame (Photo 6). Finish the framing by installing the shelves (Photo 7).

6 **Mount the top frame.** Slide the top into place over the columns. Line up the columns so the shelves fit and screw them to the top frame. Then screw the top frame to the wall.

Rough-in the wiring

Before you start your project, contact your local inspections department to find out if an electrical permit is required. In most cases the wiring will need to be inspected before you cover it with drywall. The new electrical code requires an AFCI (arc-fault circuit interrupter) in many areas when new wiring is added. Ask your inspector if an AFCI is required in your situation. If so, simply replace the existing outlet with an AFCI receptacle, and run power from the "load" side of the AFCI outlet to the new TV outlet and then on to the switch and lights. Any new receptacle outlets must also be tamper resistant.

Figure A
Shelf framing

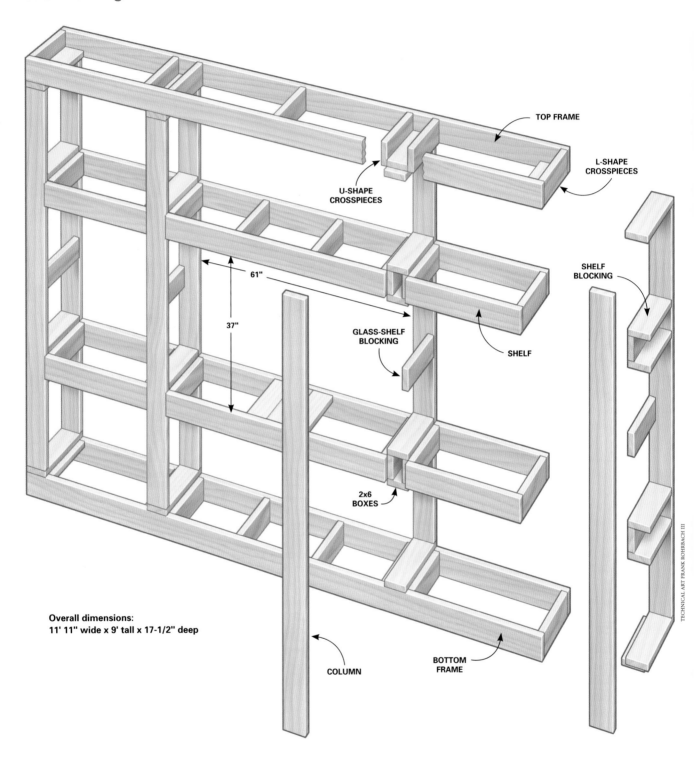

TOP FRAME

L-SHAPE
CROSSPIECES

U-SHAPE
CROSSPIECES

SHELF
BLOCKING

61"

37"

GLASS-SHELF
BLOCKING

SHELF

2x6
BOXES

Overall dimensions:
11' 11" wide x 9' tall x 17-1/2" deep

COLUMN

BOTTOM
FRAME

TECHNICAL ART FRANK ROHRBACH III

Start wiring by nailing a switch box to the frame in a convenient location, and then drilling 3/4-in. holes through the framing to make a path for the new cables (Photo 8 and Figure B). Run lengths of cable from the TV outlet to the switch, from the switch to the first light fixture, and between the light fixtures. Leave a 2-ft. loop of extra cable at each light fixture location. For details on rough-in wiring, go to familyhandyman.com and search for "wiring."

We ordered our 3-in. recessed light fixtures online because the fixtures we found at a home center were too tall to fit in the drywall space and still meet the electrical code requirement of 1/2-in. space between the fixture and the combustible surfaces. We chose remodel-type fixtures, which are installed after the drywall is finished. You can choose any non-IC (insulation contact) fixture you like, as long as there's at least 1/2 in. between the fixture, and any combustible material and insulation are kept more than 3 in. away. You can use any IC-rated fixture that will fit in the space.

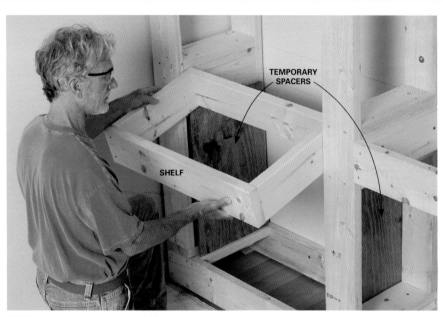

7 Position the shelves with spacers. Cut scraps of plywood as spacers. Rest each shelf on the spacers and screw them to the columns. This will ensure that the shelves are lined up precisely. You'll need another set of spacers for the top shelves.

Shelf materials list

ITEM	QTY.
2x6 x 8' SPF (spruce, pine, fir)	22
2x6 x 12' SPF (spruce, pine, fir)	4
4' x 8' x 1/2" drywall	8
8' drywall corner beads	14
Scraps of 1/2" plywood	
Shims	2 pkgs.
16d nails	2 lbs.
3" construction screws	2 lbs.
1-1/4" drywall screws	2 lbs.
1-1/4" ring-shank drywall nails	2 lbs.
1"-long, 1/4"-crown staples (optional)	1 box
45-minute setting-type joint compound	2 bags
Premixed joint compound	1 bucket
Paper tape	1 roll
Mesh tape	1 roll

Optional

1/4" glass shelves	2
Glass-shelf supports	8

8 Rough-in the electrical wiring. Drill holes and run the cable to the switch box and then to the recessed light fixture locations. Leave at least 2 ft. of extra cable at each light. Secure the cables with 1/2-in. plastic staples.

Figure B
Electrical diagrams

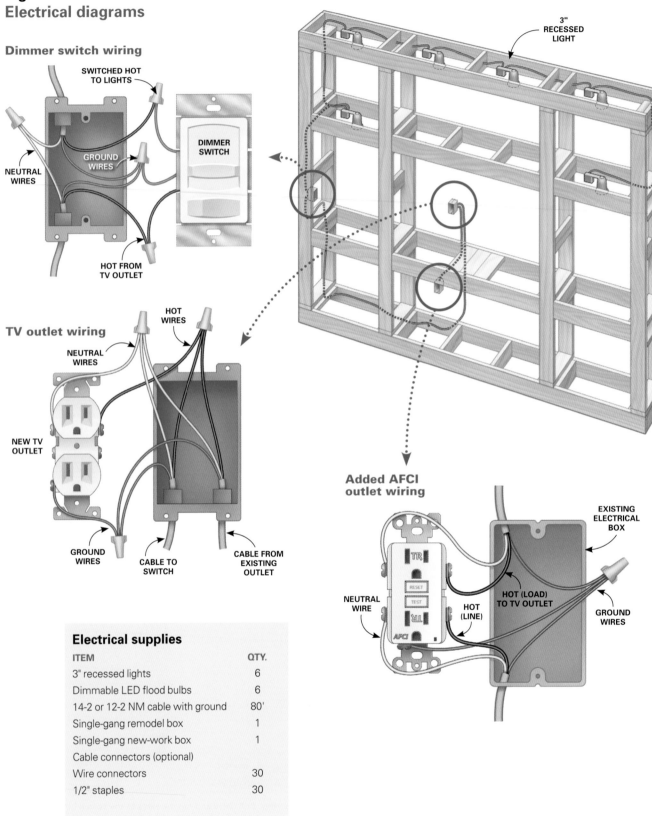

Dimmer switch wiring

SWITCHED HOT
TO LIGHTS

DIMMER
SWITCH

GROUND
WIRES

NEUTRAL
WIRES

HOT FROM
TV OUTLET

3"
RECESSED
LIGHT

TV outlet wiring

HOT
WIRES

NEUTRAL
WIRES

NEW TV
OUTLET

GROUND
WIRES

CABLE TO
SWITCH

CABLE FROM
EXISTING
OUTLET

**Added AFCI
outlet wiring**

EXISTING
ELECTRICAL
BOX

TR

RESET

TEST

TR

AFCI

NEUTRAL
WIRE

HOT
(LINE)

HOT (LOAD)
TO TV OUTLET

GROUND
WIRES

Electrical supplies

ITEM	QTY.
3" recessed lights	6
Dimmable LED flood bulbs	6
14-2 or 12-2 NM cable with ground	80'
Single-gang remodel box	1
Single-gang new-work box	1
Cable connectors (optional)	
Wire connectors	30
1/2" staples	30

9 Install the drywall. Attach the drywall with screws. If you plan to caulk the back edges, get a tight fit between the drywall and wall. Shave off overhanging edges at the front so they don't interfere with corner bead installation.

10 Nail on the top and bottom corner beads. Notch one of the corner beads as shown here. Push it into the corner and mark the opposite end. Notch the other end the same way. Fit the corner bead into the opening and staple or nail it. Repeat on the opposite side of the opening.

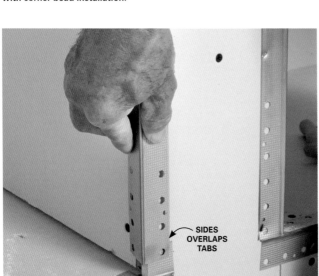

11 Add corner beads to the sides. Cut the side pieces to fit between the top and the bottom notched corner beads so they overlap the metal tabs. Line up the corners and attach the beads with nails or staples.

12 Attach corner bead with a stapler. Using a 1/4-in.-crown, pneumatic stapler and 1-in.-long staples, drive staples every 6 in. and wherever the corner bead is buckled out. Then cover the edge of the bead with mesh tape.

When the wiring is in place, call for a rough-in wiring inspection. After the wiring is approved, move on to the drywall and corner bead.

Cover the frame with drywall

You can cut the drywall the usual way by scoring one side with a utility knife, bending it to break at the scored line, and then cutting the paper backing. But for fast, super-clean cuts, we used a table saw to cut the drywall. We have a table saw with a good dust collection system, so it wasn't too dusty. But you could also cut the drywall outdoors with a circular saw and a straightedge. Stack four pieces of drywall and cut all of them in one pass. We started by cutting a 2-1/2-in.-wide strip from the edge of each sheet to remove the tapered section. We did this to avoid having a tapered edge under the corner bead or at the back where we wanted to caulk the back edges rather than tape them (Photo 15). If you're using the score-and-break method, clean up the cut edges with a rasp.

Once the pieces are cut to width, it's easy to cut them to length and screw them to the framing. Mark the length and use a

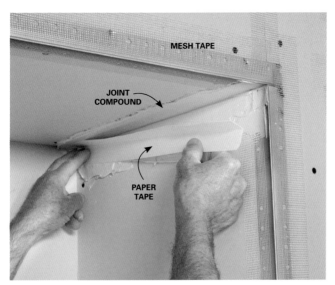

13 Tape the inside corners. Spread a layer of joint compound on both sides of the corner. Cut a piece of paper tape and fold it to fit in the corner. Press the tape in with your fingers. Then embed it with your taping knife. Spread a thin layer of compound over the top of the tape.

14 Fill the bead. Mix about a half bag of setting compound with water. Spread a thick layer of compound between the corner beads and smooth with an 8-in. taping knife. Fill both sides of all beads. Recoat after the compound firms up.

drywall square to score them. All drywall cuts should be 1/8 in. to 1/4 in. less than the actual measurements. You can easily fill gaps, but drywall will break along the edge if you try to force it in. Attach the drywall with 1-1/4-in. drywall screws. Use a special drywall screw gun, or buy a special bit for your cordless drill that sets the screws just under the surface without driving them too deep.

Nail on the corner bead

There are several types of corner bead. You can buy perforated plastic corner bead that attaches with spray adhesive, or paper-faced corner bead that you embed in a layer of joint compound. But we decided to use conventional metal corner bead. To speed up the process, we used a 1/4-in.-crown, air-powered stapler to fasten the beads (Photo 12). You can buy a stapler or simply fasten the corner bead with 1-1/4-in. ring-shank drywall nails.

You'll need a tin snips to cut the corner bead. Photos 10 and 11 show an easy method for cutting the metal beads to length and creating a strong corner. The key to installing corner beads is to press them in until the outside corner is just slightly proud of the drywall before driving the fasteners. Also, adjust the position of the bead so the corners of adjoining beads line up. For extra insurance against cracking, cover all the corner bead edges with adhesive-backed mesh tape.

Tape the corners and fill the bead

To save time, we decided to confine our taping to the intersection of the sides and tops of the drywall recesses (Photo 13). We caulked the back edges later (Photo 15). Start by taping the inside corners. Then fill the corner beads with joint compound. Use 45-minute setting-type compound for this. Mix the powder with water according to the instructions on the bag. Then use an 8-in.

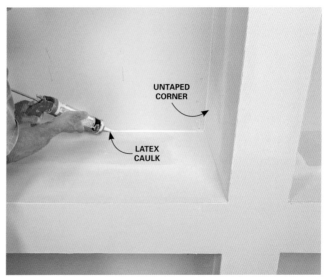

15 Caulk the back corners. Avoid a lot of tricky corner taping by caulking the back inside corners. Cut the tip of the latex caulk tube carefully to create a very small hole. Then apply a neat bead of caulk and smooth it out with your finger.

taping knife to fill the corner beads (Photo 14). We used almost two full bags of setting compound for this project. When the joint compound has firmed up to the consistency of soap, carve off any lumps and high spots with your taping knife. You can add another coat as soon as the compound hardens. You don't have to wait for it to dry completely.

Don't rush this part of the job. Plan on spending a few hours a day for several days. Use premixed joint compound for the final coats, letting it dry between each coat. Trowel on thin coats until you've got a smooth, flat surface. Let the final coat dry. Then sand carefully with 120-grit drywall sandpaper mounted on a drywall

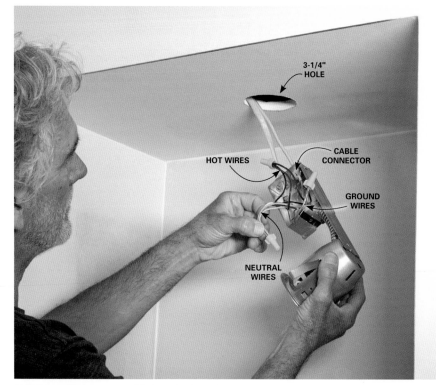

16 **Install the recessed lights.** Cut holes for lights using the template provided and a keyhole saw, or a large hole saw mounted in a drill (we used a 3-1/4-in. hole saw). Remove the cover and knockouts and add cable connectors if they're not built into the fixture. Push the cable(s) through the connectors and connect hot, neutral and ground wires with appropriate wire connectors.

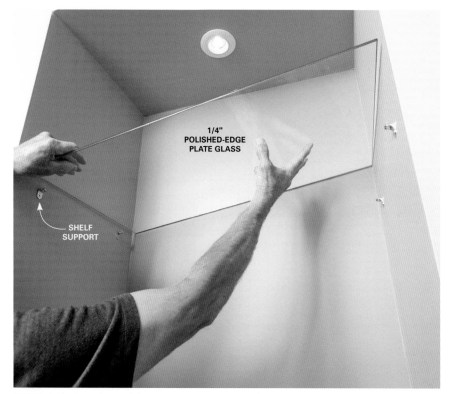

17 **Add glass shelves.** Screw shelf supports into the 2x6 backer, making sure they're level with each other. Set the 1/4-in. polished-edge glass shelves on the supports.

sander. Use a fine sanding sponge with an angled edge to sand the inside corners. Vacuum all the dust from the surfaces and check your work with a strong raking light. Fill any imperfections, resand, and you're ready to prime and paint.

Finish the wiring

When you're done sanding the drywall, you can install the recessed lights. Then when the painting is complete, finish the wiring by adding the outlets and connecting the switch or dimmer switch. For more help with installing switches and outlets, go to familyhandyman.com and search for "switch" or "outlet." Figure B shows how to wire the outlets and dimmer switch. Photo 16 shows how to install the recessed lights.

We used 6-watt dimmable LED flood bulbs in our fixtures. If you're using LED bulbs and want to install a dimmer, check the manufacturer's instructions to make sure the switch is compatible with the brand of LED bulb you're using. When the wiring is complete, turn on the circuit breaker to check your work. Then call the electrical inspector for a final inspection.

Finishing touches

Since we wanted to use the shelves as an entertainment center, we cut holes for low-voltage old-work brackets in the back wall of the TV compartment and the compartment below it. That way we could run HDMI and other audio/video cables through the wall from the components to the TV. Make sure the cables are rated for in-wall use—look for CL2- or CL3-rated cables.

We also installed 1/4-in. polished-edge plate-glass shelves in two compartments (Photo 17). To protect the drywall from wear and moisture (such as from potted plants), consider having more glass pieces cut that you can use to cover the bottoms of the other compartments. Reinstall the baseboard molding and you're ready to move in and enjoy your dramatic new display wall.

Modular masterpiece

A stunning wall unit that's infinitely flexible—customize it to suit your space and your stuff

Back when I was just starting out in my first apartment, I piled up milk crates to store all my worldly goods. It was a simple idea, and it worked like a charm.Fast-forward many years: Faced with a need to store and display lots more stuff, I made plywood boxes in two sizes and mixed them up, adding doors to some and painting the inside backs of others the same color as my wall. The result was a stunning showcase that's adaptable to any situation and includes useful storage space.

It's just a bunch of boxes

A complicated puzzle? Nope. This wall unit is just a collection of plywood boxes. Building all those boxes is time-consuming and fussy—but not difficult. If you have the patience to build precise boxes, you can do it!

1 **Design with building blocks.** Here's an easy way to design your wall unit: Use LEGO blocks to represent single and double boxes. Take photos of various patterns, then compare the photos to decide which arrangement works best.

2 **Lay out parts with templates.** Your wall unit may require dozens of parts, but there are only three rough sizes. Cut full sheets of plywood into 16-in.-wide strips, then mark the parts using a set of three cardboard templates, based on the rough sizes given in the Cutting List.

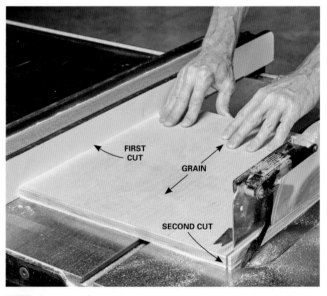

3 **Cut the rough-sized blanks.** Crosscut the plywood strips using a table saw sled or guide for a circular saw.

4 **Cut twice for a perfect edge.** To ensure that one edge of each blank is dead straight, rip it twice. Make one cut, rotate the piece 180 degrees, reset the fence and cut again. The second cut will result in a perfectly straight edge. Mark it.

Create your own design

To plan the unit, I used my kid's LEGO blocks to play around with different patterns (Photo 1), but you could just use paper or cardboard. Before you start, note any outlets or vents along the wall (see "Dealing with Outlets and Vents," p. 159).

Once your design is set, figure out how much plywood you'll need. Each box is composed of five parts: a back (A and E; see Cutting List, p. 162), top and bottom (B and F), and two ends (C and G). You can also add doors (D and H).

Count the number of single and double boxes in your design, then take a look at how many of these pieces you can get from one sheet of plywood (Figure B). The sheet shown here yields two single boxes and one double box, but you could cut one sheet into all singles or all doubles or any mix of the two sizes.

WHAT IT TAKES

TIME: 8 days
SKILL LEVEL: Intermediate
TOOLS: Table saw, drill/driver, brad nailer, clamps, basic edge-banding tools

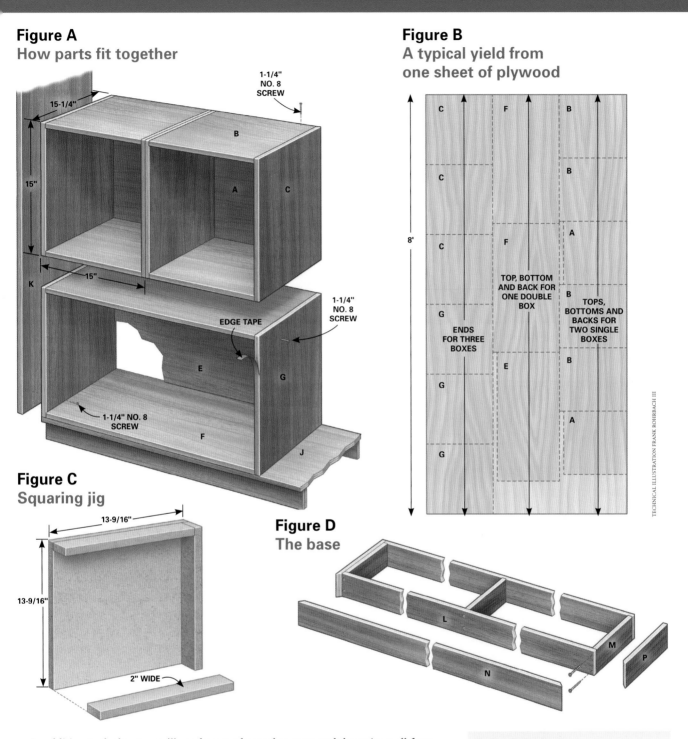

Figure A
How parts fit together

15-1/4"

1-1/4"
NO. 8
SCREW

B

15"

A

C

K

15"

1-1/4"
NO. 8
SCREW

EDGE TAPE

E

G

1-1/4" NO. 8
SCREW

F

J

Figure B
A typical yield from one sheet of plywood

C   F   B

C   B

8'

C   F   A

G

TOP, BOTTOM
AND BACK FOR
ONE DOUBLE
BOX

ENDS
FOR THREE
BOXES

B   TOPS,
BOTTOMS AND
BACKS FOR
TWO SINGLE
BOXES

E   B

G

A

G

TECHNICAL ILLUSTRATION FRANK ROHRBACH III

Figure C
Squaring jig

13-9/16"

13-9/16"

2" WIDE

Figure D
The base

L

M

P

N

In addition to the boxes, you'll need more plywood to surround the unit on all four sides (J and K; Figure A). These pieces aren't essential, but they give the unit a clean, finished look by hiding all the seams. And they make all the members look equal in thickness.

You may also need plywood to build a base for the boxes to stand on (L – P; Figure D). This part isn't essential either (you could stack the boxes directly on the floor), but I definitely recommend it for a large unit like this one. Starting out with a level base—rather than an uneven floor—makes aligning the boxes much easier when you stack them.

Materials list
- 3/4" birch plywood
- Edging tape
- 1-1/4" deck screws
- 1-1/4" coarse-thread drywall screws
- Electrical tape (for shimming)

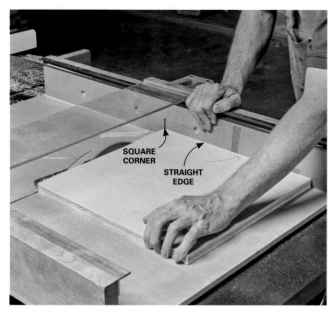

5 Cut one perfect corner. Place the marked straight edge of each blank against the sled's fence, then crosscut one end of the blank. Mark the square corner.

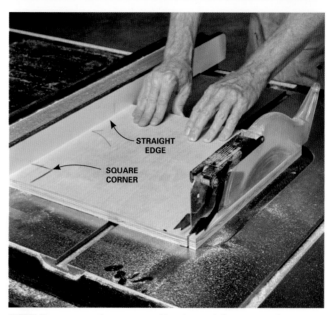

6 Two cuts make a square. Use the saw's fence to cut the single-box backs to final size. Make one rip cut, then rotate the piece 90 degrees and make a crosscut. The result will be a perfect square.

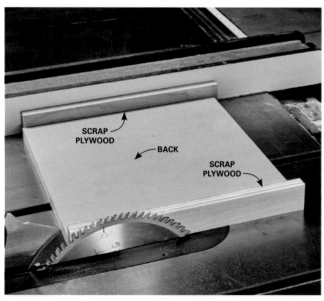

7 Set your fence to cut the ends. The length of each end piece equals a back plus two thicknesses of plywood. Unplug your saw and flip up the guard. Place these pieces next to the saw blade, then butt the fence up to them. Cut the remaining pieces to width and length using the fence as well.

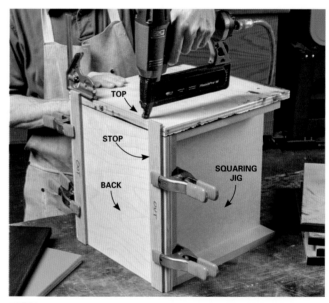

8 Join the top and bottom to the back. Begin assembling each unit by fastening a top and bottom to a back. Use two simple jigs and a pair of stops to align the parts. Shoot three brads to lock the parts in place, then drill pilot holes and drive in screws.

Cut the plywood to rough size

Building plywood boxes is usually no big deal, but these have to fit together just right. Every square box has to be absolutely square—that is, its height must be exactly the same as its width. And a double box must be exactly twice as long as a single.

If that level of precision sounds intimidating, don't worry. I've worked out a method of cutting, building and assembling the boxes that guarantees success.

Here's the best strategy for cutting the plywood: Break down your sheets into oversize backs, tops, bottoms and ends first, then cut each of these pieces to final size in batches.

MEET THE BUILDER

Tom Caspar is a professional furniture maker and former editor of *American Woodworker* magazine.

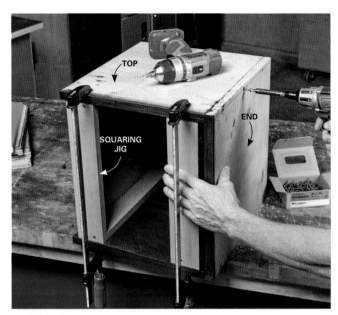

9 Add the ends. Use the jigs again to hold the parts square. Make sure all the front edges are flush before fastening the parts together.

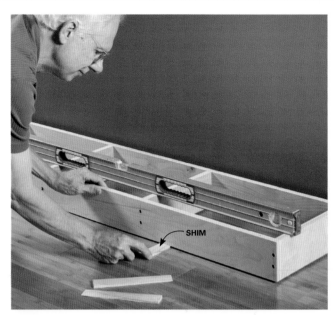

10 Build a level base. Build a base from plywood and level it with shims to ensure your wall unit will be plumb. Wrap the base with "skins" (parts N and P) and cover it with the platform (J).

11 Clamp, then fasten. Use small clamps to assemble a couple of rows of boxes. Shift the boxes as needed to align them, then fasten them together from the inside.

You'll be making "rip cuts" and "crosscuts." Rip cuts go with the grain and determine a piece's width; crosscuts go across the grain and determine a piece's length.

Start by making three cardboard templates using the rough dimensions given in the Cutting List. Cut each piece of plywood into three 16-in.-wide strips, then use the templates to draw every crosscut you intend to make (Photo 2). Label the parts and tally them to be sure you have enough of each kind. Add two extra single-box backs to your list. You'll need these to build a pair of jigs that are essential for assembling the boxes (Figure C).

Dealing with outlets and vents

Don't cover electrical outlets and air vents—work around them. Plan ahead so a box's edge won't cover an outlet. The outlet must sit "inside" a box, accessible through a hole in the box's back. Cut the hole when you're stacking the boxes to be sure you put it in the right place.

To allow airflow from a floor vent, add an elbow and extend the duct to the front of the base. Cut a hole in the front of the base to receive the duct and then fasten the vent cover to the base.

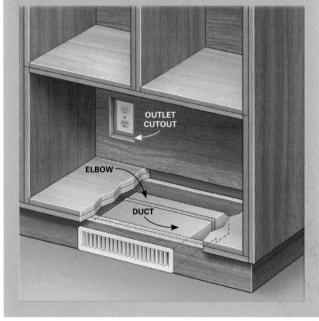

12 Add end caps. Build up one side of the entire assembly first, then fasten end cap to cover the seams. Add the remaining boxes a couple of rows at a time before fastening them together. Then add the other end cap and top.

END CAP

SUPPORT

Endless possibilities

You can mix and match boxes in any pattern, any size. Think big and you can fit a TV and speakers in between them. Think small and you can fill a short wall with just a few boxes.

Crosscut each strip using a sled on your table saw (Photo 3). Use a 60-tooth or higher crosscut blade to avoid chipping out the face veneers. For tips on building and using a sled, go to familyhandyman. com and search for "table saw sled." Sort the parts into clearly marked piles.

The next step is to make one perfectly straight edge on each part, following the grain. The best method is to rip each part twice—the cut edge will become straighter, and smoother, with each cut you make. First, set your saw's fence to cut 15-3/4 in. wide, then rip all the pieces from their straightest side (Photo 4). Mark these edges, then reset the fence to 15-1/2 in. and rip each piece again, running the marked edge against the fence. Make a different mark on this new edge to indicate it's the best one.

Next, cut one square corner on each piece (Photo 5). Make test cuts first to be sure your sled is cutting absolutely square (see "Super-Tune Your Sled," p. 161). Be fussy—accuracy will pay off when you assemble the boxes.

Cut the parts to final size

The backs determine the overall size of each box, so make them first. Start with the smallest ones—the single-box backs. Begin by setting the saw's fence to 13-9/16 in., then make a rip cut from the good edge of each single-box back (Photo 6). Rotate each piece 90 degrees and make a crosscut from the other good edge.

This dimension—13-9/16 in.—is repeated in a number of other parts, so it's best to cut them all at the same time. Crosscut all the single-box tops and bottoms, then rip all the double-box backs at this setting.

Next, cut all the double-box backs to length. It's better to use actual parts, rather than a ruler, to figure out this dimension (about 28-9/16 in.). The length of a double's back equals the sum of two single backs plus the thickness of two pieces of plywood. Place these four parts next to your saw's blade, then butt the saw's fence next to them. (Use two scraps to represent the plywood's thickness.) Crosscut all the backs to this length. Cut all the double-box tops and bottoms to this length as well.

Use a similar method to figure out the precise length of all the end pieces (Photo 7). This dimension equals the width of a single-box back plus the thickness of two pieces of plywood. Place these pieces next to the saw's blade and butt the fence to them. Crosscut all the ends at this setting (about 15 in.).

The final cuts determine the outside depth of both boxes. Set the fence to 15-1/4 in. and rip the ends, tops and bottoms at this setting.

Build the boxes

Apply iron-on edging to the fronts of all parts. For tips on that, see p. 261 or visit familyhandyman.com and search for "edge band."

It's much easier to finish the boxes before building them than after! I chose a dark stain to hide any small gaps between boxes; using a dark color, gaps just look like shadows.

Build two jigs to help with assembly (Figure C). Start assembling the single and double boxes by attaching a top to a back (Photo 8). Support the top with the jigs. Butt the top up to two stops clamped to the back. Be sure both pieces are aligned side-to-side, then shoot three 1-1/2-in. brads to lock the pieces into place.

Next, drill three pilot holes and drive in screws. The nails prevent the pieces from shifting; the screws pull the parts together. (Tight joints are essential for the boxes to nest together properly.) I used deck screws that have a smooth shank right under the screw's head. To drill the pilot holes, I used a combination bit and countersank the holes halfway into the top piece of plywood so none of the screw's threads would engage it—that's the key to pulling parts tight.

Leave the jigs in place, then turn the assembly over and repeat the procedure for attaching the box's bottom piece.

Next, reverse the jigs and clamp the open end of the U-shape

Super-tune your sled

I always use a sled to cut plywood panels on my table saw. It's easy to build—to see how, search for "table saw sled" at familyhandyman.com.

A sled is supposed to guarantee a square cut, and truly square cuts are essential for the boxes of this wall unit to stack properly. Was my sled really that accurate? I've checked panels I've cut with a combination square and they seemed OK, but before building these boxes I put my sled to the ultimate test (Photos 1 and 2).

The result? My sled was off just a teensy bit. The best solution is to readjust the sled's fence, but, in a hurry, I just shimmed it with a few layers of tape (Photo 3). Now it's dead-on perfect.

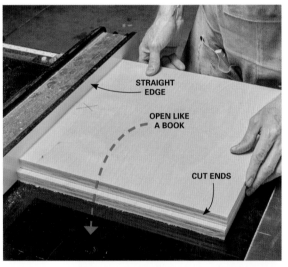

STRAIGHT EDGE

OPEN LIKE A BOOK

CUT ENDS

1 Cut two pieces. To check your sled's accuracy, cut two large pieces of plywood from the same side of the sled's fence. Stack the pieces on top of each other with the newly sawn edges facing the same way. Lay the stack against the table saw or other straight edge, then flip the top piece over—like opening a book.

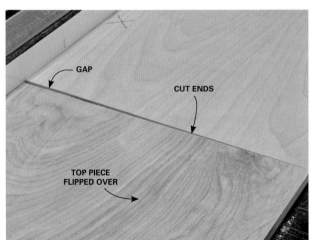

GAP

CUT ENDS

TOP PIECE FLIPPED OVER

2 Look for a gap. If there's no gap, your sled is producing perfect cuts. A gap shows you twice the amount of error the cut deviates from 90 degrees.

3 Adjust with tape. To correct the angle, add tape to the sled's fence one piece at a time. Repeat the flip test and add or subtract tape until the gap disappears.

Easy, invisible hinges

To complement the unit's sleek, modern look, I wanted the door's hinges to be hidden from the outside. Euro-style hinges are the way to go.

Euro hinges may look complicated, but that's just because they're fully adjustable. After you install them, you can easily even up the gap around a door simply by turning some small screws on the hinges.

Installing Euro hinges is pretty darn simple, but you'll need a 35mm (1-3/8-in.) Forstner bit. A template for locating the hinge holes is handy too. You can get both in one package at woodcraft.com (DrillRite Hinge Jig and Bit, No. 143958). I used Blum 110-degree soft-close hinges (B071B3650) and Blum 9mm clip mounting plates (B175H719). Both are available online.

assembly (Photo 9). Nail and fasten the top of one end piece, making sure front edges are flush. Turn the assembly over. Use a clamp, if necessary, to nudge front edges flush again, then finish nailing and screwing the end. Repeat the procedure for the other end, then remove the jigs.

Assemble the wall unit

As with building a house, the foundation of this wall unit must be level and straight before you start stacking boxes. The easiest way to do that is to make a ladder-like base (Photo 10 and Figure D). Size the base so that the wall unit will overhang it by 1 in. on all four sides. My base is 4 in. high—just tall enough to raise the wall unit above my baseboard molding. My wall unit was so long that I had to make two bases and screw them together.

After leveling the base, make a "skin" of stained and finished plywood pieces to cover the screw holes in the base. Rip the skin pieces extra wide so you can scribe them to the floor, covering the gaps where the base is shimmed. The skin is mitered at the corners and nailed to the base.

Screw one plywood piece or pieces to the base to create a shelf for stacking the boxes. The length of this shelf must equal the length of the bottom row of boxes. To figure it out, temporarily clamp together a row of boxes and measure it.

Assemble the first couple of rows on the shelf (Photo 11). Use clamps to temporarily hold the boxes together, then shift individual boxes as needed to align their front edges. When things look good, fasten the boxes together with drywall screws. Their black heads will be almost invisible.

Complete stacking one end of your wall unit and add an end cap (Photo 12). Fasten the cap from inside the boxes.

Fill in the remaining boxes, working from the end cap over. You may need to shim here and there to keep edges aligned. I used rubber electrical tape for shimming. It's a hefty 1/32 in. thick, black all the way through, and sticks anywhere.

Fasten a few of the boxes to studs in your wall so there's no

chance of the unit toppling forward. Top the boxes with another piece of plywood to preserve a "double wall" look throughout the unit.

Cutting list

PARTS	ROUGH WIDTH X LENGTH	FINAL WIDTH X LENGTH
Single box		
A - Back	16" x 14-1/2"	13-9/16" x 13-9/16" (a)
B - Top and bottom	Same as A	15-1/4" x 13-9/16"
C - End	16" x 16"	15-1/4" x 15"
D - Door	Same as A	13-3/8" x 13-3/8" (b)
Double box		
E - Back	16" x 29-1/2"	13-9/16" x 28-9/16"
F - Top and bottom	Same as E	15-1/4" x 28-9/16"
G - End	Same as C	15-1/4" x 15"
H - Door	Same as E	13-3/8" x 28-3/8"
Surround		
J - Platform and top		15-1/4" wide (c)
K - End cap		15-1/4" wide (d)
Base		
L - Front and back		4" wide (e)
M - Cross members		4" x 11"
N - Skin, front		4-1/2" wide (f)
P - Skin, return		4-1/2" wide (f)

Notes: ALL PARTS ARE CUT FROM 3/4" PLYWOOD. (a) All dimensions assume two layers of plywood equal 1-7/16" thick. (b) Final dimensions allow for a 3/32" gap all around the door and include edging on all four sides of the door. (c) Length equals one row of boxes. (d) Length equals height of column of boxes plus 1-7/16". (e) Length is 3-7/16" shorter than part J. (f) Width includes 1/2" for scribing.

Chapter 4

OUTDOORS

Ultimate garden shed 164

Quick & easy shed 176

Mini shed 184

Garden storage closet 191

Outdoor tips 194

Ultimate garden shed

Two sheds in one, this rustic cedar gem will keep everyone happy

This cedar garden shed is the perfect storage solution for every gardener and family member who enjoys working and playing in the backyard. At 8 ft. x 9-1/2 ft., the storage area has loads of room for all your lawn and garden equipment. And you can access it easily through the 46-in.-wide sliding door in the back. With the addition of workbenches and shelves, the smaller 5-1/2-ft. x 8-ft. room makes a perfect potting shed. The concrete paver floor, natural cedar siding and steel roofing add up to a low-maintenance shed that will last for generations.

NOTES FROM THE BUILDER

This was one of the first sheds I built (way back in 2003). It was such a success—by far the most popular shed I've ever built—that I decided to revisit it. This article gives the original plan and steps, plus a few notes on what I might have done differently, additional information, and options for methods and materials. I hope you enjoy this shed as much as others have. And if you decide to build it yourself, please send us some photos.

–Jeff Gorton

Figure A: Shed details   Overall dimensions: 16' x 9' 6"

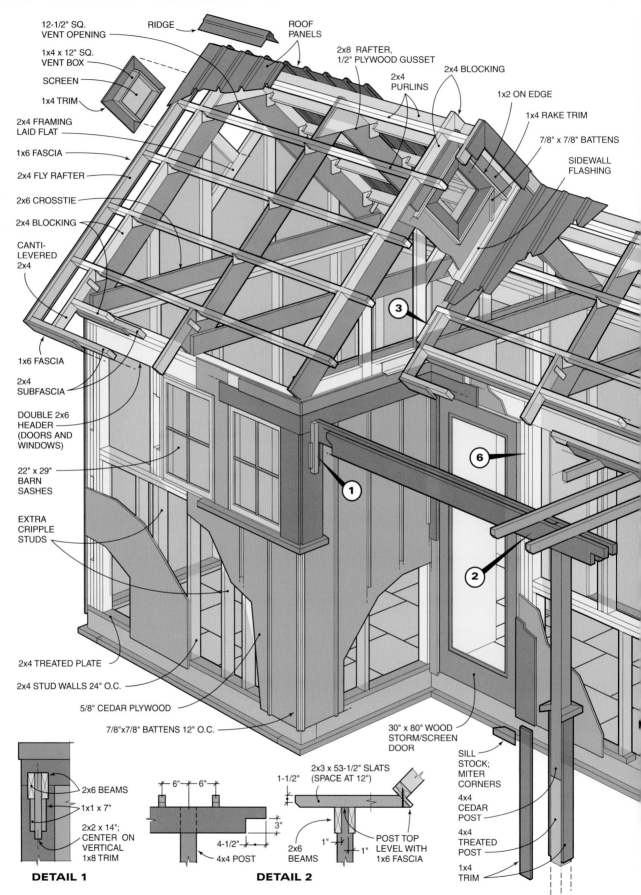

12-1/2" SQ. VENT OPENING

RIDGE

ROOF PANELS

2x8 RAFTER, 1/2" PLYWOOD GUSSET

2x4 PURLINS

2x4 BLOCKING

1x4 x 12" SQ. VENT BOX

SCREEN

1x4 TRIM

2x4 FRAMING LAID FLAT

1x6 FASCIA

2x4 FLY RAFTER

2x6 CROSSTIE

2x4 BLOCKING

CANTI-LEVERED 2x4

1x6 FASCIA

2x4 SUBFASCIA

DOUBLE 2x6 HEADER (DOORS AND WINDOWS)

22" x 29" BARN SASHES

EXTRA CRIPPLE STUDS

2x4 TREATED PLATE

2x4 STUD WALLS 24" O.C.

5/8" CEDAR PLYWOOD

7/8"x7/8" BATTENS 12" O.C.

1x2 ON EDGE

1x4 RAKE TRIM

7/8" x 7/8" BATTENS

SIDEWALL FLASHING

30" x 80" WOOD STORM/SCREEN DOOR

SILL STOCK; MITER CORNERS

4x4 CEDAR POST

4x4 TREATED POST

1x4 TRIM

2x6 BEAMS

1x1 x 7"

2x2 x 14"; CENTER ON VERTICAL 1x8 TRIM

DETAIL 1

6"   6"

4-1/2"

4x4 POST

2x6 BEAMS

1"

1-1/2"

3"

2x3 x 53-1/2" SLATS (SPACE AT 12")

POST TOP LEVEL WITH 1x6 FASCIA

DETAIL 2

TECHNICAL ART EUGENE THOMPSON

166 OUTDOORS

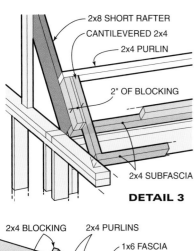

2x8 SHORT RAFTER
CANTILEVERED 2x4
2x4 PURLIN
2" OF BLOCKING
2x4 SUBFASCIA

DETAIL 3

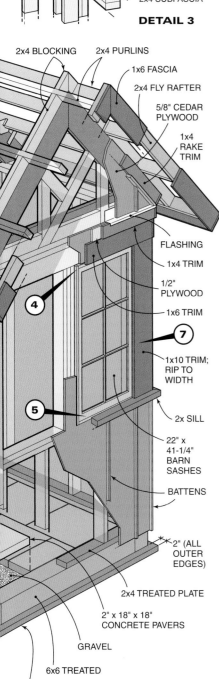

2x4 BLOCKING
2x4 PURLINS
1x6 FASCIA
2x4 FLY RAFTER
5/8" CEDAR PLYWOOD
1x4 RAKE TRIM
FLASHING
1x4 TRIM
1/2" PLYWOOD
1x6 TRIM
1x10 TRIM; RIP TO WIDTH
2x SILL
22" x 41-1/4" BARN SASHES
BATTENS
2" (ALL OUTER EDGES)
2x4 TREATED PLATE
2" x 18" x 18" CONCRETE PAVERS
GRAVEL
6x6 TREATED
2x10 TREATED

④ ⑦ ⑤

Building this shed isn't complicated, nor does it require more than basic carpentry experience. Still, it's a big job, and if you've built a deck or done other major remodeling, you'll find this project the next step up in skill level. It'll take you and a helper three or four weekends to build plus another few days to seal the siding and put on the finishing touches.

If this shed is a little beyond your budget, you could easily save several hundred dollars by simplifying the exterior trim details and using less expensive flooring material.

In addition to basic hand tools, you'll need a circular saw, drill, table saw and power miter saw. You'll also need 6-ft. and 10-ft. stepladders to work on the roof and tall gable ends. If you really want to speed up the work and simplify your job, rent scaffolding with a set of casters. **For more building details and a complete materials list, go to familyhandyman.com/2014shed.**

Check with the city—you may need a permit

Most cities require a building permit for large sheds. Call the building department to find out. This shed is 120 sq. ft. Also check for restrictions on where the shed can be placed on the lot. If you're planning to build near the edge of your lot, you may have to hire a surveyor to locate the lot lines. Start this planning process at least a month in advance in case there's a snag. A few days before you intend to start digging, call 811 to have buried utility lines located and marked.

You may have to special-order the roofing

Most of the materials for this shed are readily available at home centers and lumberyards. You may have to order the barn sash windows and the grooveless cedar plywood, however. If your lumber supplier doesn't sell the metal roofing material, check local roofing or farm supply retailers. A few colors are stocked, but you'll have to special-order the roofing materials to get a custom color or have the panels cut to the exact length you need.

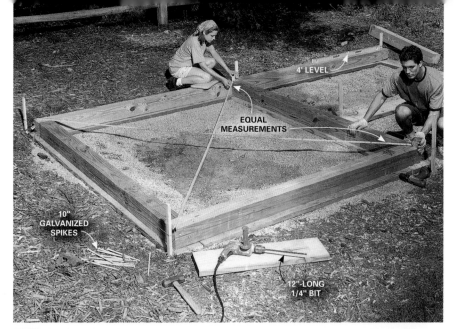

1 **Build the foundation.** Cut treated 6x6s to form the perimeter of the shed. Check with a level and slip treated shims under them at low spots. Drill pilot holes and nail the corners together with galvanized timber spikes. Adjust the 6x6s until the diagonal measurements are equal. Toe-screw the 6x6s to the 2x10s to hold them in place.

Start by outlining the shed with stakes and string

The first step in the construction process is to accurately stake out the perimeter (Photo 1). We're using 2x10s as our foundation with 6x6s resting on them. The 2x10s will stick out beyond the 6x6s about 2 in., so set your stakes 2 in. beyond the shed dimensions to mark their outer edges. Use a line level to level the strings. Then double-check the distance between stakes and make sure the diagonal measurements of each rectangular section are equal before you start digging.

2 **Prepare for pavers.** Add 3-in. layers of gravel and pack each layer with a hand tamper to within 2 in. of the top. Drag a notched 2x4 over the gravel to create a flat, level base for the concrete pavers.

NOTES FROM THE BUILDER

Great floor—but a little extra work

Knowing that the smaller section would be used as a potting area, I thought it would be nice to have a floor that allowed drainage. I came up with the plan to set pavers between a foundation of treated 6x6s. But leveling the 6x6s and cutting the thick pavers to fit in was more work than I expected. Poured concrete would have been a lot simpler. Also, if your shed site is sloping, a platform on posts would be a better choice for the shed floor.

NOTES FROM THE BUILDER

Ditch the line level

We used a line level attached to a string to level the foundation. But now that affordable, self-leveling laser levels are available, I would use one of these instead. You can buy a self-leveling laser at home centers or online.

Remove all the sod or other organic material inside the perimeter of the strings. Then dig the trench and set the 2x10 footing plates on a bed of gravel. Roughly level the 2x10s by measuring down from the string. Then fine-tune

3 **Make rafter patterns.** Mark and cut a pair of long and a pair of short rafters from the dimensions in Figure C, online. Check the fit (Photo 6), then use them as a pattern for the rest.

with a 4-ft. or longer level. Take your time here. An out-of-level foundation will cause you problems later.

Complete the wood foundation by adding the 6x6s (Photo 1 and Figure B, online). The edge of the 6x6s should be about 2 in. inside the string line and the top should be level with the string. Square the 6x6s (Photo 1) and level them with shims. Pack gravel around the perimeter to hold everything in place. You'll need about 3-1/4 yards of 3/8-in. to 1/2-in. crushed gravel.

Loose-laid pavers are easy to install and allow water to drain

You can choose any size or style paver you like for the floor. Notch the 2x4 screed board to match the thickness of the pavers you choose (Photo 2). We chose 18-in. square cement pavers. We used a circular saw and diamond blade to cut the 2-in. thick pavers to fit, but if I had it to do over, I'd rent a larger, masonry-cutting saw instead. We offset the joints for a more interesting look and to avoid having to keep the pavers precisely aligned.

Build the roof trusses before you build the walls

First cut the rafters and crossties according to the dimensions in Figure C, online. Arrange the truss parts on the shed floor as shown in Photo 4. The angles at the top should fit tightly together. Tack positioning blocks at the top and mark the bottoms on the 6x6 as a guide for building the remaining trusses. Repeat this process at the narrow end to build the three small trusses.

Connect the pairs of rafters at the top with a plywood gusset and ten 6d nails. Connect the bottoms with a 2x6 nailed to each rafter with three 10d nails. On the end trusses, cut and nail additional 2x4 framing as shown to provide nailing for the plywood siding and square openings for the screened vents (Photo 4). Mark the location of the purlins along the top of each truss (Figure C, online). Cut the purlins to length and mark the truss locations on them as well (Figure E, online).

4 **Build the trusses.** Align the rafters with the outside edges of the 6x6s as shown to build three large trusses. Do the same on the narrow end to build three small trusses. Use temporary wood blocks to center the tops of the rafters on the end wall while you nail them together with triangular plywood gussets. Add flat 2x4s 24 in. on center to create one small and two large gable end trusses. Build one large and two small trusses without the studs.

5 **Lay out the plates.** Cut treated 2x4 bottom plates and 2x4 top plates and tack them into place around the perimeter. Mark window and door rough openings and the edge of each stud according to the dimensions in Figure D.

NOTES FROM THE BUILDER

Change window sizes easily

The walls with windows have continuous support beams, called headers, over the windows. This means that if you would like to use windows that are a different width, all you have to do is adjust the position and size of the window spacers. If you want to use windows that are a different height, simply adjust the length of the cripples under the windows.

6 **Assemble the walls on the floor.** Nail the full-length studs between the top and the bottom plates. Assemble the 2x6 headers and nail them into place. Add trimmers under the ends of the headers. Cut the cripples and rough sills to complete the window openings. Build the short posts that separate the windows and toenail them into place.

7 **Stand the walls.** Stand and brace the front and back walls first, making sure the tops tilt out slightly to allow room for the walls that fit in between. Align the outside edges of the walls with the 6x6s and nail down through the bottom plates. Build the end and center walls and stand them up. Remove the temporary braces and nail the corners together, making sure the top plates are aligned with each other.

Frame the walls on the floor and stand them up

Cut the plates to length (Figure D, online) and tack them to the 6x6 exactly where they'll go to check the fit. Leave them tacked while you lay out the stud and opening locations on the plates (Photo 5).

Then cut the studs and other wall framing parts to length according to the dimensions shown in Figure D, online. Build the headers by sandwiching a layer of 1/2-in. plywood between 2x6s and nailing them together with pairs of 10d sinkers spaced every 8 in. Choose a pair of straight 2x4s for each corner and nail them together with short lengths of scrap 2x4s as spacers. Once all the parts are cut and the headers and corners are built, you're ready to assemble the walls.

Build the long back wall first. We're using a framing nailer (Photo 6) to speed things up. This is a dangerous tool. We recommend you avoid this tool and hand-nail this entire project unless you have experience using a framing nailer. Stand and brace the back wall (Photo 7), then the front walls, and finally the end walls. Tie them together with doubled top plates and finally plumb and brace the corners (Photo 8).

Stand the trusses and connect the purlins

Once the walls are plumbed and braced and the trusses are built, you're ready to frame the roof. It'll take shape quickly, but you'll need some help lifting and positioning the trusses. Also line up a few tall ladders or scaffolding. The key to this roof is to make sure truss positions are marked on the top plates, purlin positions on the rafters, and rafter positions on the purlins. Then all will go together smoothly. Start by nailing a long 2x4 brace to the end walls. It should extend up to the rafter (Photo 9). Once these are in place, you can install the two end trusses and connect them with a purlin (Photo 9). Then install the intermediate truss. Toenail everything with 8d nails and add metal hurricane ties where there's space to do so (Photo 10).

Complete the roof framing by building the cantilevered overhangs. Connect them to the trusses with metal tie plates (Photo 10 inset). Then complete the

8 **Plumb and brace the corners.** Tape a level to a long straight board with equal spacers at each end. Push or pull the wall until it's plumb and hold it in this position while your helper nails on a temporary diagonal brace. Repeat this process for each wall. Plumb both end walls first. Then sight down the long back wall to make sure it's straight before you nail the diagonal brace across the center wall.

9 **Set the trusses.** Erect the two end trusses and brace them with 2x4s nailed to the walls. Line up the outside edges with the walls and toenail them into place. Align the one long purlin and toenail it into place. Tip up the remaining trusses and toenail them to the purlin. Toenail the ends of the trusses to the top plates.

PURLINS

2x4 BLOCKING

HURRICANE TIE

LEAVE 1-1/2" SPACE

CANTILEVERED 2x4

2x4 SUBFASCIA

PURLIN

H-1 HURRICANE TIE

CANTILEVERED 2x4

METAL TIE PLATE

2x4 SUBFASCIA

10 **Add the purlins. Nail on the remaining purlins using hurricane ties (inset photo) where possible. Complete the roof framing as shown by adding the cantilevered 2x4s that support the overhang and nailing on the 2x4s that form the rough fascia. Finally, add 2x4 blocking between the purlins on the end walls to keep out birds.**

overhangs by cutting and nailing up the 2x4 rough fascias. Finally, cut and install the blocking to complete the roof framing.

Install the metal roofing

Since this design doesn't include a metal fascia that would typically cover the edge of the metal roofing at the gable ends, you'll have to cut the first rib from the starting sheet to leave a flat spot (Photo 11). We tried tin snips and abrasive metal-cutting blades but settled on a standard 24-tooth carbide blade mounted in a circular saw as the best method for making the long, straight cuts in the metal sheets. Be careful, though. The

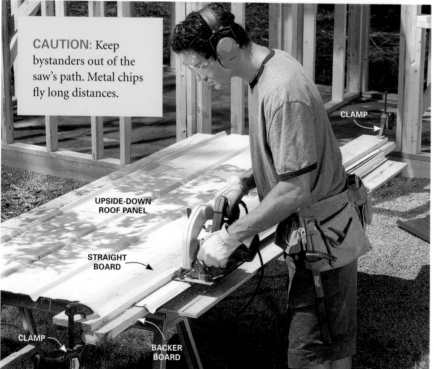

CAUTION: Keep bystanders out of the saw's path. Metal chips fly long distances.

CLAMP

UPSIDE-DOWN ROOF PANEL

STRAIGHT BOARD

CLAMP

BACKER BOARD

11 **Cut the roof panels. Cut metal panels with a 24-tooth carbide blade in a circular saw. Clamp the panel between a straight board to guide the saw and a 2x4 that backs up the cut. Cut the first rib from the starting piece to create a flat edge (see Photo 12).**

CUT EDGE

FULL ROOF PANEL

OVERLAP SEAM

1x6 CEDAR FASCIA

12 **Install the metal roofing. Nail 1x6 cedar fascia boards to the 2x4 subfascia boards. Overhang the metal panel 1 in. on the end and 2 in. on the bottom and attach it to the purlins with special self-sealing hex head screws. Overlap the second panel onto the first and screw it into place (Photo 13). Measure and cut the last panel to overhang the cedar trim by 1 in. Finally, cap the top with the metal ridge cap (Figure A).**

blade throws metal chips quite a distance. Keep bystanders away and make sure to wear safety glasses, hearing protection and leather gloves. Smooth the cut edges with a mill bastard file to remove sharp burrs.

Photos 12 and 13 show how to install the sheets. Screw down each sheet before moving to the next. Use special hex head roofing screws that have a built-in rubber washer to seal the hole. Set the last sheet into place, overlapping at the seams as usual, and mark it 1 in. past the fascia for cutting. On the back side of the roof, you'll have to notch one panel where the roof transition occurs. If your last panel is a few inches short of the end as ours was, rather than cutting a 2-in. strip, cut a piece 13 in. wide and run it underneath the previous panel so the seam won't show from below.

It's difficult to reach the top of the roof to install the ridge cap after all the roofing is on. One solution is to complete one side of the roof, then cut the ridge and screw it down over the completed side. Slide the panels on the opposite side of the roof under the ridge and screw down the ridge as you fasten each panel.

NOTES FROM THE BUILDER

Consider shingles

Metal roofs look great and last almost forever. But over the last decade, asphalt shingles have improved in both looks and longevity. So shingles are a great option for this or any shed.

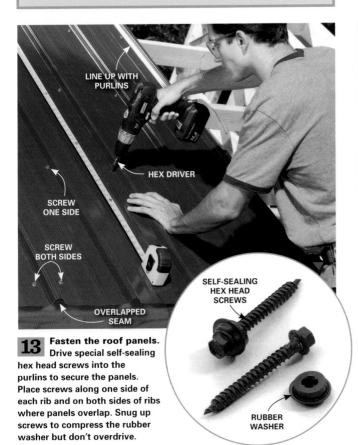

LINE UP WITH PURLINS

HEX DRIVER

SCREW ONE SIDE

SCREW BOTH SIDES

OVERLAPPED SEAM

SELF-SEALING HEX HEAD SCREWS

RUBBER WASHER

13 **Fasten the roof panels.** Drive special self-sealing hex head screws into the purlins to secure the panels. Place screws along one side of each rib and on both sides of ribs where panels overlap. Snug up screws to compress the rubber washer but don't overdrive.

Finish the exterior with cedar plywood panels and cedar battens

Since all of the cedar plywood panels for the walls are the same height, you can start by marking and cutting them all to 91 in. long. A drywall square works great for marking the 4x8 sheets. Mark and cut from the back side of the sheets. The studs are spaced so you'll be able to start each wall with a full-width sheet and cut the last sheet to fit.

Drive 6d galvanized nails every 6 in. around the perimeter of the panels and at 8-in. intervals along the studs (Photo 14).

Build your own windows

Adding the windows, doors and trim can be time consuming. But it's these details that make the shed look sharp. Patience pays off here. Construct the window frames by screwing together 1x4 cedar boards to form a box that's about 1/4 in. wider and taller than the window sash. You'll have to pull out your table saw to cut out the 1/2-in. x 7/8-in. stops, as well as the sills (15-degree angles), battens and window trim. Mount the larger barn sash in the frames with a pair of 3-in. screen door hinges at the top. We chose to mount the smaller sashes between stops and leave them permanently closed. Then mount storm window hold-open hardware 10 in. up on each side to hold the windows open or closed. Finally, shim and install the windows (Photo 15).

Add the trim and battens. Position the battens so every other one falls over a stud (24 in. on center). That way, you can use 8d galvanized finish nails. Fasten intermediate battens with 4d nails and construction adhesive. A layout stick (Photo 17) speeds up the layout. After you've completed the siding, trim and drip cap

MARK STUDS

5/8" CEDAR PLYWOOD

6d GALVANIZED SIDING NAILS

14 **Nail on the siding.** Cut 5/8-in. cedar plywood panels to fit and nail them to the studs with galvanized siding nails. Lap the bottom of the panels 1 in. over the 6x6. Complete the lower panels and window and door installation and trim before installing the panels on the gable end trusses.

NOTES FROM THE BUILDER

Save money on siding

We used 5/8-in. rough-sawn plywood with no grooves for the siding. The only source I know for this type of plywood is a company called Roseburg. The siding is called Breckenridge. At most lumberyards this is a special-order item and it's quite expensive. You could save several hundred dollars by substituting the more commonly available grooved siding and then eliminating the battens.

LINE UP TOPS

EQUAL DISTANCE

1x4 CEDAR FRAME

22" x 41-1/4" BARN SASH

15 **Build and install the windows.** Build 1x4 cedar frames for the barn sash, allowing for a 1/8-in. gap around the sash. Hinge the sash at the top and nail 1/2-in. x 7/8-in. stops around the inside. Level the frames in the openings and adjust with shims until the gap between the sash and the frame is even and the space between pairs of windows is equal on the top and bottom. Nail through the frame and shims from inside to secure the windows. Cut off the shims.

NOTES FROM THE BUILDER

Recycled windows are a great option

You could use old windows instead of barn sash. Get in touch with someone who does window replacements—you'll probably find all kinds of cool, divided-lite sash for free. Of course, you'll have to plan ahead and build the openings to fit.

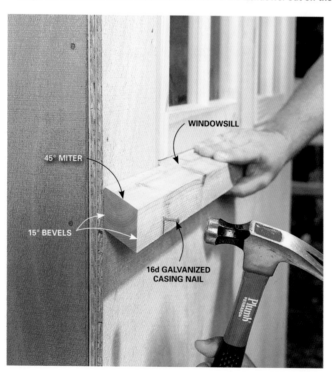

WINDOWSILL

45° MITER

15° BEVELS

16d GALVANIZED CASING NAIL

16 **Attach a beveled sill.** Rip 2-in.-wide cedar sills with 15-degree bevels on each side with a table saw. Cut 45-degree miters where the sills wrap around the walls. Nail the sill pieces below the windows with 16d galvanized casing nails.

on the lower walls, seal the gap between the small front roof and the gable end wall with sidewall flashing.

The optional cedar arbor is a great place to hang plants or grow vines

You can be as creative as you want with this part of the project. Figure A shows how we built our arbor. The key is to temporarily brace the post and level across from the bottom of the fascia to mark the height and cut the notches. Then it's a simple matter to plumb the post, attach the beams and finally top them with the 1-1/2-in. x 2-1/2-in. cedar lattice pieces. We screwed the lattice through the fascia and into the 2x4 subfascia with 4-in. galvanized deck screws run in at a 45-degree angle.

17 **Add trim and battens.** Cut cedar boards to fit around windows and doors and nail them into place. Continue the top 1x6 cedar board across the end of the shed. Shim out the 1x4 board over this with 1/2-in. plywood strips and add a metal drip cap overtop before cutting and installing the gable end plywood. Mark the batten locations every 12 in. and nail them up with galvanized siding nails.

18 **Build the sliding door.** Glue and screw 1x3s flat and then 1x3s on edge to the perimeter of a 48-in. x 80-1/2-in. sheet of 5/8-in.-thick cedar plywood to create a sliding door. Screw pocket door wheel brackets to the top 4 in. from the ends and centered in the top 1x3.

Add simple shelves and benches

We fitted the smaller side of the shed with two full-length workbenches and 1x6 wall shelves. The workbenches are simply 2x4 frames screwed to the studs and supported by angled 2x4 braces. We covered the tops with three 1x6 boards for a width of 16-1/2 in. For the shelves, we notched 1x6 boards to fit around each stud and supported them by nailing 2x4 spacers to the studs under each shelf.

Build the sliding door

Referring to Figure G, online and Photo 18, build the sliding door from a sheet of 5/8-in. cedar plywood. Mount the heavy-duty sliding door track to the wall of the shed and hang the door. To keep the bottom of the door from bumping into the battens, cut 1-1/2 in. from the bottom of each batten that's under the track and nail on a horizontal 1x2 for the door to ride against. Keep the bottom of the door from swinging by mounting a metal 2x4 bar holder to the foundation 6x6 just to the left of the door (Figure G, online). Install a gate latch to hold the door shut.

Protect the cedar with exterior finish

We finished the outside of this shed with an exterior-grade penetrating oil finish. Recoating every few years with a cedar-tinted stain should maintain the natural beauty of the cedar.

Quick & easy shed

Build a home for all your garden gear

If you need more space to store and organize your lawn and garden gear, consider this simple, elegant 5 x 12-ft. shed. It's large enough for wheelbarrows, lawn mowers and even a moderate-size garden tractor. And there's still plenty of room left over for garden hoses, tools and supplies, pots and other stuff. We also included a built-in bench for potting plants.

The shed will look good for years because it's built from durable cedar siding, pressure-treated wood and a 30-year steel roof. The front is attractive,

but the back is all business—it's wide open for easy access and storage. But if leaving it open won't work in your yard, you can install doors (see p. 178).

Another nice feature of this shed design is that you can easily enlarge the plan. Build it up to 12 ft. deep and as long as you like. Even in larger sizes, the shed uses exactly the same techniques and materials. Just keep the post spacing under 6 ft., adding more posts as needed.

The following pages will show you how to assemble this shed, which requires no more skill than building a fence. We simplified the tough spots—laying

out the posts, assembling the roof and marking the angles—so that you can successfully build it even if this is your first shed. This project costs about the same as a store-bought kit, but ours is better and prettier. You can complete the project in three easy weekends.

Siting your shed

If you build the shed and leave the back open, it's best to position the open back against a backdrop of foliage, a fence or a garage wall. That'll keep the finished side most visible and the clutter out of sight. Still, if security is an issue, you may not

Easy as building a fence

Build the shed walls from posts, rails and boards—just like a fence. We'll show you fast, foolproof roof-building tricks too!

You can leave the back wide open for instant access to yard tools and equipment, or enclose it using any of the options in "Adding Doors," p. 178.

1 Build a 2x4 template to the shed dimensions, square it and mark the post locations with stakes. Set the template aside and dig 3-ft.-deep postholes.

ANGLE BRACE

STAKE POSTHOLES

LAYOUT TEMPLATE

TOE-SCREW

2 Drop the posts into the holes, position them using the template, plumb them and screw them into place. Fill the holes with concrete.

Adding doors

If you want to enclose your shed, you have a few options. You could build a wall covering half the back, framing and siding it just as you did the front. Then cover the other half with a pair of swinging doors or install one sliding door. For easier access, skip the wall and cover the whole back with two sliding "bypass" doors. Some home centers carry sliding door hardware designed for farm buildings. To shop online, go to hardwarestore.com and search for "barn door hardware." If your shed has board-on-board cedar siding like ours, you can make doors that match the siding using rough-sawn plywood framed with rough-sawn boards.

want to store any valuable items there.

It's best to position your shed on a level site. The greater the slope, the more work you'll have leveling the floor. Our site sloped about 6 in. from one end to the other. The floor in this shed is simple concrete pavers laid over a 6-in. layer of level sand. It's inexpensive, drains well and can be cleaned with a few squirts from the garden hose. Other options are pouring a concrete slab or even framing in a deck-like floor. Whatever floor you choose, make sure it's higher than the surrounding yard to keep runoff water out of the building.

Materials list

QTY.	ITEM & USE
6	4x4 x 10 (treated) for posts
1	2x4 x 10 (treated) for bottom rail (end walls)
1	2x4 x 12 (treated) for bottom rail (front wall)
2	2x4 x 10 for end wall framing
3	2x4 x 12 for front wall and window framing
5	2x8 x 12 for beams
6	2x4 x 10 for rafters
1	2x6 x 16 for ridge beam
6	2x4 x 16 for purlins
10	1x12 x 10 (cedar) for end wall siding
8	1x6 x 10 (cedar) for end wall siding
8	1x12 x 8 (cedar) for front wall siding
10	1x6 x 8 (cedar) for front wall siding
2	1x6 x 8 (cedar) for window jambs (all trim for two windows)
2	1x6 x 6 (cedar) for window jambs
4	1x4 x 8 (cedar) for window trim
8	60-lb. bags of concrete mix for footings

Metal roofing

10	56-in.-long sheets of steel roofing (roof panels)
2	10-ft. residential ridge cap
2	1-lb. boxes of roofing screws

Hardware

34	1-1/2 x 2-in. angle brackets (framing-to-post connections)
18	Hurricane ties (beam-to-post and rafter-to-beam connections)
2	Boxes of 1-1/4-in. joist hanger screws
2	1-lb. boxes of 16d nails
2	24-in. x 43-1/2-in. barn sash windows with handles
2	Pairs of storm window hanger brackets
2	Pairs of storm window adjusters

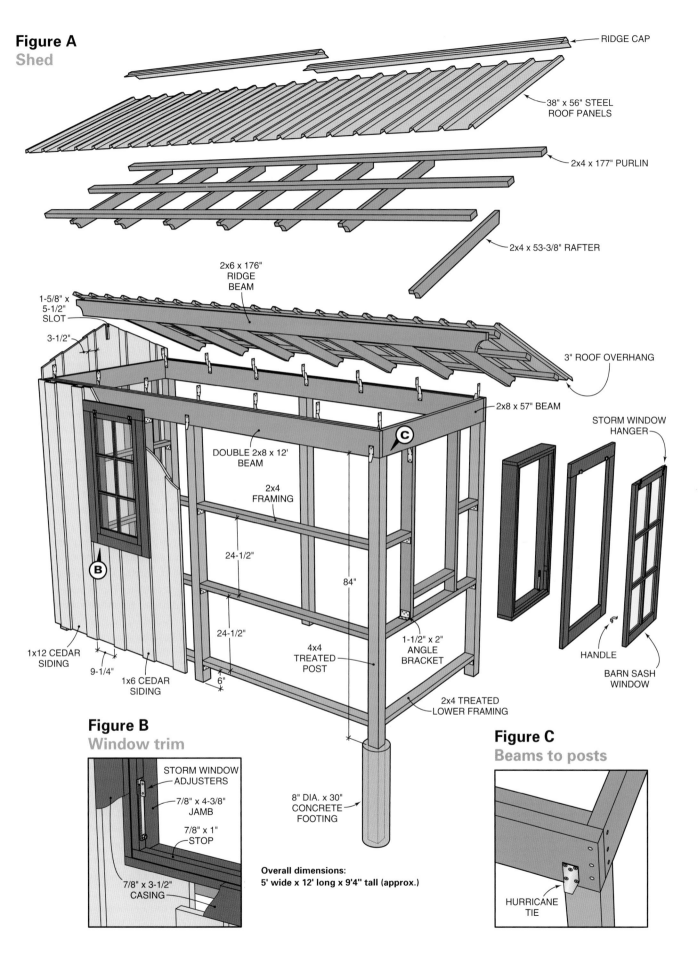

Figure A
Shed

RIDGE CAP

38" x 56" STEEL
ROOF PANELS

2x4 x 177" PURLIN

2x4 x 53-3/8" RAFTER

2x6 x 176"
RIDGE
BEAM

1-5/8" x
5-1/2"
SLOT

3-1/2"

3" ROOF OVERHANG

2x8 x 57" BEAM

STORM WINDOW
HANGER

DOUBLE 2x8 x 12'
BEAM

2x4
FRAMING

24-1/2"

84"

24-1/2"

4x4
TREATED
POST

1-1/2" x 2"
ANGLE
BRACKET

HANDLE

BARN SASH
WINDOW

1x12 CEDAR
SIDING

9-1/4"

1x6 CEDAR
SIDING

6"

2x4 TREATED
LOWER FRAMING

Figure B
Window trim

STORM WINDOW
ADJUSTERS

7/8" x 4-3/8"
JAMB

7/8" x 1"
STOP

7/8" x 3-1/2"
CASING

8" DIA. x 30"
CONCRETE
FOOTING

Overall dimensions:
5' wide x 12' long x 9'4" tall (approx.)

Figure C
Beams to posts

HURRICANE
TIE

You probably won't need a building permit for this shed because in most communities it will fall under the minimum size that requires a permit. But check with the building permit department at city hall to be sure.

Remember to keep your shed to the proper setback distance from your neighbor's property line. Even if you don't need a permit, it's important to check with your local building department to learn the setback rules and shed building requirements. In any case, call 811 before you dig to have underground utilities marked.

One-stop shopping for materials

You can buy everything you need at a home center and take it home in one (rather large) pickup load (see the Materials List, p. 178). All of the framing is standard construction lumber; just make sure to get treated posts and treated 2x4s for the bottom horizontal rail (Photo 5).

If the home center stocks metal roofing, it'll probably only have green, brown or white, but you can special order about 25 other colors and have the panels cut to length for a small extra charge. If you're comfortable cutting panels to length and are happy with stock colors, just buy 8-ft. lengths. Our roofing was special order and took a couple of weeks to arrive, so plan accordingly. Be sure to order *residential* ridge caps to match (Photo 13). Otherwise, you'll get the large ridge caps used on farm buildings. Also order the special roofing screws that are colored to match your roof.

Our siding is vertical "board-on-board" cedar; 1x12s overlaid with 1x6s. This is by far the most expensive feature of our shed. Substitute any type of siding you wish, either to save money or to match the siding on your home. The construction details are the same if you're using plywood siding. But if you use horizontal lap siding, substitute a 4x4 for the 2x4 around the bottom. Then add vertical studs every 16 in. between that and the top beam instead of the horizontal 2x4 framing we show.

You can use any window you wish, wherever you wish. We chose an

3 Slide the template up 5 ft. and level it, screwing it to the posts. Recheck the posts for plumb and brace the assembly. Let the concrete harden overnight.

STAGGER ENDS

HURRICANE TIE

DOUBLED FRONT BEAM

4 Cut the post tops to length. Then cut and assemble the 2x8 beams. Anchor them with hurricane ties.

HURRICANE TIE

ANGLE BRACKET

WINDOW OPENING

ANGLE BRACKETS

TREATED BOTTOM RAIL

5 Cut the rails to fit and fasten them between the posts with angle brackets. Frame the window openings to suit your windows.

inexpensive "barn sash" type window (Photo 10). Add storm window hanger brackets and storm window adjusters and you'll have low-cost windows that open like awnings to let the breeze flow through.

Position the posts with a template

Screw a 2x4 template together as a guide for locating the posts (Photo 1). Make the inside dimensions of the frame exactly 5 x 12 ft. Square the template by racking until the diagonal measurements are equal and then add an angled brace to hold it square. Measure and mark the posthole positions on the template. Drive stakes at the post marks, remove the template and dig 8-in.-diameter holes with a posthole digger.

Screw the posts to the template to hold them plumb while you mix and pour the concrete. To make sure the tops of the posts are also perfectly aligned, unscrew the template and move it up about 5 ft. before the concrete hardens. Carefully level the template as you screw it to the posts; you'll use it later to gauge the post cutoff heights. Then plumb and brace the whole assembly (Photo 3). Leave the braces in place overnight and get back to work the next morning after the concrete has set up.

Set the beams and frame the walls

Choose the post that's closest to the highest point on the ground and mark it 6 ft. 8 in. above your estimated finished floor height. You'll have to guess somewhat at this. The idea is to keep from bonking your head when you enter the shed. Cut off the post at the mark by cutting from two opposite sides with a circular saw. Then measure from the top of the template to the newly cut top. Match that distance to mark and cut the other posts to the same height. (This is why that template had better be level!) Preassemble the doubled 2x8 beams, toenail them on top of the posts and add the end 2x8s (Photo 4). Set 2x8 beams on the posts, toenail them in place and then anchor them with hurricane ties (Photo 4).

Now add the rest of the wall framing, using Figure A as a guide. It's easiest to

6 Cut a slot, then center and nail a 1x12 siding board to each end wall. Then drop the ridge board into the slots and center it.

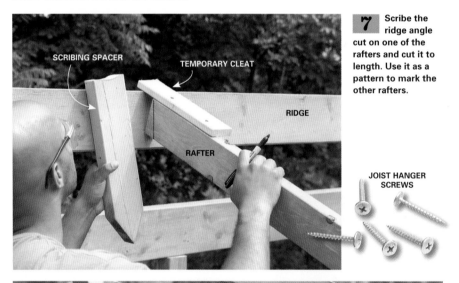

7 Scribe the ridge angle cut on one of the rafters and cut it to length. Use it as a pattern to mark the other rafters.

8 Lay out the rafter positions on the ridge and beams. Then toenail the rafters to the ridge and anchor the other ends to the beam with hurricane ties.

CUT FLUSH
WITH RAFTER

3-1/2"
GAP

9 Space and nail the siding to the end walls (Figure A). Trim it even with the rafters. Add the rest of the 1x12 siding.

STORM
WINDOW
HANGER

WINDOW
STOP

10 Mount the storm window brackets to the window and trim and then hang the window. Nail 1x1 window stop tight against the window.

toenail the 2x4s into place, then anchor them with angle clips (Photo 5).

Size window openings to fit your windows. If you're using barn sash windows, measure the width and height of the window sash and add 1-7/8 in. to each dimension to arrive at the rough opening size.

Frame a super-simple roof

Hand-framing a roof is usually challenging, but we've made the job foolproof with a simple trick: You use the siding to center and support the ridge board while you scribe, cut and install the rafters.

Start the roof by cutting a 5-1/2-in.-deep by 1-5/8-in.-wide slot at the ends of two 10-ft.-long 1x12s. Then cut the boards to length so the bottoms will be at least 2 in. above grade and the top will project past the beam 16 in. (Photo 6). Center, plumb and nail those boards to each end wall.

Cut a 2x6 ridge board to length and cut coves (we used a 1-qt. can for a pattern) at the ends with a jigsaw. Drop the ridge board into the slots, making the overhang equal at both ends (Photo 6). Eyeball the ridge board from one end. If there's a bow, straighten and brace it from the beams with a 2x4 (Photo 8).

Scribe the first rafter angle by screwing a short cleat on the top. Then rest the board on the ridge and scribe the angle

with a scrap 2x4 (Photo 7). Cut the angle and test the fit. Then cut it to length and add the decorative end cut. Use this rafter as a pattern to mark the rest and then cut and install them (Photo 8).

Finish the siding

To save time, finish the ridge board, the rafter and all of the siding on all four sides before installation (we even stained the interior framing to brighten the inside of the shed). To inhibit rot, coat the freshly cut bottom ends of the siding boards before nailing the boards into place.

Begin siding by nailing up the 1x12 boards on the ends. Raise them 2 in. above the ground and run them long at the top (Photo 9). Fasten them in the center of each board with a single nail at each framing member (the overlapping 1x6s will hold the edges). Use a 2x4 block to space the boards 3-1/2 in. apart. That way the 1x6s will overlap 1 in. on both sides. Determine the length of each siding board on the front of the shed by measuring from the ground to the top of the beam and subtracting 2 in.

Install the window frame and exterior trim before you install the 1x6s. Rip the 1x6 jamb boards to 4-1/4 in. wide so they'll be flush with the outside of the 1x12s and the wall framing on the inside of the shed. (Use the leftover strips for the window stops; see Photo 10.) That way you can add the window trim around the openings and surround them with 1x6 siding for a nice, clean look (Photo 10).

Draw marks 1 in. from the edge of the 1x12s to help align the 1x6s. You can cheat the 1x6s left or right a bit if it helps them clear window openings or arrive at corners at a better point. Small variations won't be noticeable. Just make sure you have at least a 3/8-in. overlap and that you plumb each one with a level. Nail each side of the 1x6s through the 1x12 below it and into the framing. Use a reciprocating saw to cut off the long siding boards at the end walls flush with the end rafters (Photo 9). Or snap a chalk line on the outside and use a circular saw. Use the leftover pieces to fill in above or below the windows.

Hang the windows

Screw the hanger brackets to the windows. Then center the window in the opening to position and screw the bracket clips to the window trim. Shim the window sash so it's 1/4 in. back from the window trim and centered in the frame. Nail the 1x1 window stops to the jambs, holding them snug against the window sash (Photo 10). Add the storm window adjusters, following the instructions on the packaging.

Screw down the metal roofing

Cut the 2x4 purlins to length and nail them to each rafter with two 16d nails (Photo 11). If they're twisted and won't lie flat, screw them down. Otherwise the metal roofing will deform or kink when you screw it down.

Nail together a 2x4 "L", push it against the bottom purlin and screw it into place from the underside so you can remove it later (Photo 12). This will hold the metal roof panels in place while you screw them to the purlins. If you need to cut roof panels, before installation cut them from the underside with a jigsaw and metal-cutting blade.

Starting at one end, lay the first panel in place, hanging one edge 3 in. over the purlin ends. Center the screws in the flat areas between the ribs and over the purlins. The screws are self-tapping; push down firmly as you run the screw gun and they'll drill their way through the metal and into the wood. Tighten them up until the special neoprene washer mushrooms against the metal. Measure carefully and keep all the screws exactly in line. It'll look bad if lines of screw heads wander all over the place. And if you drive a screw in the wrong place and miss the purlin, there's no good way to repair a screw hole.

Cut both pieces of ridge cap to length with a tin snips so they overlap 6 in. near the middle. Center and clamp the ridges while you screw them to the ribs of the underlying panels (Photo 13). It's best to predrill these holes with a 1/8-in. bit.

PURLIN   3" FROM END

11 Cut the purlins to length, then center and nail them to each rafter with two 16d nails.

PURLIN

TEMPORARY 2x4 "L"

12 Screw a 2x4 "L" to the rafter tails tight against the bottom purlin. Then rest the roof panels against it and screw the panels to the purlins.

RESIDENTIAL RIDGE CAP

13 Cut both ridge caps to length, then center and clamp them into place. Screw them to every third rib.

Mini shed

A convenient storage locker for yard gear—and relief for your overstuffed garage

Running out of space in your garage? The solution is a mini shed on the exterior wall of the garage for yard tools.

We used cedar trim boards and shingles, but you could save money if you used pressure-treated trim boards and three-tab shingles. The project took about 20 hours to build, a few hours at a time. We wanted to build as much of this project as possible in the comfort of the shop, so we made each section an individual unit. You can build two sections like this one or stack a whole bunch of them together. Ours is filled with garden tools, but it would also work great for pet supplies, grilling accessories, toys or whatever.

Cut the box components

Start by cutting the sides (A) and backs (B) to the dimensions given in the Cutting List on p. 189. Clamp two sides together, and crosscut them to length at the same time with a circular saw. Crosscut one back at a time with your circular saw set to a 20-degree angle. This will match the angles you'll be cutting on the sides to achieve the slope of the roof. For all your cuts, make sure the surface of the plywood with the least flaws faces inside the locker. Measure down 6 in. from the top of one of the sides and mark the slope of the roof. Again, clamp two sides together and cut them at the same time.

Rip the three shelves (C) down to size and clamp them all together before crosscutting them. Rip the bottoms (D) to size and crosscut them together as well. The only plywood pieces left to cut are the top braces (F).

Cut the cedar parts that will be installed inside the boxes. These include the door stops (L), hinge supports (M) and the door latch blocks (N). Crosscut one of the 12-ft. cedar 1x6s in half, and then rip down the door stops and the hinge supports out of one of the 6-ft. halves. Always square up the factory edges before cutting any of the boards to length.

Sand and paint the inside parts

Paint all the interior parts of this project before assembling them. Fill any voids and holes in the plywood with wood filler. Spot-sand the really rough spots with 80-grit paper but don't sand any of the exterior surfaces.

Only the plywood surfaces that face the inside of the storage locker need painting. Paint all but one of the 3/4-in. sides on the door stops, hinge supports and door latch blocks. The plywood that forms the roof can be painted if you wish, but it really isn't noticeable, and the top braces (F) will be completely covered by trim, so there's no need to paint them. We rolled on a product that was a combination of exterior paint and primer, and were able to get full coverage with one thick coat.

Assemble the boxes

Set the sides next to each other and mark the location of the shelves with a framing square. Then mark a guideline for the screws on the exterior of the sides. Measure up from the bottom of the sides and mark the top line of the shelves at 22-3/4 in., 37-3/4 in. and 51-3/4 in. These measurements were based on some specific items we wanted to store. Make your shelves any height you wish, add more shelves, or eliminate them altogether.

Attach one of the sides to the back with 1-1/2-in. stainless or exterior-grade screws. Save time and buy self-drilling

WHAT IT TAKES
TIME: 2 weekends
SKILL: Intermediate
TOOLS: Miter saw or circular saw, 18-gauge brad nailer, compressor, drill, hammer, stapler, level, caulking gun

1 **Assemble the boxes.** Paint all the plywood components, then assemble them with self-tapping, trim-head screws. Screw one side to the back, then add the shelves and finally the other side.

2 **Trim the sides.** Mount the boxes on their bases, then add trim and siding to the sides that will be exposed. Fasten the trim and siding with construction adhesive, plus a few brads to hold them in place while the adhesive sets.

screws that don't require a predrilled hole. Space the screws about 16 in. apart. Once one of the sides is attached, transfer the shelf lines to the back with a framing square. Secure the bottom and the shelves with the same type of 1-1/2-in. screw (Photo 1). Install three screws per shelf side.

Flip the box on its side, and mark a screw guideline on the back of the back. Secure the bottom and shelves to the back with three screws in each. Flip the project on its back again and attach the other side to the back, and then finish securing the bottom and shelves.

The top braces create a solid surface to fasten the top front trim board to. Screw them to the boxes with one screw in the center of each end, and then go back and tack two more 1-1/4-in., 18-gauge brads, one above and one below the screw. Two screws would likely split the plywood.

The hinge supports add extra strength to the trim board that the hinges will be fastened to. Attach the hinge supports and the door stops by driving 1-1/2-in. screws every 16 in. through the plywood sides into the back of the cedar strips. Install the two door catch blocks with two screws driven through the back side. Space them about 6 in. down from the top and up from the bottom, on the back side of the door stop in the box that has no shelves. The door catches on the other side will be fastened to the shelves.

Build and install the base

Cedar is naturally resistant to rot, but it doesn't do so well in direct contact with the ground. Build the base out of pressure-treated wood and keep the cedar trim at the bottom 3/4 in. from the ground. Screw the base fronts, backs and sides (J and K) together with two 3-in. screws in each connection. Attach the boxes to the base with 2-in. exterior grade screws. Install two screws on each of the four sides of the box. Make sure all screws used with treated wood are compatible with treated lumber.

Install the trim and siding on the sides

Cut the side trim board (P) to length and install it with construction adhesive and 1-1/4-in., 18-gauge brads. The brads just hold the board in place while the adhesive dries, so you don't need more than one in each corner and one in the middle.

Create the smaller trim pieces by ripping the 12-ft. cedar (or treated) boards in half. Find the length of the two side trim boards (Q) by setting them on the side bottom trim board and marking the top angle on the back side of the board. Install them with adhesive and two brads every couple of feet. Make the side top trim board (R) by cutting one 20-degree angle and then marking the other angle in place. Install the side center trim board (S) so the top side is 42-3/4 in. off the ground.

For siding, we chose 1/4-in.-thick cedar planks often used as wainscoting (BB). Look for it at home centers near the paneling, not the lumber. If this product isn't available in your area, you could use pine paneling, vinyl siding, fiber cement panels, cedar shingles or whatever is available to you. Just make sure the siding profile is less than 3/4 in. or it will stick out past your trim boards. It just so happened that three of the cedar siding planks we bought fit in between the trim boards on the side without having to be ripped down. There was about a 3/16-in. gap on either side, which we caulked later.

Avoid a big mess by cutting all the siding planks to length and dry-fitting them before applying the adhesive. Tack them in place with 3/4-in. brads (Photo 2). Just shoot a couple of brads at the very end of the planks and a few on the edges. After they're all in, pound each plank flat with a rubber mallet or your fist and add one more brad in the center of each groove. The brads are only holding the siding in place until the adhesive sets up. Now repeat all these steps to build the other box.

Join the boxes

You can create an attractive platform out of pavers. Or, you could pour a small slab, tamp down some gravel or build a pressure-treated wooden platform. If you build a small platform, make sure it's level; larger patios should always slope away from the building.

Push the boxes into their permanent location and clamp the two sections together. Before fastening them, measure and cut the top plywood (E) so it's flush on all four sides. Temporarily set the top in place to see that it sits flat. Slip composite shims under one or both bases until the top is flat, the fronts are aligned and each side of the unit is relatively plumb. Secure the boxes to each other with eight 1-1/4-in. exterior grade screws, four through each side.

Trim the front

Install the two outside side trim boards (Q) first. Overlap them so they're flush with the trim boards on the sides. Keep them 3/4 in. off the ground like the trim on the sides. These trim boards will be shorter on top than the side trim to accommodate the slope of the roof. Find the length by holding a straight-edge on the roof slope and measure up to that. The drip edge (AA) installed under the shingles will overlap all the top trim boards and cover any imperfections. Install the trim boards with 1-1/4-in. brads and construction adhesive.

Cut and install the front bottom trim board (U). It should be flush with the top of the plywood that makes up the bottom of the boxes. Cut and install the top trim board (V). After you cut the center trim board (W) to length, apply the adhesive. Then center it over the door stops and tack it on with just a couple of brads to hold it in place (Photo 3).

Build the doors

Start by cutting the four temporary braces (H) that will hold the door slabs in place while you install the trim. Attach the braces to the back of the door stops and hinge supports. One 1-1/4-in. screw through each side will be enough to temporarily hold the doors.

The door slabs (G) sit flush with the door stops and the hinge supports. Cut each door slab so there's at least a 1/4-in. gap around all sides. The gap can be a little bigger, but a smaller gap may cause the doors to bind. Screw the slabs into place with two screws into each temporary brace (Photo 4).

Now install the door trim with construction adhesive and 1-1/4-in. brads. Install the sides first (X), then the tops and

3 **Add the front trim.** Trim the front after the boxes are attached. Double-check that both door openings are the same size before you permanently attach the center trim board.

4 **Mount the door slabs.** Screw the door slabs to temporary braces. This will let you build the doors in place for a perfect fit. Keep the screws at least 4 in. from the edge of the slab so they won't get covered up by the trim.

Figure A
Mini shed

Overall dimensions:
Approx. 79" tall x 55" wide x 18" deep

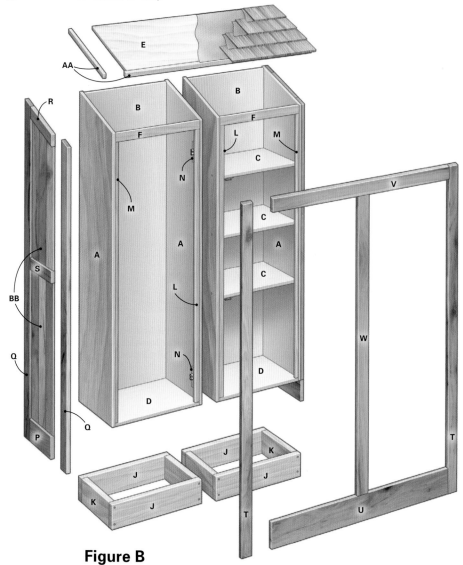

Figure C
Door construction

Figure B
3/4" plywood cutting diagram

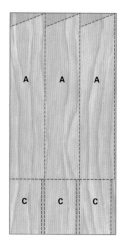
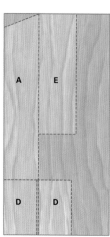
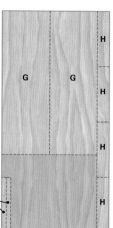
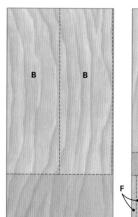

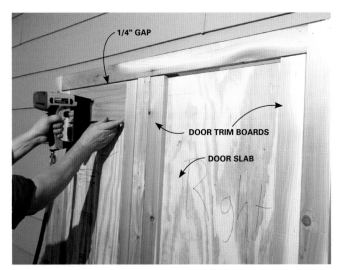

1/4" GAP

DOOR TRIM BOARDS

DOOR SLAB

5 **Build the doors in place.** Nail and glue the trim to the slabs, leaving an even gap around the edges. Then screw on the hinges, remove the temporary screws in the slabs, and install the siding back in your garage.

Cutting list

KEY	DIMENSIONS	QTY.	NAME
3/4" BC sanded plywood			
A	15-3/4" x 72"	4	Sides
B	23-3/4" x 72"	2	Backs
C	14-1/4" x 23-3/4"	3	Shelves
D	15" x 23-3/4"	2	Bottoms
E	17" x 52-1/8"	1	Top*
F	2" x 23-3/4"	2	Top braces
G	21-1/4" x 62-1/4"	2	Door slabs*
H	5-1/4" x 23-1/2"	4	Temporary door brace
Pressure-treated lumber			
J	1-1/2" x 5-1/2" x 25-1/4"	4	Base fronts and backs
K	1-1/2" x 5-1/2" x 12-3/4"	4	Base sides
Cedar (or pressure-treated)			
L	3/4" x 1-1/4"	2	Door stops*
M	3/4" x 3/4"	2	Hinge supports*
N	3/4" x 1-1/4" x 4"	2	Door latch blocks
P	3/4" x 5-1/2"	2	Side bottom trim boards*
Q	3/4" x 2-3/4"	4	Side trim boards*
R	3/4" x 2-3/4"	2	Side top trim boards*
S	3/4" x 2-3/4"	2	Side center trim boards*
T	3/4" x 2-3/4"	2	Front side trim boards*
U	3/4" x 5-1/2"	1	Front bottom trim board*
V	3/4" x 2-3/4"	1	Front top trim board*
W	3/4" x 2-3/4"	1	Front center trim board*
X	3/4" x 2-3/4"	4	Door side trim boards*
Y	3/4" x 5-1/2"	4	Door top and bottom trim boards*
Z	3/4" x 2-3/4"	2	Door center trim boards*
AA	3/4" x 1-1/8"	3	Drip edge*
BB	1/4" x 3/1/2"		Cedar planks*

*Cut to fit

bottoms (Y; Photo 5). Leave a 1/4-in. gap between the outside edge of the door trim and the trim on the face of the locker. Install the door center trim board (Z) so the top is 42-3/4 in. up from the ground, the same height as the center trim board on the sides.

Install the hinges before removing the doors. Cheap hinges tend to sag, which makes the doors a real challenge to hang, so buy good heavy-duty strap hinges. Center the hinge on the top and bottom door trim. These hinge screws required predrilled holes. Hold the hinges in place and mark all the hole locations with a pencil. Punch a starter hole in each spot with a nail set before predrilling the holes with a 1/8-in. bit. Mark the depth on the drill bit with a little masking tape so you don't drill too deep.

Once the hinges are installed, take out the screws that hold the slab to the temporary braces, and make sure the doors open and close without binding. Now remove the hinges, and take the doors back to your garage. Doors take a lot of abuse, so install additional 1-1/4-in. screws through the plywood slab into the door trim for a little extra support. Space them every 16 in. or so.

Install the siding the same way you did on the sides. It looks best if the first and last siding planks are close to the same size. You may need to rip about 1/4 in. off the first and last pieces to make them come out even. If you don't want to do the math, just snap a bunch of pieces of siding together, center them over the opening and mark how much to take off each side.

Materials list

ITEM	QTY.
4' x 8' x 3/4" sanded pine plywood	4
1x6 x 12' cedar	6
2x6 x 8' pressure-treated lumber	2
1/4" x 4" x 8' tongue-and-groove cedar paneling (six-pack)	3
Bundle of cedar shingles	1
1-1/4" exterior-grade trim-head screws (100-pack)	1
1-1/2" exterior-grade trim-head screws (100-pack)	1
2" exterior-grade screws (1-lb. box)	1
3" exterior-grade screws (1-lb. box)	1
1-1/4" 18-gauge brads (small box)	1
3/4" brads (small box)	1
1-1/4" 6d galvanized nails (1-lb. box)	1
Roll of 15-lb. felt paper	1
Construction adhesive (tube)	3
Polyurethane caulking (tube)	2
Composite shims (small bundle)	1
8" decorative T-hinges	4
Door handles	2
Roller door catches	4
1-1/2" fender washers	2
4" structural screws	2
Wood filler (small container)	1
Paint and/or exterior sealant	

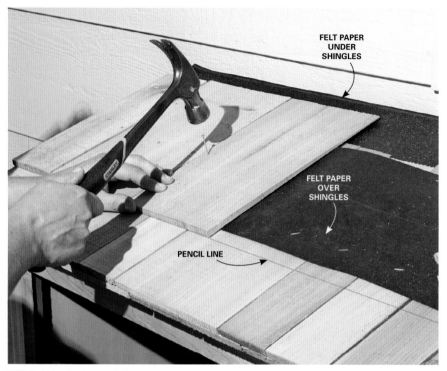

FELT PAPER UNDER SHINGLES

FELT PAPER OVER SHINGLES

PENCIL LINE

6 **Shingle the roof.** Cover the roof with felt paper. Prevent water from leaking between the shingles by covering every row with a strip of additional felt paper.

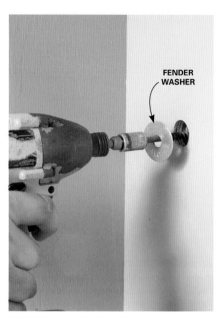

FENDER WASHER

7 **Prevent tipping!** This shallow locker can tip forward easily, so once you've applied your finish to the exterior, fasten the locker to wall studs with a couple of screws. An oversize hole and a fender washer on your screws will allow the locker to move up or down slightly with ground movement.

Install the roof

There is a difference between cedar shakes and cedar shingles. We tried using shakes on our first attempt, but they looked too gnarly on such a small surface. Fasten the top plywood with two 1-1/2-in. screws along the outside edges and middle, and four more along both the back and the front edges.

Cover the whole roof with 15-lb. felt paper. Install the first row of shingles so they overhang 1-1/2 in. past the trim on the front and sides. Drive in two 1-1/2-in. galvanized 4d nails per shingle about 3/4 in. from each edge and about 1-1/2 in. above the exposure line. Lay down a layer of felt paper about 8 in. wide and cover the whole first row almost to the bottom of the shingles. Install the second row directly over the first, staggering the seams as you go. Install another 8-in. strip of felt paper over this second row about 5-3/4 in. up from the bottom of the shingles. That's an inch higher than the exposure line. In this case, each of the four rows will have a 4-3/4-in. exposure. Use a straightedge and a pencil line to mark each row as you go (Photo 6).

Overlap the rest of the rows with felt paper in the same manner. You'll need to trim the back side of the shingles on the last two rows. It's easier to do this if you pull the locker away from the wall and mark each shingle as you go. The exposed nail heads on the last row will get sealed later on.

Install the drip edge (AA) under the shingles. Install the sides first, then the front. Secure them with construction adhesive and 1-1/4-in. brads spaced every 8 in.

Seal the exterior

Seal the exterior before you push the storage locker back up against the wall and reinstall the doors. Start with a polyurethane caulk similar to the final color of your project. Seal all the areas where the siding meets the trim. Fill any knotholes or voids in the siding and trim, and don't forget to cover the exposed nails on the shingles. Let the caulk dry overnight before applying the finish.

Coat the storage locker with an exterior wood finish, which darkens the wood just a bit (we used a Sikkens product). This product holds up well, but it's also really stinky. Wear a respirator and finish the doors outside. Lay the finish down with a roller and back-brush it. Force a little extra sealant into the holes made by the brads. If you don't want your shingles to turn a weathered gray, cover them with sealant as well. We applied one coat and will add another coat next year.

Finish it up

The profile of this storage locker is tall and thin, so secure the locker to the wall to prevent it from tipping over. Push it back into place and reinstall the shims so it's tight up against the wall and the sides are plumb. Soil can rise and fall in cold climate regions because of the freeze/thaw cycle. To give the unit a little wiggle room, drill a 3/4-in. hole through the back and secure the locker to your garage wall with two 4-in. screws and 1-1/2-in. fender washers (Photo 7), one on each side. An easy way to find the studs in the garage wall is to locate the nails in the siding.

Reinstall the doors and install the door catches. Install them where you attached the support blocks. On the other side, install one underneath the top and bottom shelves. All that's left is to trim off the shims, attach the handles and fill up your locker.

Garden storage closet

If you don't have room in your yard for a large, freestanding shed, you can still create plenty of space for garden tools with a shed attached to the back or side of the house. If you're an experienced builder, you can build this shed in a couple of weekends. Save money by using treated lumber, pine, and asphalt shingles instead of cedar as shown here.

Frame the walls and roof

Nail together the side walls, then square them with the plywood side panels. Overhang the panels 3/8 in. at the front—this will hide the gap at the corner when you hang the doors.

Join the two sides with the top and bottom plates and rim joists. The sides, top and bottom are all mirror images of each other except for the top front rim joist, which is set down 1/2 in. from the top so it stops the doors (Photo 1). Use screws to fasten the framework together except in the front where fasteners will be visible—use 2-1/2-in. casing nails there.

Screw the 4x4 footings to the bottom plates, then nail on the plywood base. Cut and screw together the two pairs of rafters, then nail on the fascia and ridge boards. Nail on the roof sheathing and the soffit, butting the corners together (Photo 2). Screw on the collar ties at the points shown in Figure A, then screw on the

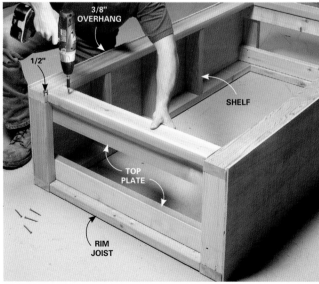

1 Frame and sheathe the walls, then join them with plates and joists. Use the best pieces of lumber in the front where they'll show.

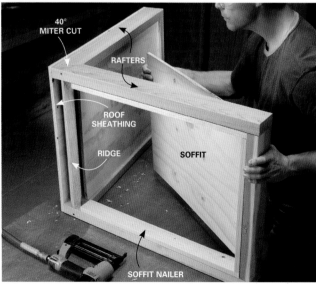

2 Build the roof on your workbench. Start with an L-shaped 2x4 frame, then add the nailers, soffit, sheathing and trim. Shingle with cedar or asphalt shingles.

Figure A
Garden closet construction details

The shed is made from three components—the roof, the walls and the doors, with edges covered by trim boards.

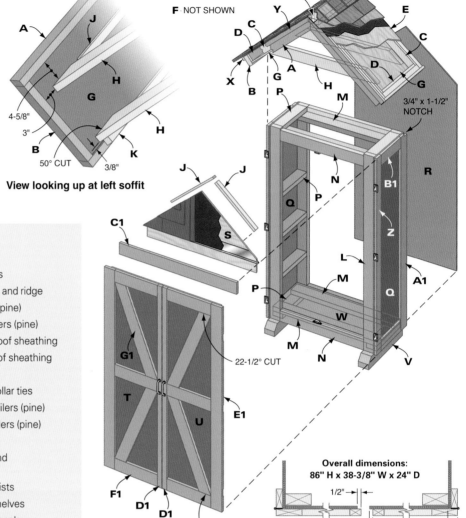

View looking up at left soffit

Overall dimensions:
86" H x 38-3/8" W x 24" D

Door Detail - Top View

LEFT DOOR   RIGHT DOOR

Cutting list

KEY	QTY.	SIZE & DESCRIPTION
A	4	1-1/2" x 3-1/2" x 32" rafters
B	3	1-1/2" x 3-1/2" x 20" fascia and ridge
C	4	3/4" x 2-1/2" x 27" nailers (pine)
D	2	3/4" x 2-1/2" x 18-1/2" nailers (pine)
E	1	1/2" x 23" x 31-7/8" right roof sheathing
F	1	1/2" x 23" x 32-1/4" left roof sheathing
G	2	1/2" x 20" x 28" soffit
H	2	1-1/2" x 3-1/2" x 38-3/8" collar ties
J	2	3/4" x 1-1/2" x 18" front nailers (pine)
K	2	3/4" x 1-1/2" x 23" rear nailers (pine)
L	4	1-1/2" x 3-1/2" x 64" studs
M	4	1-1/2" x 3-1/2" x 36" top and bottom plates
N	4	1-1/2" x 3-1/2" x 29" rim joists
P	10	1-1/2" x 3-1/2" x 13-1/2" shelves
Q	2	3/8" x 16-7/8" x 64" side panels
R	1	3/8" x 36-5/8" x 79-1/4" back panel
S	1	3/8" x 36" x 19-1/2" front panel
T	1	17-5/16" x 60-1/8" left door
U	1	18-5/16" x 60-1/8" right door
V	2	3-1/2" x 3-1/2" x 19-1/2" footings
W	1	13-3/8" x 35-7/8" plywood base
X	2	3/4" x 1-1/2" x 23" roof trim
Y	2	3/4" x 1-1/2" x 33-1/8" roof trim
Z	2	3/4" x 2-1/2" x 64" side battens
A1	2	3/4" x 3-1/2" x 64" rear side battens
B1	4	3/4" x 3-1/2" x 11-1/8" horizontal side battens
C1	1	3/4" x 3-1/2" x 38-3/8" front trim
D1	2	3/4" x 1-1/2" x 60-1/8" door edge
E1	2	3/4" x 3-1/2" x 60-1/8" door edge
F1	6	3/4" x 3-1/2" x 14-1/8" horizontal door trim
G1	4	3/4" x 3-1/2" x 28-3/8" (long edge to long edge) diagonal door trim

Materials list

ITEM	QTY.	ITEM	QTY.
3/8" x 4' x 8' rough-sawn exterior plywood	3	2-1/2" exterior screws	2 lbs.
		1-5/8" exterior screws	1 lb.
1/2" x 4' x 8' BC grade plywood	1	2-1/2" galv. finish nails	1 lb.
1x2 x 8' pine	1	1-1/2" galv. finish nails	1 lb.
1x2 x 8' cedar	3	1" narrow crown staples (for cedar shingles)	1 lb.
1x3 x 8' pine	2	30-lb. felt	1 roll
1x3 x 8' cedar	2	10" x 10' roll aluminum flashing	1
1x4 x 8' cedar	7	2-1/2" x 2-1/2" rust-resistant hinges	3 prs.
Cedar shakes	1 bundle	Magnetic catches	1 pr.
2x4 x 8' cedar	11	Handles	1 pr.
4x4 x 4' pressure treated	1		

Note: Shown are rough-sawn cedar boards—which usually (but not always!) measure 7/8 in. thick—for the trim. If you substitute pine, which measures 3/4 in., subtract 1/8 in. from each door width.

3 Set the completed roof on the shed base. Screw on the front and back panels to join the roof and the base.

ROOFING FELT

1" MINIMUM OVERLAP

FLASHING

4 Cover the front panel with roofing felt and shingles. Place metal flashing over the trim so water won't seep behind it.

front and rear nailers. Nail on the roof trim, staple on a layer of roofing felt, then shingle the roof. If you use cedar shingles, fasten them with narrow crown staples or siding nails. Leave 1/8-in. to 1/4-in. gaps between cedar shingles for expansion, and nail a strip of aluminum flashing across the ridge under the cap shingles.

Tip the shed upright, then set the roof on, aligning the front collar tie with the front rim joist and centering it side to side (Photo 3). Nail the cedar trim to the sides, aligning the 1x3s on the sides with the overhanging edge of plywood along the front edge. Glue and screw on the back and front siding panels to join the roof and base together. Use the back panel to square the structure and make it rigid.

Nail on the front trim piece, aligning it with the horizontal side battens (Z). Attach flashing and felt to the front panel, then cover it with cedar shakes (Photo 4).

Hang the doors

Finally, construct the doors (see Figure A, Door Detail, p. 192), cut the hinge mortises (see below) and hang the doors. Leave a 1/8-in. gap between the doors and trim along the top. Paint or stain if desired, then set the shed against the house on several inches of gravel. Add or take away gravel under the footings until the shed is tight against the siding and the gap above the doors is even. Screw the shed to the studs in the wall to keep it from tipping. Drill two 1/2-in. holes for the screws through the plywood near the rim joists, then loosely fasten the shed to the wall with 2-1/2-in. screws and large fender washers so the shed can move up and down when the ground freezes and thaws.

How to mortise a hinge

Mark the hinge locations on the doorjamb, then on the door, less 1/8 in. for clearance at the top of the door. Separate the hinge leaves, then align the edge of the leaf with the edge of the door or jamb. Predrill and fasten the leaf, then cut along all three edges with a razor knife to about the same depth as the hinge leaf (Photo 1).

Remove the hinge and make a series of angled cuts to establish the depth of the mortise (Photo 2). Turn the chisel over and clean out the chips using light hammer taps.

Holding the chisel with the beveled front edge against the wood, chip out the 1/4-in. sections. Check the fit of the hinge leaf and chisel out additional wood until the leaf sits flush.

If the hinges don't fit back together perfectly when you hang the door, tap the leaves up or down (gently) with a hammer.

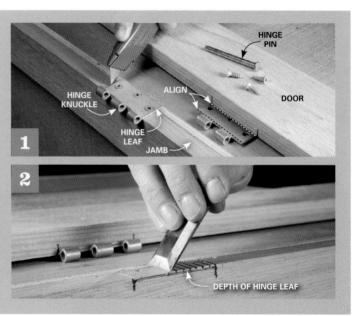

HINGE PIN

HINGE KNUCKLE

ALIGN

DOOR

HINGE LEAF

JAMB

1

2

DEPTH OF HINGE LEAF

Outdoor tips

Clothespin hamper

Need a clothespin hamper? An empty plastic plant hanger basket is a good one. It just needs a thorough cleaning and a couple of extra 1/4-in. drainage holes drilled into the bottom. The plastic hook slides easily along the line, and the basket has more than enough room for clothespins.

Add a remote hose connection for easier watering

If you're constantly dragging long lengths of hose from the house to the far corners of your yard, consider adding a remote faucet instead. Depending on how much time and expense you want to put into it, this can be as simple as a length of garden hose connected to a fence with pipe straps, or an underground pipe complete with a vacuum breaker at the house. Either way, you'll save a ton of time and effort by not having to deal with long hoses.

Hose caddy

Here's an easy way to store unwieldy garden hoses without strangling yourself. Coil them up in a round laundry basket or plastic bucket. Then hang the basket or bucket on the garage wall or slide it into an obscure corner.

Seed library

Now that CDs are being replaced with smartphones and other devices, you can use your old CD case to organize and store your seed packets. It works great to store them by seed type or even alphabetically. It's a convenient reference to have for the following year. Write notes on the packets to remember which seed variety worked and which didn't.

Propane tank carrier

When you take your 20-lb. propane tank to be filled, does it always roll around in the trunk of your car? To solve the problem, stick it in an old milk crate. The crate's wide, flat base keeps the tank stable.

Garden tool hideaway

A mailbox near your garden provides a convenient home for tools. A small mailbox like this one costs about $10 at hardware stores and home centers. King-size models cost about $25.

Garden/garage tool caddy

I had some leftover wood and plastic lattice from a fence I was building. Rather than toss the scraps, I decided to use them to build a caddy to organize my garden shovels, hoes and brooms. I installed casters, so it scoots easily into a corner of my garage. Works great!

–Philip J. Gruber

Bulb storage solution

Tender bulbs that must be overwintered indoors are hard to keep organized. These include canna lilies, freesias, caladiums, gladioluses, dahlias and tuberous begonias. Keep track of who's who by storing them in egg cartons, with each bulb identified on the top of the carton. The cartons even have ventilation holes that help prevent rot and mildew.

Cord reel solution

Zip ties are great to have on hand for quick repairs and fastening jobs around the shop. I like to zip-tie one end of an electrical cord so it stays with the cord reel. I keep the connection loose enough that I can pull out enough cord to reach an outlet.

–Oliver Rodriguez

Hose and sprinkler bucket

Storing hoses and cords on thin hooks or nails can cause them to crack or lose their shape. Five-gallon buckets fitted with a scrap of 3/4-in. plywood in the bottom and then screwed to the wall make great multipurpose holders. The plywood can be any shape, but to give it a more finished look, cut a circle slightly smaller than the diameter of the bucket.

Mount the bucket by driving screws through plywood. Without plywood, the screws will pull through the bottom of the bucket.

Chapter 5

GARAGE

Ultimate garage cabinets 198

Super-sturdy drawers 208

Bin tower 214

Flexible garage storage................................ 218

Garage wall system 222

One-day garage makeover 228

Garage tips 232

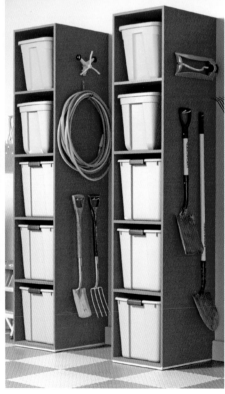

Ultimate garage cabinets

Inexpensive, enormous and surprisingly easy to build

If you're looking for easy, attractive, economical cabinets, you've found them. Keep in mind that this cabinet system can easily adapt to your situation: You can build one cabinet or a dozen, adjust the height or width to suit your space, or combine closed cabinets and open shelves in different ways. You can even configure this system for a laundry room, closet or basement.

DEEP UPPER CABINETS provide space for oversize items. But they're completely optional; you could cover the lower cabinets with a shelf.

OVERLAY HINGES are inexpensive and make door installation a cinch.

MELAMINE particleboard is economical and has a tough plastic coating that's easy to clean and lets you skip painting.

OPEN SHELVES between cabinets cut materials costs and labor. They also provide instant access to often-used items.

SIMPLE DOORS, which are just slabs of melamine, keep dust out and hide clutter.

BASIC BOX CABINETS are incredibly simple to build; just screw them together. You can add doors, or not.

OPEN SPACE under cabinets allows for easy sweeping and prevents water damage.

WHAT IT TAKES

TIME: 1 to 3 weekends
SKILLS: Intermediate
TOOLS: Basic hand tools, drill, circular saw

1 **Iron on the edge banding.** Cut melamine to width and iron on the edge banding. Position the banding so it overhangs the ends and sides. Let the banding cool before trimming.

EDGE BANDING

2 **Trim the ends.** Hold a wood block firmly over the end and carefully slice off the excess banding. Use a sharp new blade in your utility knife.

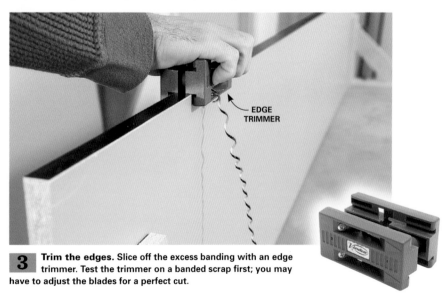

EDGE TRIMMER

3 **Trim the edges.** Slice off the excess banding with an edge trimmer. Test the trimmer on a banded scrap first; you may have to adjust the blades for a perfect cut.

Tools, materials & money

You could build this system with just a few hand tools, a drill and a circular saw, but a table saw would save you lots of time. The skills you'll need are as basic as the tools. If you can make long straight cuts and screw parts together, you can build this system.

This whole system is made from just two materials: plastic-coated particleboard, usually called "melamine," and construction-grade pine 1x4s. (Melamine is the type of plastic used as the coating.) You could use 3/4-in. plywood or particleboard, but we chose melamine because it didn't require a finish.

The materials for this floor-to-ceiling system cost less than we would have paid for wimpy "utility" cabinets at a home center. Our garage walls were 10 ft. tall. If your ceiling is about 8 ft. tall, you can eliminate the deep upper cabinets. That will lower the cost per linear foot. If you opt for completely open shelving and skip the cabinet doors, your cost will drop to about $20 per linear foot.

Plan the system to suit your stuff

Roughly block out the cabinet locations on the wall, using masking tape. Remember to space the garage cabinets to leave room for shelves in between. Experiment with different cabinet widths and spacing until you find a layout that works well. Follow these guidelines:
- Each cabinet must have at least one stud behind it so you can fasten the cabinet securely to the wall.
- Limit door widths to 24 in. or less. To cover a wider opening, install double doors. We limited most of our doors to 12-in. widths so that we could open them even when the car was parked in the garage.
- Shelves longer than 2 ft. often sag. If you make yours longer, stiffen the melamine by screwing 1x4 cleats to the undersides.
- Size your cabinets to make the most of a full sheet of melamine. By making our cabinets 16 in. deep, for example, we were able to cut three cabinet sides from each sheet with no wasted

Figure A
Upright cabinet construction

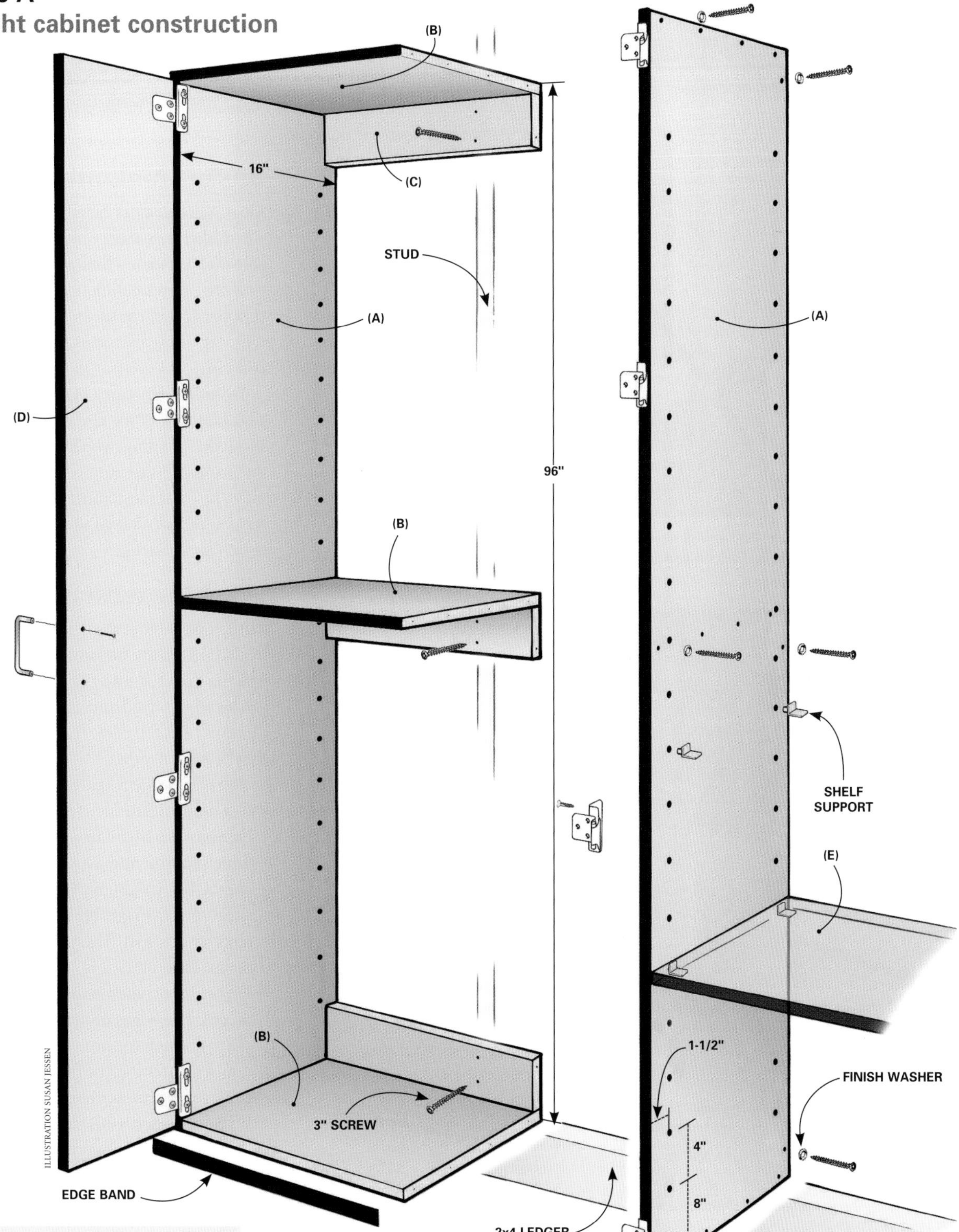

(B)

16"

(C)

STUD

(A)

96"

(B)

(D)

(A)

SHELF
SUPPORT

(E)

(B)

1-1/2"

FINISH WASHER

4"

3" SCREW

8"

ILLUSTRATION SUSAN JESSEN

EDGE BAND

2x4 LEDGER

2" SCREW

Parts list

KEY	SIZE & DESCRIPTION
A	16" x 96" (side)
B	16" x 23-5/8" (fixed shelf)
C	3-1/2" x 23-5/8" pine (cleat)
D	12" x 95-1/4" (door)
E	16" x 23-5/8" (adjustable shelf)

Overall dimensions:
96" tall x 25-1/8" wide x 16-3/4" deep.
Your dimensions may differ.

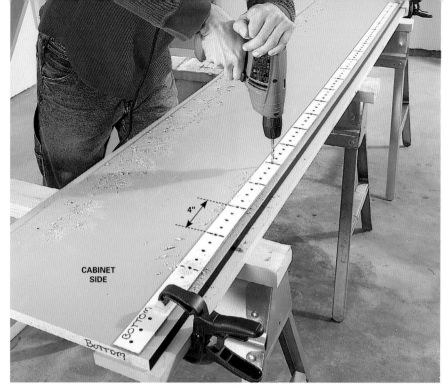

4 **Drill shelf support holes.** Drill 1/4-in. shelf support holes through cabinet sides using a scrap of pegboard as a guide. For end panels that won't support shelves on one side, place a stop collar on the drill bit.

CABINET SIDE

4"

STOP BLOCK

2x4 SUPPORTS

CROSSCUT GUIDE

5 **Crosscut the parts.** Cut parts to length using a crosscut guide. A stop block screwed to the guide lets you mass-produce identical lengths fast. Support the melamine on both sides of the cut with 2x4 scraps.

Figure B
Crosscut guide

This guide takes a few minutes to make but saves time when you're cutting the fixed shelves (Photo 5) and even more time later when you're cutting shelves (Photo 14). Our system required 30 shelves. To make a crosscut guide, screw a guide strip to the base and run your saw against the guide strip to trim the excess off the base. Add a squaring strip positioned perpendicular to the guide strip. Position the stop block to set the length of your parts.

SQUARING STRIP

STOP BLOCK

1/2" GUIDE STRIP

3/4" BASE

material (see Figure A for other dimensions). Don't forget that your saw blade eats up about 1/8 in. of material with each cut. Some sheets of melamine are oversized by about 1 in. to account for this.

Buying melamine

Most home centers carry melamine in 4 x 8-ft. sheets, usually only in white. For colors other than white, try a lumberyard that serves cabinetmakers. These suppliers often charge more and might sell only to professionals, so call before you visit.

Home centers carry plastic iron-on edge banding. Some also carry peel-and-stick edge banding, which lets you skip the ironing. Either way, white will be your only choice at most home centers. If you want another color, go to fastcap.com and search for "Fastedge."

Working with melamine

With your cabinet dimensions in hand, begin cutting the melamine into parts. Cut the material into equal widths for the sides and the fixed and adjustable shelves, but don't cut the parts to length until they're edge banded.

Here are some pointers:
- **Get help.** Melamine is too heavy to handle solo. If you have a large, stable table saw, you and a helper can cut full sheets. But it's usually better to slice a sheet into manageable sections with a circular saw first. Then make finish cuts on the table saw.
- **Wear gloves when handling large pieces.** The edges of melamine are sharp enough to slice your hands.
- **Avoid scratching the melamine surface.** If your workbench has a rough surface, cover it with cardboard or old carpet. Pad sawhorses the same way. Run a few strips of masking tape across the shoe of your circular saw so it doesn't mar the melamine.
- **Be careful with edges.** They're easy to chip. When you stand parts on edge, set them down gently. Don't drop sheets or drag them across the floor.
- **Plan for chip-out.** Saw blades often leave slightly chipped edges in the melamine coating. A new carbide blade will chip less than a dull one, but

you can't completely prevent chips. Chipping is worse on the side where the saw teeth exit the material. When you run melamine across a table saw, the underside of the sheet is particularly prone to chipping. When you're using a circular saw or a jigsaw, chipping is worse on the face-up side. Plan your cuts so that all the chipped edges are on the same side of the part. Then you can hide them during assembly by facing them toward the inside of cabinets.

Iron on the edge band

Set your iron to the "cotton" setting and iron the banding on in two or three passes (Photo 1). On the first pass, run the iron quickly over the banding just to tack it into place. Center the banding so it overhangs on both sides. Make a second, slower pass to fully melt the glue and firmly adhere the banding. Then check the edges for loose spots and make another pass if needed.

Trim the ends of the banding with a utility knife (Photo 2) before you trim the edges (Photo 3). If you damage the banding while trimming, just reheat it, pull it off and start over. For more information, see p. 261 or visit familyhandyman.com and search for "edge banding."

Drill shelf support holes

The adjustable shelves rest on shelf supports that fit into holes drilled into the cabinet sides (Photo 4). Drill all the way through the sides that will support shelves inside and outside the cabinet. Drill holes 3/8 in. deep in cabinet sides that form the outer ends of your shelf system. Tape wrapped around a drill bit makes a good depth marker when you're drilling just a few holes, but a stop collar is better for this job.

Check your shelf supports before drilling. Some require 1/4-in. holes; others require 5mm holes. Use a brad-point drill bit for a clean, chip-free hole. To limit blowout where the bit exits the melamine, set a "backer" underneath. You can make a drilling guide from just about any material, but a strip of pegboard is a perfect ready-made guide. Label the bottom of your guide and the bottoms of the cabinet sides so all the holes will align.

6 **Assemble the cabinets.** Predrill and screw 1x4s to melamine to form the fixed shelves. Screw all the fixed shelves to one cabinet side, then add the other side to complete the cabinet.

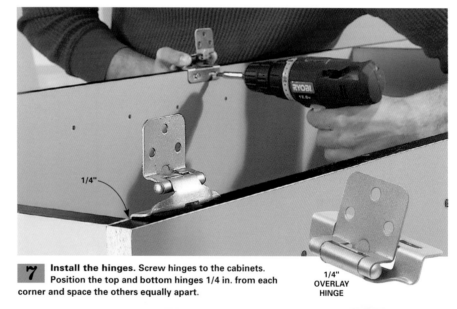

7 **Install the hinges.** Screw hinges to the cabinets. Position the top and bottom hinges 1/4 in. from each corner and space the others equally apart.

1/4"
1/4"
OVERLAY HINGE

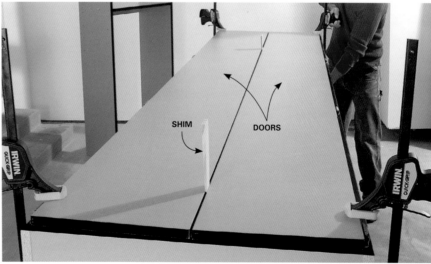

8 **Position the doors.** Position the doors over the hinges using shims to maintain a 1/8-in. gap. Use clamps or weights to hold the doors in place.

SHIM   DOORS

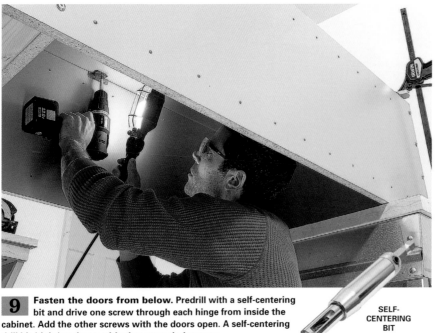

10 install a ledger. Fasten a 2x4 ledger to the wall framing with 3-in. screws. Choose a straight 2x4 and make sure the ledger is level.

9 Fasten the doors from below. Predrill with a self-centering bit and drive one screw through each hinge from inside the cabinet. Add the other screws with the doors open. A self-centering drill bit (right) makes positioning screw holes easy.

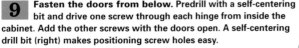

SELF-CENTERING BIT

Build fixed shelves and assemble the cabinets

The fixed shelves that fit between the cabinet sides (A) are made from melamine panels (B) and pine 1x4s (C). Paint the 1x4s to match the melamine. Cabinets less than 4 ft. tall need only top and bottom fixed shelves. Taller cabinets also need a middle fixed shelf (Figure A). To make the fixed shelves, just cut melamine and 1x4s to identical lengths and screw them together.

Assembling the cabinets is a simple matter of fastening the sides to the fixed shelves (Photo 6). Predrill and drive a screw near the front of each fixed shelf first, making sure the banded edges of the fixed shelf and side are flush. Then drill and drive another screw near the back of the cabinet to hold the fixed shelf in position before you add the other screws. Handle the completed cabinet boxes with care—they're not very strong until they're fastened to the wall.

Hang the doors

Make the doors *after* the cabinet boxes are assembled. To hang the doors, first screw hinges to the cabinets (Photo 7). The type of hinge we chose is called a "wrap" hinge because it wraps around the corner at the front edge of the cabinet. If you don't find them at a home center, search online for "1/4 overlay wrap hinge." This design has two big advantages: It mounts more securely to the cabinet and it lets you position the doors perfectly (Photo 8) before you fasten them (Photo 9).

1/2" OR MORE CLEARANCE FROM WALL

LEDGER

11 Hang the cabinets. Set the cabinet into place and screw it to the ledger. Then level the cabinet and fasten it to the wall with pairs of 3-in. screws driven through the upper and middle cleats into studs.

Making screws work in melamine

Screws are the only fastening method used in this entire project. They make fast, strong joints. But screwing into melamine presents a few complications:

■ **Strip-out:** As with any other particleboard product, melamine strips easily if you overdrive screws. Go easy on the drill trigger as you drive screws home. Use coarse-thread screws only. Fine-thread screws will strip every time. Longer screws also minimize stripping. If this project had been built from plywood, 1-5/8-in. screws would have worked fine. But we used 2-in. screws to assemble the boxes.

■ **Splits:** Particleboard splits easily. Never drive a screw into particleboard without drilling a pilot hole. We drilled 7/64-in. holes and used No. 8 screws. Even with a pilot hole, screws will split particleboard if you place them close to ends. Keep them at least an inch from the ends of parts.

■ **Countersinking:** Tapered screw heads will sometimes sink into melamine, but often they'll strip out before the head is flush with the melamine surface. Next to an edge, they'll crush out the particleboard. Always drill countersink holes to create a recess for screw heads. You can drill countersink and pilot holes in one stroke with a countersink bit.

■ **Appearance:** Even with a clean countersink hole, screw heads are a blemish in melamine's perfect surface. For a neater look, use finish washers (photo below) with screws that will be visible. Finish washers would eliminate the need for countersink holes.

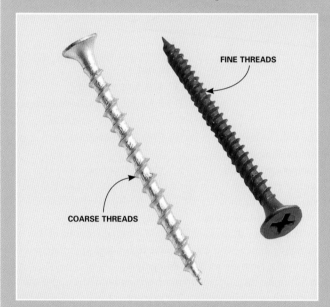

FINE THREADS

COARSE THREADS

FINISH WASHER

SPLIT

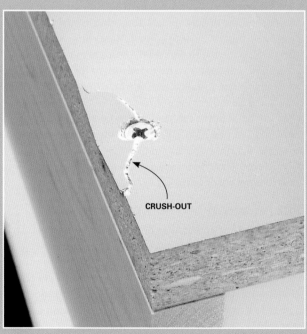

CRUSH-OUT

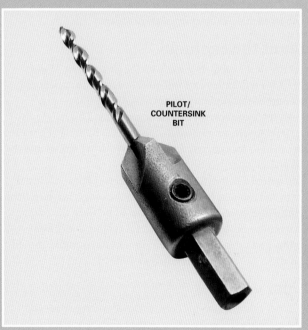

PILOT/ COUNTERSINK BIT

Figure C
Upper cabinet construction

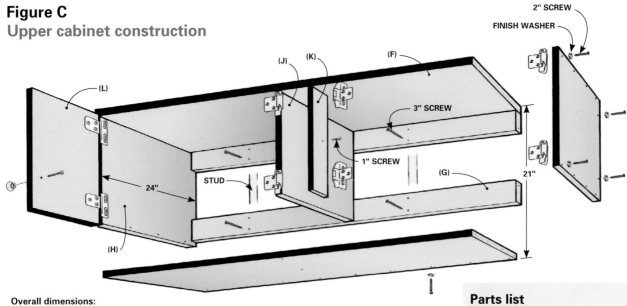

2" SCREW
FINISH WASHER

(J) (K) (F)

(L)

3" SCREW

1" SCREW

STUD

(G)

24"

21"

(H)

Overall dimensions:
21" tall x 72" wide x 24" deep.
Your dimensions may differ.

Parts list		
KEY	SIZE & DESCRIPTION	
F	24" x 70-1/2" (top/bottom panel)	
G	3-1/2" x 70-1/2" pine (cleat)	
H	21" x 24" (side panel)	
J	19-1/2" x 23-1/4" (divider)	
K	4" x 23-1/4" (hinge spacer)	
L	17-7/16" x 20-1/4" (door)	

We used four hinges for each of our 12-in.-wide double doors. If you opt for a single wide door, use at least five hinges. The hinges themselves are strong enough to hold much more weight, but they're fastened with just two screws each. The particleboard core of melamine doesn't hold screws very well. So when in doubt, add more hinges.

With the hinges in place, measure between them to determine the door width (with double doors, allow a 1/8-in. gap between them). To determine the length, measure the cabinet opening and add 3/4 in. Cut the doors and set them in place to check the fit before banding the edges. When the doors are complete and screwed to the hinges, label each door and cabinet. Then unscrew the doors to make cabinet installation easier.

Mount the cabinets

Don't install the cabinets directly on the garage floor. Water puddles from dripping cars will quickly destroy particleboard. We mounted these cabinets about 6 in. off the floor—just enough space to allow for easy floor sweeping. This height also let us level the ledger and fasten it to the wall framing (Photo 10) rather than to the concrete foundation. We drove screws into the studs and sill plate.

You'll need a helper to install the cabinets (Photo 11). Install the two end cabinets first, then position the others between them, leaving equal spaces for the shelves that fit between the cabinets. Watch out for obstructions that prevent cabinet doors from opening. End cabinets that fit into corners, for example, should stand about 1/2 in. from the adjacent wall.

Upper cabinets

The upper cabinets provide deep, enclosed storage space and tie the upright cabinets together so they can't twist away from the wall. Instead of installing upper cabinets, you could simply run a long shelf across the tops of the upright cabinets.

The upper cabinets are simply horizontal versions of the upright cabinets; you use the same techniques and materials (see Figure C). Here are some building tips:

- Minimize measuring and math errors: Build the upper cabinets after the upright cabinets are in place.
- To allow easy installation, leave a 1/2-in. gap between the ceiling and the upper cabinets. You could leave the resulting gap open, but we chose to cover it. Here's how: We ripped 1x4s into 1-in.-wide strips, painted the strips to match the edge band and screwed the strips to the tops of the cabinets. After the uppers were installed, we cut trim strips from 1x4, painted them and used them to cover the gap.
- You can build upper cabinet sections up to 8 ft. long. For strength and ease of installation, size the sections so they meet over the upright cabinets, not over open shelves.
- Remember to add hinge spacers (K) to dividers (J) so you can install hinges back to back.

Shelves and hardware come last

Cut the shelves at the very end of the project (Photo 14). That way, you can take exact measurements inside and between shelves and use up any scraps. The number of shelves is up to you; we made four for inside each cabinet and six for each between-cabinet space. Install cabinet knobs or pulls after the doors are in place to make drilling a hole in the wrong location just about impossible.

12 **Assemble the upper cabinets.** Build the upper cabinets with the same techniques and materials used for the uprights. Install a blank panel where cabinets will meet at a corner.

13 **Install the upper cabinets.** Set the upper cabinets on top of the lower cabinets and screw the uppers together with 1-1/4-in. screws. Then screw them to the wall studs and to the lower cabinets.

14 **Add shelves between cabinets.** Measure the spaces inside and between cabinets. Subtract 1/4 in. and cut shelves using the crosscut jig.

CABINET BUMPER

SHELF SUPPORT

Super-sturdy drawers

Super big, super tough, super easy

This heavy-duty storage system is modeled after old metal filing cabinets, but these cabinets will hold more weight.

We decided to build a bunch of them and add shelves and a continuous top. The first one (the prototype) took one full day to build and a couple hours to paint and finish, but we built the other five in just two more days. This isn't a project that requires a high-end furniture maker's craftsmanship: If you can build basic plywood boxes, you can build these drawer units.

Getting started

We'll focus on how to build one unit, but you can build as many as you like and arrange them whichever way works best. Refer to the cutting diagram, and cut all the plywood components except the back (C), drawer bottoms (D) and hardwood drawer fronts (L, M, N). Cut these parts to size as you need them in case one or

more components get a little out of whack. Many home centers will help you cut your plywood so it's easier to haul home, but don't wear out your welcome and expect them to make all the cuts for you.

Cut and install the drawer supports

Lay the two sides (A) next to each other on your workbench. Position them so the surface with the most flaws faces up—this will be the inside and won't be visible once the drawers are installed. Also, determine which of the plywood edges have the fewest flaws and voids, and arrange the pieces so the best edges face toward the front. Measure up from the bottom on each side 14 in., 26 in. and 38 in., and make a pencil mark near the outside edge of each side. Use a straightedge, and draw a line between your marks and across the face of both sides at the same time. These will be the guidelines for the tops of the drawer supports (P).

WHAT IT TAKES

(for four units)

TIME: 2 days

SKILL: Beginner to intermediate

TOOLS: Circular saw (table saw preferable), drill, 18-gauge brad nailer, router/round-over bit, clamp

Cut 18 in. off the 6-ft. pine 1x4, and set it aside to be used as the [cen]ter brace (Q). Rip down what's left of the 1x4 into 1-in. strips to be [use]d as the six drawer supports, and cut them to length (see Cutting [List, p. 212]).

[I]nstall the drawer supports with glue and 1-1/2-in. brads (Photo [1]. The drawer supports should be 1/2 in. short on the front side [to ac]commodate the thickness of the hardwood drawer fronts. Flip [the] sides over and install three 1-1/2-in. screws in each support. [Cou]ntersink all the screws a bit on the outside of the entire carcass so [the] holes can be filled with wood filler before painting.

[As]semble the carcass

[App]ly wood glue and tack on the top or bottom (B) to the sides [with] three or four brads. Even if you picked the straightest plywood [avai]lable at the home center or lumberyard, it will probably cup and [bow]l a bit after it's cut up. So whenever you join two pieces of plywood,

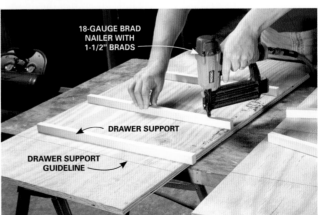

18-GAUGE BRAD NAILER WITH 1-1/2" BRADS

DRAWER SUPPORT

DRAWER SUPPORT GUIDELINE

1 **Mount the drawer supports. Attach the drawer supports to the side panels before assembling the cabinet. Glue each support and tack it down with brads. Then flip the panel over and drive 1-1/2-in. screws into the supports.**

2 Assemble the carcass. Fasten the sides to the top and bottom with glue and brads, and then add screws. To avoid splitting the plywood, drill pilot holes for the screws and stay 1-1/2 in. from the ends.

In image: STAY 1-1/2" FROM END · 1-1/2" TRIM-HEAD SCREWS

3 Add the back. Use the back to square up the cabinet. Fasten the whole length of one side, and then align the other sides with the back as you go.

start on one end and straighten out the plywood as you go.

Secure each joint with three 1-1/2-in. screws before moving on to the next one. Whenever drilling close to the edge of plywood, avoid puckers and splits by predrilling 1/8-in. holes for the screws. And stay at least 1-1/2-in. from the end of the plywood that's being drilled into (Photo 2). If a screw is installed too close to the end, it will just split the plywood instead of burying into it.

Spread glue on the back edge of the carcass and fasten the back with 1-1/2-in. brads along one whole side first. Then use the back as a guide to square up the rest of the carcass (Photo 3). Finish attaching the back with screws every 16 in. or so.

The center brace keeps the plywood sides from bowing in or out. Measure the distance between the drawer runners at the back of the carcass. Cut the center brace that same length. Install the brace between the two middle runners 4 in. back from the front. Make sure the brace is flush or just a little lower than the drawer supports or the drawer will teeter back and forth on it. Hold it in place with a clamp and secure it with two 3-in. screws through each side (Photo 4). Install a brace at more than one drawer support location if your plywood is particularly unruly.

Assemble the drawers

Lay out each drawer so all the best edges face up. Then, just as you did with the carcass, assemble the drawers with glue, brads and screws. Cut the drawer bottoms after the sides (F, H, K) and fronts/backs (E, G, J) are assembled. That way you can cut the bottoms exactly to size. A perfectly square bottom will ensure your drawers are also square. Make sure the bottom is flush or a little short on the front side of the drawer; otherwise the hardwood drawer fronts won't sit flat on the front of the drawer (Photo 5).

Fasten the drawer fronts

The home center carried three options of hardwood plywood: oak, birch and one labeled just "hardwood." We went with the generic hardwood, but if you do the same, make sure you get enough to finish your project because the grain and color will vary

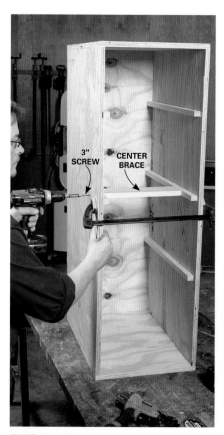

In image: 3" SCREW · CENTER BRACE

4 Install the center brace. The brace prevents the sides from bowing in or out. Clamp the brace in place, and then fasten it with 3-in. trim-head screws.

Figure A
Storage unit

Overall dimensions:
16" wide x 51-1/2" tall x 24" deep

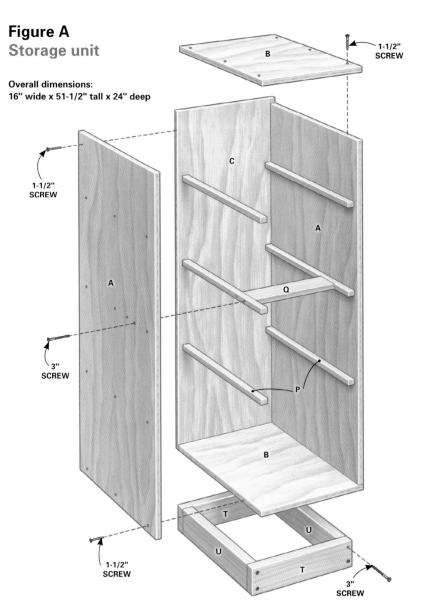

1-1/2" SCREW

1-1/2" SCREW

3" SCREW

1-1/2" SCREW

3" SCREW

B

C

A

A

Q

P

B

T

U

U

T

Materials list (for one unit)

ITEM	QTY.
4' x 8' x 3/4" BC sanded plywood	2
2' x 4' x 1/2" hardwood plywood	1
1x6 x 6' pine	1
2x4 x 8' pressure-treated lumber	1
1x2 x 4' oak	1
1-1/4" x 16" oak dowel	1
1-1/2" screws (small box)	1
3" trim-head screws (small box)	1
1-1/2" 18-gauge brads (small box)	1
1/4" x 3-1/2" carriage bolts	8
1/4" nut and washer	8
Wood filler, patch or putty	1
Paint, quart	1
Polyurethane, quart	1

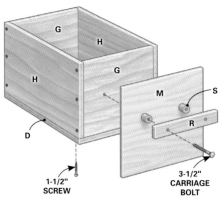

G

H

G

H

M

S

R

D

1-1/2" SCREW

3-1/2" CARRIAGE BOLT

There are three drawer sizes.
See the Cutting List for dimensions.

DRAWER BOTTOM

GLUE

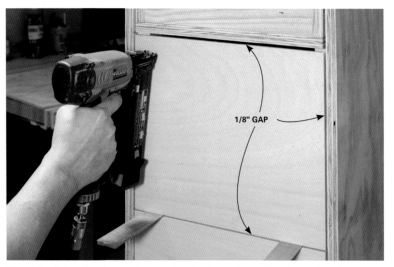

1/8" GAP

5 **Build the drawers.** Assemble the drawers just as you built the cabinets: Glue, nail and screw the sides, front and back. Then square up the box as you fasten the bottom.

6 **Position the drawer fronts.** Slip the drawer boxes into the cabinet. Center the drawer fronts and shim under them to achieve 1/8-in. gaps. Secure the fronts to the drawer boxes with glue and one brad in each corner.

from one batch to the next.

The drawers may not sit perfectly flat until they are filled with stuff, so before you secure the hardwood drawer fronts, add some weight to the drawer you're working on and the one above it. Center each drawer in the opening before you secure the drawer front.

Start at the bottom, and cut the hardwood drawer fronts to size one at a time. Cut them so there's a 1/8-in. gap between the bottom and the sides and the bottom of the drawer above it. Rest the drawer front on a couple of shims to achieve the gap at the bottom and eyeball the gaps on the side. Glue it and secure it with four brads, one in each corner (Photo 6). There's no need for screws; the handle bolts will sandwich everything together. If you're building several of these storage units and purchased a piece of hardwood plywood larger than 2 x 4 ft., you'll have the option to line up the grain on the drawer fronts the same way it came off the sheet. It's a small detail that can add a lot to the looks of your project.

Build and attach the handles

Rout the edges of the handle with a 1/4-in. round-over bit before cutting the handles (R) to length. Next, cut the dowels for the

handle extensions (S) to length.

HANDLE

Build one simple jig to align the dowels on the handles, and to position the handles on the drawer fronts. Cut a 3/4-in. piece of plywood the same width as the drawer fronts and rip it down to 4-3/8 in. Fasten a scrap of 3/4-in. material to the end of the jig. Measure in from each side and mark a line at 2-1/8 in., 3-1/8 in. and 4-3/8 in.

This jig is designed to center the top handle on the top drawer front and keep the others the same distance down from the top on all the other drawers. If you want all the handles centered, you'll have to build two more jigs or mark center lines on the other drawers.

Set the jig on your workbench and line up the handle with the two outside lines. Line up the dowels on the inside and middle lines on the jig and glue them to the center of the handle. No need for clamping—just keep pressure on them for 10 to 20 seconds. Then set them aside for an hour or so to let the glue dry. The glue is just to keep the dowels in place until the handle bolts are installed.

Figure B
Cutting diagram

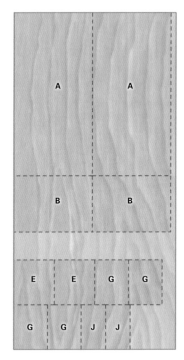
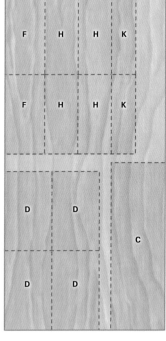

Cutting list (for one unit)

KEY	QTY.	SIZE & DESCRIPTION
3/4" BC sanded plywood		
A	2	46-1/2" x 23-1/4" sides
B	2	16" x 23-1/4" top/bottom
C	1	48" x 16" back*
D	4	22-3/4" x 14-1/4" drawer bottoms*
E	2	12-3/4" x 12" bottom drawer front/back
F	2	22-3/4" x 12" bottom drawer sides
G	4	12-3/4" x 10" middle drawer front/back
H	4	22-3/4" x 10" middle drawer sides
J	2	12-3/4" x 7-1/4" top drawer front/back
K	2	22-3/4" x 7-1/4" top drawer sides
1/2" hardwood plywood		
L	1	14-1/4" x 13-7/8" bottom drawer front*
M	2	14-1/4" x 11-7/8" middle drawer fronts*
N	1	14-1/4" x 8-3/8" top drawer front*
Cut from 6' pine 1x4		
P	6	22-1/2" x 1" x 3/4" drawer supports
Q	1	12-1/2" x 3-1/2" x 3/4" center brace
Cut from 4' oak 1x2		
R	4	10" x 1-1/2" x 3/4" handles
Cut from 1' oak 1-1/4" dowel		
S	8	1" x 1-1/4" handle extensions
Cut from 8' pressure-treated 2x4		
T	2	16" x 1-1/2" x 3-1/2" base front/back
U	2	17" x 1-1/2" x 3-1/2" base sides

*Cut to fit

Clamp the jig onto the top of the drawer front, and line up the handle with the guidelines. Drill a starter hole through each handle and the drawer front with a 1/8-in. drill bit before drilling the final holes with a 1/4-in. bit (Photo 7). The 1/8-in. bit probably won't be long enough to clear all the material, but it still helps make a cleaner hole when you drill through the second time.

Mark the bottom of each handle extension and the area near the hole on each drawer with the same number so you can install that same handle on the same drawer after you apply the finish.

Build and secure the base

If you're building only one unit, cut the base parts (T) and assemble them with glue and two 3-in. screws that are compatible with pressure-treated lumber. Secure the base to the bottom of the carcass with glue and 1-1/2-in. screws: three on the sides and two each on the front and back.

Finish the components

Patch all the screw holes, brad holes and voids on the carcass with wood filler or wood patch. We painted only the outside and front of the cabinet. We didn't bother painting the wood on the insides, backs or sides that were going to be sandwiched together. Cover the hardwood drawer fronts and edges with two coats of polyurethane, or a similar coating of your choice. Avoid discoloration around the brad hole on the drawer fronts by filling them with matching putty between coats of poly. We

stained the oak handles with a medium-tinted stain to make them "pop" a little more before finishing them with two coats of poly.

Install the handles with the carriage bolts, washers and nuts. Seat the carriage bolts with a hammer so they don't spin while you turn the nut, and turn them tight.

Install multiple units

If you're building several units, build the base and then set each unit in place individually (Photo 8). Create a toe space by building the base 4 in. narrower than the units. If your garage floor slants down toward the overhead door, you'll have to rip down the base to make the whole thing level. You may just need a few shims to make yours level. Level each storage unit as you go and screw them to the base and to one another with 1-1/2-in. screws. Angle the screws a bit so they don't poke through when you screw the units together.

Rip down a couple of cleats and screw them to the sides for the middle shelf to sit on. Leave them a couple inches short of the front so you don't see them. Attach the lower shelf to the base before you install the middle shelf (Photo 9).

Once all the units are in place, attach the top(s) so the seams fall in the middle of one unit. Screw the whole thing to the wall studs last using one screw per unit. The front side of the base may need a few shims to make it sit flush against the wall.

Touch up the exposed screw holes and scuff marks with paint. Now all that's left is to file away all that clutter.

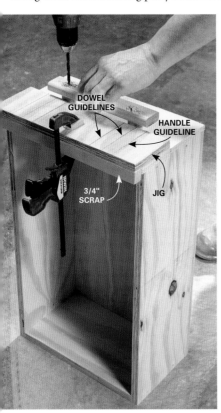

7 **Add the handles.** Build a simple jig and clamp it onto the drawer front. Hold the handle in place and drill holes for the carriage bolts.

8 **Set the carcass on the base.** When installing multiple units, build, paint and lay down the base first, and then attach each unit to the base.

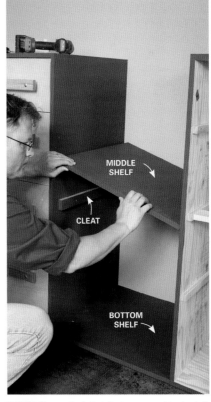

9 **Hang shelving between units.** Install the bottom shelf on the base. Install cleats to support other shelves.

Bin tower

Tons of easy-access storage—and more space to hang stuff!

WHAT IT TAKES

(for three towers)

TIME: One weekend

SKILL: Beginner to intermediate

TOOLS: Table saw/circular saw, drill, 18-gauge brad nailer (optional)

These bin towers are simple to build, don't require expensive tools, and actually add wall space without losing a lot of floor space. We designed the towers to fit 16- to 18-gallon bins with a lid size of about 18 x 24 in.

Cut up the plywood

We used "BC" sanded pine plywood for this project. The holes and blemishes on the "B" side are filled and make for a good painting surface. It's not furniture grade, but it's priced right and works well for garage projects like this one. Rip all the sheets down to 23-3/4 in. If you don't own a table saw, use a straightedge and make your cuts with a circular saw

Once all the sheets have been ripped down, cut the tops, bottoms and shelves to 18-in. lengths. If you're using a circular saw, save time by clamping two 8-ft. strips together, and cut two at a time. Some home centers will make your cuts for you, so if you don't have a ton of confidence in your cutting skills, ask the staff if they can help.

Paint the parts before assembly

Finishing the cut components before you assemble them will save you a bunch of time, but before you start slathering on the paint, figure out which edges need to be painted—the back edges of the sides don't, and only the front edges of the shelves do. Configure all the parts so the best edge faces out. Mark an "X" with a pencil on all the edges that need paint. Some of the edges will have voids in the wood that will need to be filled (Photo 1).

Make a couple of passes with 100-grit sandpaper before you paint. We covered the wood with a paint/primer in one (Photo 2). If you choose a traditional wood primer, have the store tint it close to the final color.

Assemble the towers

Use an 18-gauge brad nailer with 1-1/2-in. brads to quickly attach the shelves to the sides, three brads on each side. If you don't have a brad nailer, that's OK; you can assemble everything with screws only. Cut a piece of plywood 18-5/16 in. wide to align the shelves (Photo 3). The spacer board may scuff up the paint a little bit, but you can touch it up when you paint over your fastener holes after everything is all put together. Arrange the sides so the good surface faces out. The good surface on the bottom four shelves should face up, and the top two should face down. That way, you'll see the nicer finish from almost any angle.

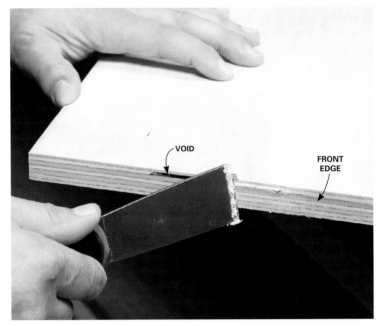

1 Fill plywood voids. Figure out which edge will be exposed on each part, and fill any voids in the plywood. When the filler dries, sand the edge with 100-grit sandpaper.

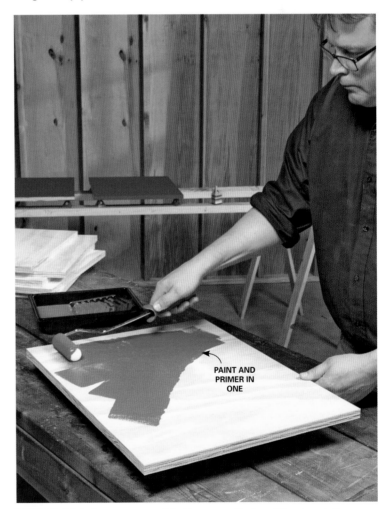

2 Finish before you assemble. Save yourself a ton of time by painting or staining the individual components of this project before you assemble them.

Figure A
Bin tower

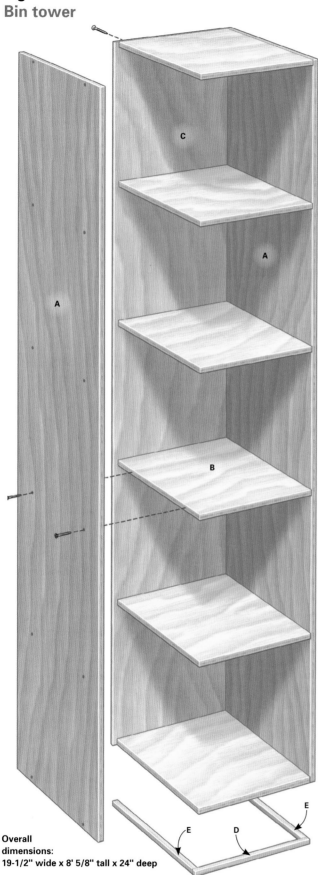

Overall dimensions:
19-1/2" wide x 8' 5/8" tall x 24" deep

Materials list (for three towers)

ITEM	QTY.
4' x 8' x 3/4" BC sanded plywood	5
4' x 8' x 1/4" underlayment plywood	2
4' x 4' x 1/4" underlayment plywood	1
1x2 x 8' pressure-treated board	1
1" 18-gauge brads	
1-1/2" 18-gauge brads	
2" trim-head screws	
Can of wood filler or patching compound	
Gallon of paint/primer	

Cutting list (for three towers)

KEY	QTY.	SIZE & DESCRIPTION
A	6	23-3/4" x 96" x 3/4" BC sanded pine plywood (sides)
B	18	18" x 23-3/4" x 3/4" BC sanded pine plywood (shelves)
C	3	19-1/2" x 96" x 1/4" sanded pine plywood (backs)
D	3	5/8" x 3/4" x 18-3/4" pressure-treated lumber (front bottom strip)
E	6	5/8" x 3/4" x 22-7/8" pressure-treated lumber (side bottom strip)

Figure B
Cutting diagrams for 3/4" plywood

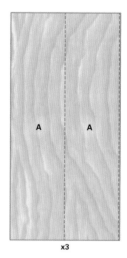

x3

x2

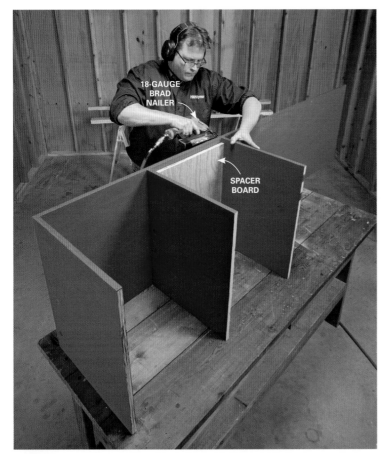

18-GAUGE BRAD NAILER

SPACER BOARD

3 **Shoot, then screw.** Tack the shelves into position with a brad nailer. Then strengthen each connection with 2-in. trim-head screws. A plywood spacer lets you position parts perfectly without measuring.

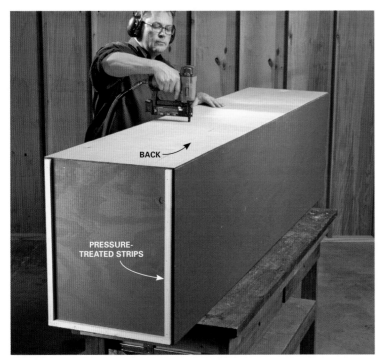

BACK

PRESSURE-TREATED STRIPS

4 **Use the back as a square.** Use the factory-cut edges of the plywood back to square up your project. Start on the top or bottom, and then work your way up the side. Check for square before finishing it off. Reinforce it all with screws.

After everything is nailed together, come back and install two 2-in. trim-head screws into each shelf (use three if you're not using brads).

Install the bottom strips

Plywood will eventually rot if it's sitting directly on a concrete floor. To avoid this, rip 5/8-in. strips from a 1x2 pressure-treated board and install them on the bottom (Photo 4). Four square blocks would also keep the plywood off the floor, but we wanted to avoid any space where screws, washers or any other little objects could get lost. Inset the strips about 3/8 in. and nail them on with 1-1/2-in. brads.

Fasten the back

Use the 1/4-in. plywood to square up the unit (Photo 4). Fasten the two factory-cut edges of the plywood to the back first using 1-in. brads. Nail the short side, and then the long side, aligning the edges as you go. Don't install a whole bunch of brads until you know everything is square. Flip the piece over and check for square using a framing square or by measuring from inside corner to inside corner on a couple of different openings—if the measurements are the same, you should be good to go. Finish fastening the back with brads spaced every 8 in. or so, then reinforce it with one 2-in. trim-head screw in the center of each shelf and five screws on each side.

Screw it to the wall

In many garages, the concrete floor slopes toward the overhead door. That means you'll probably have to shim the bottom to get the bin tower to sit straight and tight up against the wall. Use composite shims: they don't compress as much as wood, they break off cleanly, and they won't ever rot. Set the first tower against the wall and shim the front until it sits tight against the wall. Use a level to check for plumb while you shim the low side. Insert at least four shims on the side and three on the front. Go back and snug up the front shims.

Once the tower is plumb, screw it to the wall studs with 2-in. screws. Make sure each tower is fastened to at least one stud. Since tipping is a concern, install a few screws near the top; you'll only need screws down low if you need to draw the tower tight to the wall.

Mark all the shims, and pull them out one at a time. Cut them down to size and replace them. Run a small bead of clear silicone around the bottom to hold the shims in place. If the towers ever get moved, the silicone will be easy to scrape off the floor. Finally, go get all sorts of caddies, hooks and hangers, and start organizing.

Flexible garage storage

Squeeze more stuff into less space!

WHAT IT TAKES

TIME: One weekend
SKILL LEVEL: Beginner
TOOLS: Circular saw, screw gun,
18-gauge nailer

This storage system solves two challenges: first, how to design storage space for the narrow alley between the garage side wall and the family car; and second, how to create a solid mounting surface to hold shelves and hooks that are capable of carrying hundreds of pounds of stuff.

The solution is to create a framework of horizontal wood strips and inexpensive shelf standards. It can hold almost any arrangement of shelving and hooks, at any point on the wall, and it's easy to rearrange.

Planning and materials

Pull your car into the garage and measure how much space is available. Then look over what you need to store and figure out where it will fit. Generally it's best to hang narrow shelves and smaller hooks lower where space is tight, with wider shelves up near the ceiling so you don't bump your head or interfere with car doors.

Planning the layout and buying materials can take a few hours, but you can do the actual installation, including ripping the plywood shelves and strips, in less than a day. Put up horizontal strips even if you have exposed studs or block walls—they'll make it much easier to install shelf standards and hooks. Apply finish to the strips and shelves, if desired, before installing them.

We used 3-1/2-in.-wide strips of 3/4-in. plywood for the strips because plywood is always straight and never splits—but pine 1x4s also work. Birch plywood was our choice for the strips and shelves, but you can also use less-expensive BC plywood. You can rip 12 strips from one 4 x 8-ft. sheet—that's enough for an average wall. (If you don't have a table saw, see p. 236 or visit familyhandyman.com and search "circular saw" for tips on making straight cuts.) We used four sheets of plywood. For shelf edging, we used 1-1/2-in.-wide strips of solid birch (Photo 6). Total cost for our 20-ft.-long system was about $500, but you could cut that cost in half by skipping the fold-down workbench (Photo 5) and using less-expensive wood and plywood.

Just screw wood strips to the wall

Strips of plywood fastened horizontally to the studs are the key to this system. Once they're up, you can easily mount any kind of storage hardware or shelf standard without worrying about where the stud is or whether a drywall anchor will hold. Since you can drive a screw anywhere, you can pack more stuff on the wall.

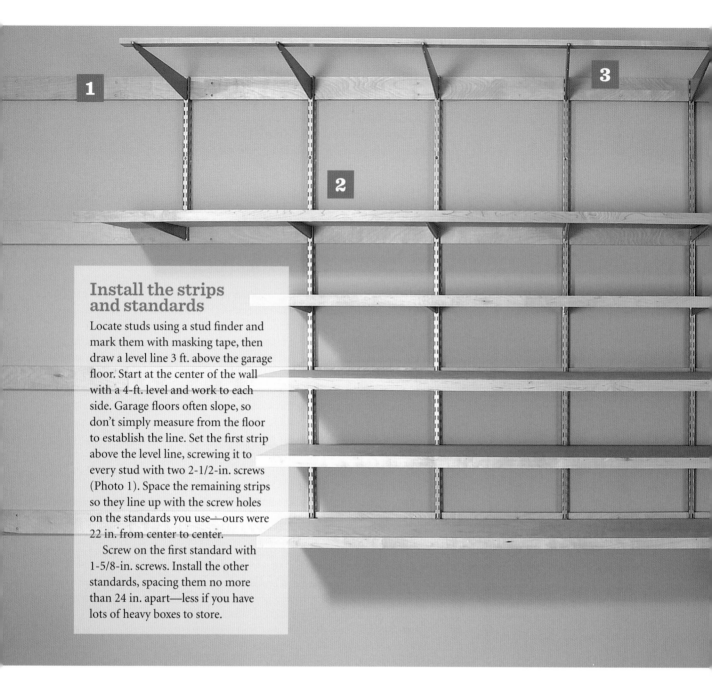

Install the strips and standards

Locate studs using a stud finder and mark them with masking tape, then draw a level line 3 ft. above the garage floor. Start at the center of the wall with a 4-ft. level and work to each side. Garage floors often slope, so don't simply measure from the floor to establish the line. Set the first strip above the level line, screwing it to every stud with two 2-1/2-in. screws (Photo 1). Space the remaining strips so they line up with the screw holes on the standards you use—ours were 22 in. from center to center.

Screw on the first standard with 1-5/8-in. screws. Install the other standards, spacing them no more than 24 in. apart—less if you have lots of heavy boxes to store.

1 Screw plywood strips to the studs. Cut them to length so the ends meet on the studs.

2 Mount the first shelf standard, then use it as a reference to locate the others. Space standards no more than 24 in. apart.

3 Lock brackets together with a wood lip to create a lumber and pipe rack. The lip keeps pipes and lumber from falling off.

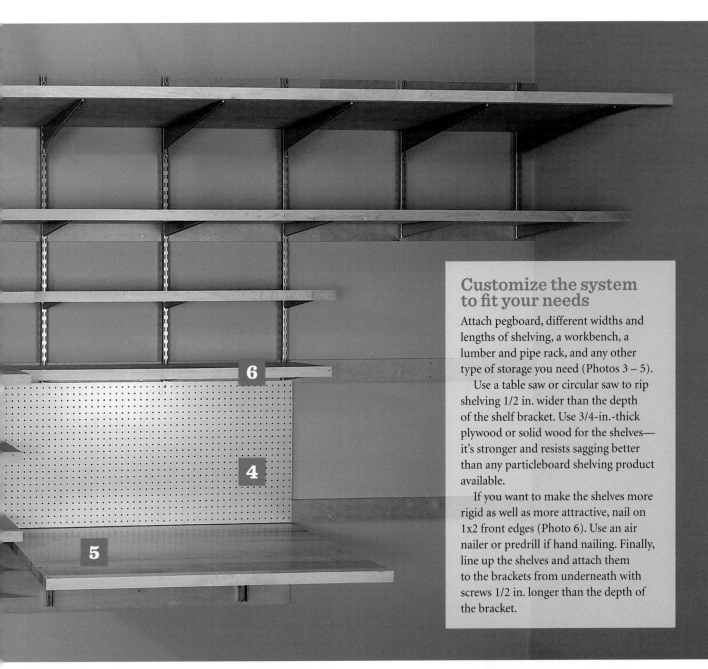

Customize the system to fit your needs

Attach pegboard, different widths and lengths of shelving, a workbench, a lumber and pipe rack, and any other type of storage you need (Photos 3 – 5).

Use a table saw or circular saw to rip shelving 1/2 in. wider than the depth of the shelf bracket. Use 3/4-in.-thick plywood or solid wood for the shelves—it's stronger and resists sagging better than any particleboard shelving product available.

If you want to make the shelves more rigid as well as more attractive, nail on 1x2 front edges (Photo 6). Use an air nailer or predrill if hand nailing. Finally, line up the shelves and attach them to the brackets from underneath with screws 1/2 in. longer than the depth of the bracket.

4 Add a section of pegboard. Frame the edges with wood strips and fasten all four sides of the pegboard.

PLYWOOD BACKER

FOLDING BRACKET

5 Mount heavy-duty folding brackets on a 3/4-in. plywood backer to create a fold-down workbench.

6 Apply a bead of wood glue to each shelf edge, then nail on edging with finish nails every 12 in.

Garage wall system

Create your own custom storage system in one weekend

You can drop a lot of cash on garage storage systems. Shelves, tool racks, special hooks, and other odds and ends can really add up. Our homemade system gives you the versatility of those store-bought systems without the big price tag. Our materials cost for the whole system you see here, covering 16 ft. of wall, was about $200. It'll be even cheaper if you have scrap plywood and other common materials lying around.

This system is so simple and fast to build that even a beginning DIYer can complete it in a weekend. You'll find everything you need at home centers or hardware stores. And the system is completely customizable to your specific garage and gear—you can easily move or add accessories by driving in a few screws. Transform your cluttered garage into one so organized you'll be the envy of the neighborhood.

Start with struts

Each of these storage accessories hangs from a simple framework of vertical struts, which are just 2x2s screwed to the garage wall studs. If you use struts, you can hang something on the wall without hunting for studs, and you can screw shelf brackets and accessory hangers to the sides of them. Of course, if you have bare stud walls, you can skip the struts. We used 2x2s rather than 2x4s because they cost slightly less and have fewer knots. Just be sure you screw them in every 16 in. for extra strength. Most home centers sell 2x2s in 8-ft. lengths.

Shorten or lengthen the struts to suit your garage. If you go with 6-footers as we did, you can use the leftover 2x2 scraps to build some of the accessories described here. It doesn't matter if the struts are centered 16 in. or 24 in. apart. Just make sure they're plumb by using a level.

Screw 2x2 struts to each wall stud. Snap a chalk line to align the tops of the struts and mark the stud locations with masking tape. Drill pilot holes or use "self-drilling" screws to avoid splitting the struts.

Strong, low-cost hooks

Plumbing hooks are designed to support pipes, but they make great storage hooks too. Use them to hold ladders, sports gear and wheelbarrows. You can easily cut them to length if space is tight. They're sized for pipe ranging from 1/2 in. to 4 in.

Yard tool rack

Weed trimmers and leaf blowers can slide around if you prop them in a corner, and fall off the wall if you try to hang them from a hook. Solve the problem with this custom storage rack, which uses 3/4-in. plywood for the brackets, top and back. Cut two 8-in. x 11-in. brackets to support the top and back of the rack. Our rack is 34 in. long and 12 in. deep—customize the dimensions to fit your yard tools. To determine the best shape for your slots, measure the diameter of your tools and cut basic slots in the top of the rack. Then play with the shape of your slots to get a snug fit.

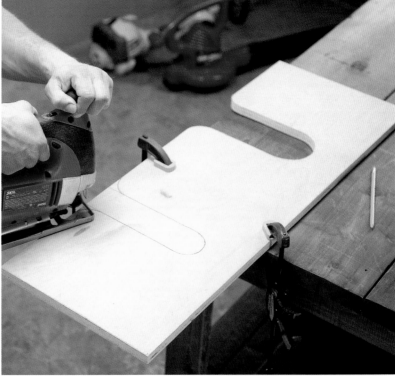

Cut basic slots in the top of the rack and test-fit the tool. Enlarge the slot or change its shape until the tool hangs securely.

Shelf brackets

Metal shelf brackets seem inexpensive, but the cost can add up quickly if you're installing several shelves. So why not make free brackets from plywood scraps? We created a simple, flexible and inexpensive shelving system using 3/4-in. plywood brackets screwed to the vertical framework. We used 3/4-in. plywood rather than 1/2-in. because it gives you a wider surface to screw into when attaching the shelves to the brackets.

For shelves, we used 3/4-in. birch

Cut shelf brackets from scrap plywood. Cut the scraps into rectangles first, using a table saw or circular saw. That keeps time-consuming jigsaw cuts to a minimum.

plywood, but you could use 1x12s or melamine-coated particleboard, or you could edge-band the plywood for a more finished look. Screw a bracket at each strut to support the shelves. You can put shelving across the entire length of the wall or stack shorter shelves on top of each other (or do both, as we did). The 1-1/2-in.-wide brackets are surprisingly strong and will easily hold 100 lbs. or more.

Vinyl gutter storage bins

Ten-foot lengths of vinyl gutter screwed to the 2x2 framework are a perfect place to store long items like hockey sticks, fishing rods, dowels, wood trim and corner

bead. Items like these often end up leaning against a wall or taking over an entire corner only to tumble over or get wrecked because they're not really supposed to be stored on end.

Shorter sections of vinyl gutter and sturdy window box liners attached the same way work well for storing hard-to-hang items like gloves, hose nozzles, fertilizer spikes and sprayers. And people who refuse to hang stuff back up on the wall can just toss it into the bin. If the gutter end caps don't fit snugly, apply PVC cement, silicone or gutter adhesive and press firmly.

Vinyl gutters are surprisingly sturdy—you can even store a few sections of rebar and metal pipe in them without a problem. Metal gutter is also an option. It's the same price, but it's harder to cut and too flimsy for heavier items.

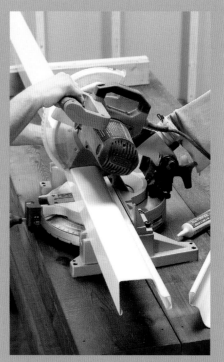

Cut vinyl gutter sections to length with a miter saw. You can use a handsaw, but you'll need to mark the cut carefully to get it square.

Long-handled tool storage

Typical brackets for storing long-handled tools stack the tools one on top of another. This is definitely an efficient use of wall space, but it's frustrating to move other tools out of the way to reach the one you're after. Or you end up devoting an entire wall to hooks that hang individual items.

Here's a better solution. Screw a pair of 3/4-in. plywood brackets to a chunk of scrap 2x2. Attach several 16d finish nails to the side of each bracket and screw the bracket assembly to the 2x2 framework. Drill holes into each of your tool handles, and you can easily hang and retrieve individual rakes and shovels without using up a lot of wall space.

5/8" COUNTERSINK BIT

Drill holes in your tool handles. Then taper the holes with a countersink bit so the tools will slip easily on and off nails.

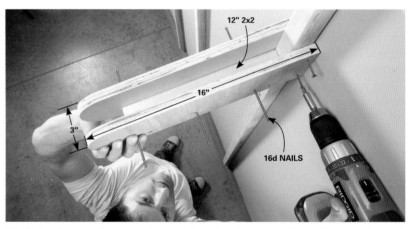

12" 2x2

16"

3"

16d NAILS

Slip the bracket over the strut and screw it into place. Be sure to drive nails into the bracket's outside edge before you install it. Leave 1-1/2 in. of the nails exposed to hang tools.

Wheelbarrow storage hub

Here's a slick way to get your wheelbarrow off the garage floor: To start, screw two plumbing hooks to the wall (we used 1-1/2-in. hooks). Tilt the wheelbarrow onto the hooks and up against the wall. Drill a pilot hole and then drive in a screw hook to hold the wheelbarrow upright. To release the wheelbarrow, just turn the hook.

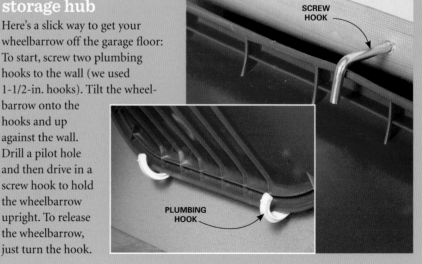

SCREW HOOK

PLUMBING HOOK

Kid-friendly ball corral

This sturdy ball corral holds a herd of balls and lets kids easily grab the balls at the bottom without unloading all the ones on top. It's built from 3/4-in. plywood and 2x2s. We made our ball corral 24 in. wide x 33 in. high x 12 in. deep.

The hooks on Bungee cords can be a safety hazard for kids and adults alike. So cut the hooks off the cords (or use elastic cord available at camping, sporting goods and hardware stores). Thread the cord through predrilled holes and secure with knots. Drill the holes slightly larger than the cords to make threading them easier.

We added plumbing hooks and short gutter troughs on the outside of the corral to make it easy for kids to stash smaller balls, helmets and mitts.

2x2

2x2

Sports gear rack

Specialty gear hooks and bat racks are expensive. Vinyl-covered utility hooks are not but they only hold single items. Each of these inexpensive sports gear hangers will hold several bats and racquets.

Each set of hangers is made from a pair of lag screws covered with CPVC sleeves to protect the gear. Customize the hangers by spacing them closer or wider apart depending on what you want to hang.

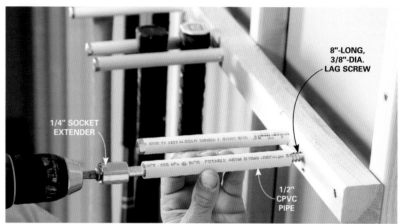

8"-LONG, 3/8"-DIA. LAG SCREW

1/4" SOCKET EXTENDER

1/2" CPVC PIPE

Screw a scrap of 2x2 to the face of a vertical 2x2 to hold the hangers. Slip a 6-in. length of 1/2-in. CPVC or PVC pipe over an 8-in.-long, 3/8-in.-diameter lag screw. This CPVC sleeve will prevent the lags from scratching the sports gear.

Simple bike rack

Closet pole-and-shelf brackets can keep your bikes up and out of the way of car doors and bumpers. Just screw the brackets to the wall studs. Line the pole carriage with self-stick hook-and-loop strips so it won't scratch your bike frame.

SELF-STICK HOOK-AND-LOOP STRIPS

CLOSET POLE AND SHELF BRACKET

One-day garage makeover

BEFORE

Does this look like your garage? Here's a quick, easy-on-the-wallet solution: simple shelves that can hold plastic storage bins. You can build the whole project in less than a day, for about $300 for 26 ft. of shelving (the bins were extra).

Timeline

SATURDAY, 10 A.M.

RAIL LOCATION

1 **Mark the frame parts for quick assembly.** Cut all your frame parts to length. Then mark where the rails are going to be screwed to each leg. Do the same thing to the 2x2s. This makes the whole thing go together in a snap.

10:45 A.M.

2 **Assemble the frames.** Working on top of a sheet of plywood helps keep each frame squared up. Use the edges of the plywood to line up and adjust things as you screw the frame together. It also really helps to pick the straightest lumber possible when you're shopping.

BEFORE

Tips

- Each storage unit is basically two frames tied together with plywood shelves. Buy your bins first so you can customize the height and depth of each shelf space. Remember to leave enough clearance space in front of your shelving units to open your car doors.

- Small bins are great for storing screws, glue and painting supplies in the middle bays of each unit. The best bins for hanging are those with snap-lock lids. They allow you to hang heavier loads without worrying that the lid will come off.

- The fussiest measurements are those for the center bay of smaller bins. If your width measurements are off by a quarter inch, the bins won't sit squarely between the cleats or will be too tight to slide easily.

- If your garage floor sometimes gets wet, nail plastic feet to the bottom of the legs. Nail-on plastic feet are available at home centers.

- You can paint the wood to give it a classy look or leave it bare. Painting it before you put it together is a lot easier than painting it once it's assembled.

Materials list

(To build one shelf unit 95-1/4 in. long x 80 in. high)

- Two 8' 1x2s
- Eight 8' 2x2s
- Eight 7' 2x4s
- Two 4' x 8' x 3/4" BC plywood sheets
- Masking tape and construction screws
  (1-1/2", 2-1/2" and 5")

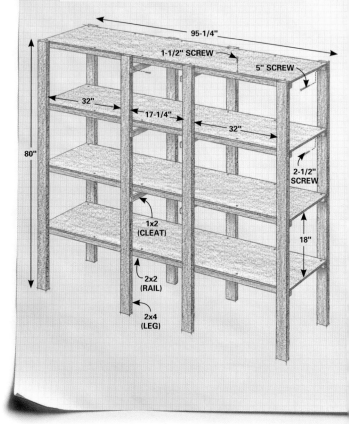

95-1/4"

1-1/2" SCREW

5" SCREW

32"

17-1/4"

32"

80"

2-1/2"
SCREW

1x2
(CLEAT)

18"

2x2
(RAIL)

2x4
(LEG)

3 **Screw on the shelves.** Installing the shelves in each frame is a lot easier if you have a helper to hold the frames. If you're working alone, lean one of the frames against the wall and hold up the other frame while you screw the first shelf into place.

TAPE MARKS
STUDS

5" CONSTRUCTION
SCREW

4 **Fasten the shelves to the wall.** Screw each unit to the wall through the top rail using construction screws (GRK is one brand) spaced every second or third stud. This shelf unit is really sturdy. But make it ultra-secure by screwing the units together through the front legs. Shim the legs if your floor is sloped or uneven.

SPACER

CLEAT

5 **Install cleats for slide-out bins.** To avoid stacking the small bins on top of one another, hang the top bins from cleats. Installing the cleats goes really fast if you start your screws in each cleat first and then use a spacer to mark the cleat's location as you screw it on.

Plastic storage bins
and simple shelves
turned chaos into
order – instantly!

I.D. bins the smart way

Think about how you'd like to identify the
contents of each storage bin. Some people use
adhesive labels or write with markers directly on
the bins. The best system lets you make changes
easily. We like the adhesive storage pouches that
come with cardboard inserts (or you can just
use index cards). Changing the label is as easy as
slipping a new card into the pouch.

Garage tips

Bike gear to go

Tired of hunting down all your biking gear when you want to go for a ride? Pick up a plastic crate to solve the problem. Simply screw some 2x4 pieces to the back of the crate (use fender washers with the screws to better grip the plastic). Then screw through the studs into the 2x4s. Next, screw a 25-in.-long 2x4 to the front of the top and add a pair of rubber-coated bike hooks. Keep biking shoes, a helmet, gloves, a tire pump and water bottles within reach so you can spend more time biking and less time looking in closets!

Pet collar cord hanger

Pet collars make a great strap for electrical cords and air hoses. The leash ring is perfect for hanging the cords on the hooks, and the quick-release fastener makes for fast strapping and unstrapping.

Clear leaf bags for storage

Clear leaf bags are great for storage. Because they're large, you can cover lawn chairs, cushions, space heaters, fans and other items to keep them dust-free in the rafters or on shelving in the garage. The best part is that you can easily find items at a glance because the bags are transparent—a feature that black garbage bags lack.

Tight-space garage storage

If your garage is too narrow for most shelving systems, here's a great way to store a lot of stuff in very little space. Hang several multilevel wire racks on the wall—the same racks you use in a pantry. They hold a ton and hug the wall, so they don't get in the way.

Garage extension cord reel

Tired of digging out your extension cord every time you want to use it in the garage? Try this easy tip: Attach a retractable cord reel to your garage ceiling and plug your cord into the unused outlet mounted near your garage door opener. Your cord will always be centrally located and easily accessible, yet out of the way when you're not using it.

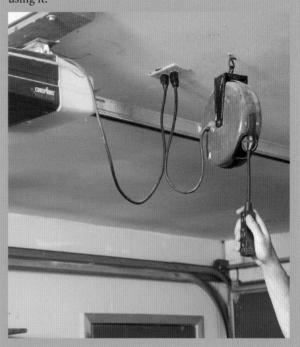

Brilliant bungee cord storage

Bungee cords always seem to end up in a tangled mess. To keep them organized, screw a scrap piece of closet shelving to the wall and hook the cords along its length. It'll be easy to find the one you need.

MARK HARDY

Hanging storage rack

Stow bulky items overhead by cementing together a simple rack from 2-in. PVC pipes and fittings. Bolt the straight pipe to the ceiling joists to support heavy loads, and screw the angled pieces from the "wye" connectors into the cross brace to stabilize the whole rack. The PVC's smooth surface makes for easy loading and unloading.

Ceiling-mounted ladder rack

An extension ladder has to be one of the most difficult things to store. When you need to use it, it has to be easy to get to. But there are long stretches when it just gets in the way of everything else in your garage. Here's a good solution: Mount it on your garage ceiling on sturdy racks made of scrap 2x4s that are screwed into the ceiling joists. Use two 3-1/2-in. screws at each joint to make the rack secure. These racks make it easy to slide the ladder out when you need it. Just make sure to position the racks where they won't interfere with your garage door.

Skills tutorial

Creating attractive, functional storage solutions for your home, garage and yard is immensely satisfying and can save you a bundle of money.

This tutorial is a collection of DIY skills that will help you complete successful storage (and other) projects that help unclutter your life.

Circular saw

12 tips for smooth, accurate cuts

Every time you pick up your circular saw, you're picking up 12 lbs. of gyrating metal with a blade spinning at 100 revolutions per second. Sure, it has knobs for controlling depth and angle—but it's 100 percent up to you to accurately guide it where it needs to go.

SCRAP SIDE OF BOARD   "V" MARK

Sharper chalk lines

The fastest way to make straight cutting lines on plywood is to use a chalk line. But before you lay the line on the plywood, give it a quick midair twang. That first twang will get rid of excess chalk, and your mark will be less fuzzy and easier to follow. This is an especially important step to do right after filling your chalk line.

CHALK LINE

Start with accurate marks

To get an accurate cut, you have to start with an accurate mark. Stretch out your tape measure, place your pencil at the correct measurement and make two marks that form a "V," with the tip of the "V" pointing at the exact measurement. A "V" is more accurate than a single line, which can stray slightly to the right or left and throw off your cut mark.

Using a square, mark your cutting line over the tip of the "V." Finally, put an "X" on the "scrap" side of the board; that's the side of the line you want to cut along. Cutting on the wrong side of your line can make a 1/8-in. difference in the length of your board; sometimes this is a big deal, sometimes not.

Light up the cut

A perfect cutting line won't do you any good if you can't see it. So before you pull the trigger, take two seconds to check the lighting. Even in the best-lit workshops or the sunny outdoors, you or your saw can cast shadows that make it hard to see your mark. Change the angle of the board or reposition your work light so the line won't disappear into the shadows as you cut.

MEET THE PRO

Spike Carlsen was an editor at *The Family Handyman* for 15 years. He has written several books including *Woodworking FAQ: The Workshop Companion* and *Ridiculously Simple Furniture Projects.*

Watch the blade, not the guides

Every saw has notches or marks on the front of the shoe to indicate where the blade is going to cut. I've never had any luck using those guides. They get covered with sawdust or the whole shoe gets bent out of whack, which throws off the guide.

We prefer to watch the actual blade and line as we cut. The problem, of course, is that sawdust covers the line. Some saws have built-in blowers to clear away dust. If your saw doesn't, use your own built-in blower—your mouth. All it takes is a light puff every few seconds to keep your view clear and open.

Tape before you mark

When cutting dark wood or laminate, mark your cutting line on masking tape rather than directly on the workpiece. You'll be able to see your line easier, and in some cases—like when you're cutting hardwood plywood—the masking tape can minimize splintering.

MASKING TAPE

Clamp before cutting angles

Blade guards tend to hang up when they contact a board at anything other than a 90-degree angle. Since you need one hand to push the saw and the other to retract the guard, clamp your workpiece down so it doesn't move around—even if that clamp happens to be your knee. When you cut angles or bevels, keep your left thumb on the blade guard retracting lever and start retracting the guard when you feel the saw hesitate a little.

Safe = accurate

What do earmuffs, safety glasses and dust masks have to do with cutting accurately? Well, it's tough to watch the cutting line with your eyes squinting and blinking through a storm of sawdust. And let's face it: Protection against noise, dust and splinters will make you more comfortable and more patient—and less likely to make a sloppy rush through the cut.

Shoulder the cord

On most saws, the electrical plug is perfectly engineered to snag on the edge of plywood. And that will throw off your cut. To prevent snags, drape the cord over your shoulder.

Quick, identical cuts

When you need to cut dozens of boards the same length, don't measure and mark them one at a time. Instead, make a simple jig. This one took less than five minutes to build and guaranteed each of the 100 fence pickets were exactly the same length.

To make one, screw a fence to a long scrap of plywood and run your saw along the fence to trim off the excess plywood. Then measure back from the cut end and screw on a cleat. The cleat location determines the length of the cut, and the fence guides your saw for perfectly square cuts every time.

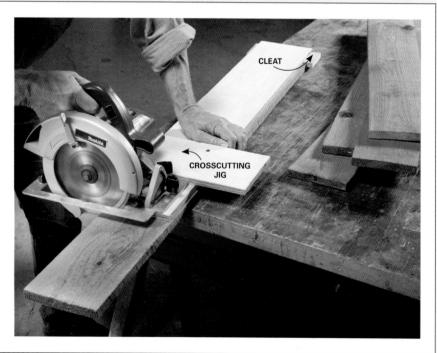

CLEAT

CROSSCUTTING JIG

Plywood cutting pad

Only NBA players have arms long enough to push a saw across an entire sheet of plywood. We find it easier to lay the plywood on a sheet of extruded foam (at home centers) and then crawl along while making the cut. You don't have to reach as far and you'll have better sight lines. Cut the foam into two or three pieces and rejoin them with duct tape. The tape creates hinges, which allow you to fold up the foam and stash it away when not in use.

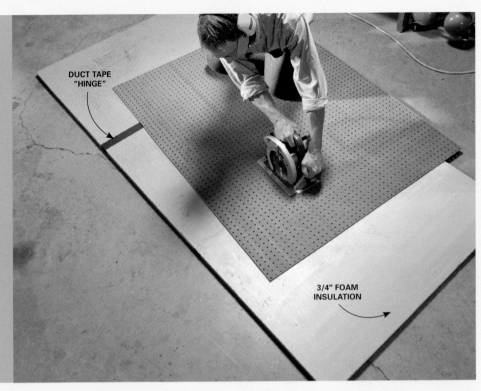

DUCT TAPE "HINGE"

3/4" FOAM INSULATION

Score a clean cut

Circular saws usually splinter the wood that's facing up and cut cleanly on the side that's facing down. So when you're cutting veneered plywood, always position the material "good side down" so the teeth of the blade are pushing the veneer up against the core rather than ripping it away. Pushing your saw more slowly than normal also helps reduce splintering. If you need both sides splinter-free, mark your cut by scoring the veneer with a sharp utility knife, then cut just a hair to the "waste side" of the line. Any splintering will occur on the waste piece. A quick swipe with sandpaper will clean up any little fuzzies left behind.

When to retire your saw

There comes a time when you should throw your circular saw a retirement party—or at least assign it a new job. Most saws cut accurately out of the box, but after years of hard use, the bearings become sloppy, the blade and motor vibrate, the shoe gets bent, and the blade guard becomes stubborn. It all adds up to a saw that just won't cut as accurately or cleanly as a new model. So as your saw enters old age, use it for rougher tasks like demolition or cutting concrete. Then invest in a new one.

Jigsaw

10 tips for smoother, cleaner, more accurate cuts

A jigsaw is one of those DIY necessities. For beginners, it's less intimidating than a circular saw and also very versatile—lots of basic projects require nothing more than a drill and a jigsaw. But DIY veterans need a jigsaw too, no matter how many other tools they own. If you fall in either category, or somewhere between, we'll help you get more from your jigsaw. We'll demonstrate a few practical tips, tell you what you need to know about blades, and point out which features to look for when you buy a jigsaw.

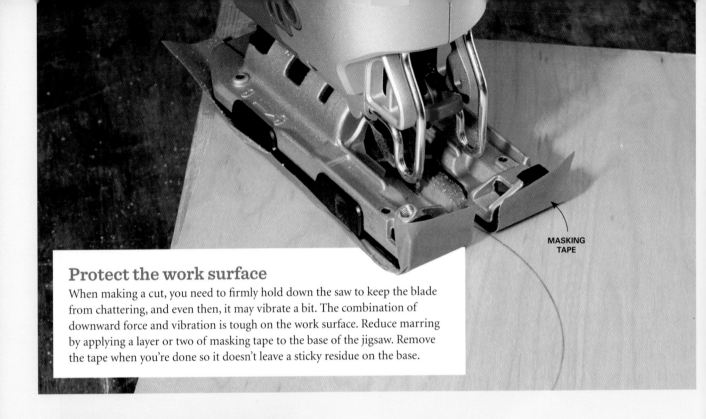

MASKING
TAPE

Protect the work surface

When making a cut, you need to firmly hold down the saw to keep the blade from chattering, and even then, it may vibrate a bit. The combination of downward force and vibration is tough on the work surface. Reduce marring by applying a layer or two of masking tape to the base of the jigsaw. Remove the tape when you're done so it doesn't leave a sticky residue on the base.

METAL-
CUTTING
BLADE

Cut anything

The main mission of a jigsaw is to cut curves in wood, and it's easy to overlook its other abilities. Instead of slaving away with your hacksaw, grab your jigsaw to quickly cut steel, copper or any metal. You can also cut plastics and tougher stuff like ceramic tile and fiber cement siding. The key to success is to match the blade to the material (more on that later).

Get the right saw for you

It's helpful to think of jigsaws in three categories: For $50 or less, you'll get a jigsaw that will do its job just fine, but you'll probably sacrifice features and power. For most DIYers, a saw in the $50 to $100 range is a good choice. It will have some special features and adequate power. Saws that cost over $100 will have large motors and all the best features.

Our favorite features are toolless blade change, toolless base plate bevel and oscillating control. Bonus features include an LED light, a blower to blow away dust, a larger base plate and a speed control dial.

If you'll be cutting a lot of material that's 1 in. or thicker, look for a saw with a higher amp rating (listed in the specifications). Smaller saws draw 5 amps or less; larger models go up to 7 amps. Larger motors also add a little "heft" to the saw, which helps cut vibration.

Some jigsaws have handles; some don't. Many pros like the no-handle "barrel-grip" style. They feel they have better control with their hands closer to the action. Folks with smaller hands often complain about the barrel being too large to grab.

OSCILLATING
CONTROL

PORTER
CABLE.

TOOLLESS
BLADE
CHANGE

BASE PLATE
BEVEL LEVER

Find the SPM "sweet spot"

Typically, there's an SPM (strokes per minute) "sweet spot" where the saw cuts the fastest and cleanest and with the least vibration. Try different speeds by changing pressure on the trigger. Once you find the best speed, set the adjustable speed dial so you can pull the trigger all the way while maintaining the desired SPM.

SQUARE

Square the blade

To get a square-edge cut, the blade has to be perfectly perpendicular to the base. So before you make a cut, make sure the blade isn't bent. If it is, just toss it or save it for jobs where a clean, square cut isn't important. With a straight, new blade in the saw, square it up. There's not a lot of surface area on the base, so a smaller square is easier to work with.

Smart starting and stopping

Be sure the blade is up to speed before you start your cut. If you start the saw with the blade touching your material, it can grab hold and rattle the material, possibly damaging it. And let the saw come to a complete stop when you pull it from the material mid-cut. If you don't, you might experience the dreaded "woodpecker effect," when a moving blade bounces off the surface, leaving behind pockmarks and a bent blade.

TEAR-OUT

TOP-SIDE TEAR-OUT

Cut with the "good" side down

Most jigsaw blades cut on the upstroke, so chips and splinters occur mostly on the top of the wood. So if you value one side of a board more than the other, make sure you keep the good side face down, and mark and cut the less important side.

You can buy "reverse cut" or "down cut" blades that do cut on the down stroke. These blades are used when you want as little tear-out on the top surface as possible. Cutting out a sink hole in a laminate countertop is one common use for reverse-cut blades.

Oscillation education

Most jigsaws offer oscillating action: While the blade moves up and down, it also lunges forward with each stroke. Typically, you can turn off the oscillation or select from three levels of oscillation. The higher the setting, the faster you cut.

But faster isn't always better. More oscillation means rougher, less-accurate cuts. So turn the oscillation way down or off when you need clean or precise cuts or when you're working with delicate materials like veneers. Turn the oscillating feature off when you're cutting metal. Practice on a scrap to find the best setting for the material.

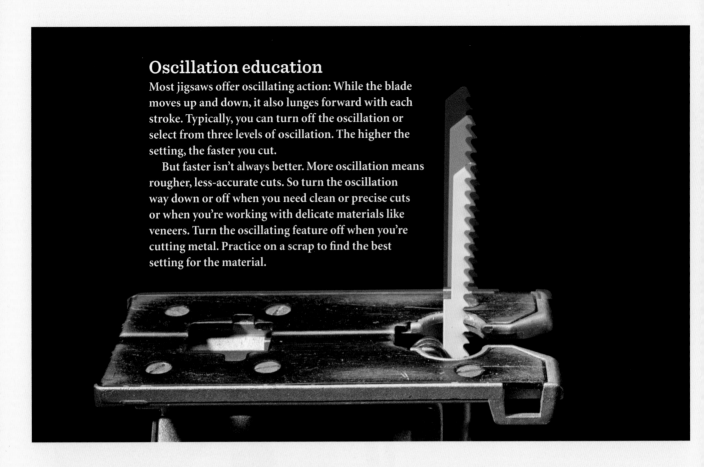

Make a metal sandwich

Jigsaws are great at cutting sheet metal, but it's difficult to clamp the material down so the saw blade doesn't just rattle the material up and down instead of cutting through it. One way to solve this problem is to sandwich the metal between two sheets of 1/4-in. plywood. Once the plywood is clamped down, the metal has nowhere to go, so you get a fast, easy, clean cut. You don't have to spend a bunch of money on plywood either; inexpensive 1/4-in. underlayment works fine.

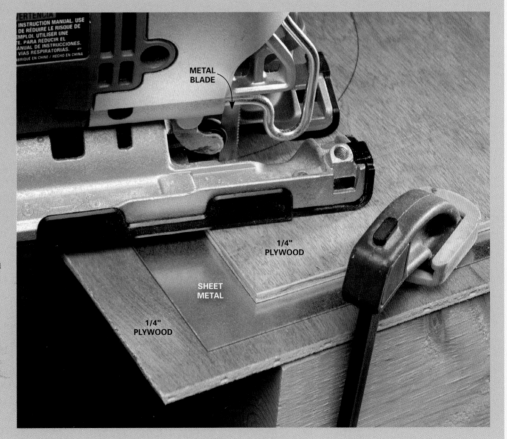

METAL BLADE

1/4" PLYWOOD

SHEET METAL

1/4" PLYWOOD

RELIEF CUTS

Make relief cuts for sharp turns

There's a limit on how sharp a curve a jigsaw can cut, and that depends on the blade—the narrower the blade, the sharper the turns it can make. If you try to force the blade into a turn tighter than it's capable of, you'll either veer off your line or break the blade.

If you're not sure about a particular shape, mark it out on a scrap and practice on that. If you have a curve you know is too tight, make relief cuts. The sharper the curve, the more relief cuts you'll need. And be sure you don't cut past your line. Play it safe and leave at least a blade's width of material between the relief cut and your pencil mark.

Drill starter holes

If you need to cut out a hole in the center of the work surface—like a hole for a heat register in a sheet of bead board wainscoting—drill a hole slightly bigger than your jigsaw blade in two opposite corners. That way, you can make four neat cuts starting from the two holes.

ACCESS HOLE

ACCESS HOLE

A blade for every occasion

There are a couple of basic things to know about blades: The larger the teeth, the more aggressive and rougher the cut. And the narrower the blade, the tighter the turns it can make. Narrow, double-sided blades are especially well suited for sharp turns because the teeth on the back side widen the kerf as you turn.

Match the type of blade with the material you're cutting—don't use a wood blade to cut metal. Most manufacturers have taken the guesswork out of blade selection—the description of the blade and what it does is usually written on the blade itself. Buy a combo pack and you'll be ready for most jobs. A 15-pack of quality blades costs less than $20, and you'll avoid making a special trip to the store.

There are also specialty blades designed for very specific jobs: blades for cutting tile and fiber cement, and flush-cut blades that extend the cut right up to the front of the base. Specialty blades are usually sold individually and can cost more than $10 each.

FIBER CEMENT

DOUBLE-SIDED

CERAMIC

FLUSH-CUT

Let the tool do the work

Pushing as hard as you can on the saw doesn't necessarily make it cut faster; sometimes the exact opposite is true. And pushing too hard into a curve can cause you to veer off your line, burn the material or break a blade. Ease off on the pressure until the saw cuts smoothly with little vibration.

Gluing wood

Even the most experienced carpenters and woodworkers occasionally break into a sweat when it comes time to glue up a project, especially one that takes lots of clamps after the glue is applied. You only get one shot at it, so there's little room for mistakes. Before your next glue-up, read our top 10 tips for gluing wood and save all that sweating for the gym.

Do a dry run

To head off any glue-up catastrophes, be sure to dry-fit and clamp together all the parts and pieces of your project *before* you apply glue. Do this no matter what type of glue you choose.

Plain old wood glue is best

Dozens of glues claim to work well on wood and a variety of other materials. But regular wood glue is the best choice for raw wood-to-wood joinery. Most wood glues are a type of polyvinyl acetate (PVA). Also sometimes called carpenter's glue, wood glue is formulated to penetrate wood fibers, making glue joints that are stronger than the wood itself.

Wood glue can last for years

You may have heard that PVA glue goes bad after freezing or sitting around for a long time, but the truth is that it might still be OK. Try stirring it with a stick to mix all the glue particles (don't just shake it). If it's a little thick, add some water–up to 5 percent. If glue flows freely from the bottle and feels slippery between your fingers—not stringy or clumpy—it's probably OK to use. But if in doubt, throw it out. It's not worth taking the chance.

Slow-setting glue buys you time

Most wood glues set up quickly, which can be a blessing or a curse. Sometimes you want a quick bond, but on a complicated glue-up, you might want more time before the glue starts to set up. Slow-setting glues have labels that say "longer assembly time" or "longer open time."

Use waterproof glue for outdoor projects

If your carpentry project might get wet, use glue that stands up to water. Glues labeled "water resistant" are fine for things that'll only get wet occasionally. For most outdoor projects, however, choose "waterproof" glue, which comes in both PVA and polyurethane formulas. Both types are plenty strong and stand up to the weather, but polyurethane glue has the added benefit of being able to bond materials like stone, metal and glass. It's messy stuff, though, so wear gloves while using it.

Use enough glue, but not too much

Use too much glue and you'll have a big mess on your hands, but too little can give you a weak joint. You'll know you have the right amount of glue when you see a fairly even bead of squeeze-out—about the thickness of a penny—the entire length of the joint.

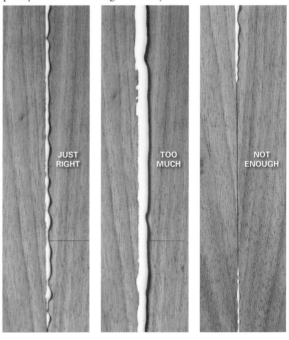

Rub the joint

One good way to ensure a strong glue joint is to use the "rub joint" method. Simply apply glue to the edges of one or both boards and rub them together to help spread the glue evenly before clamping.

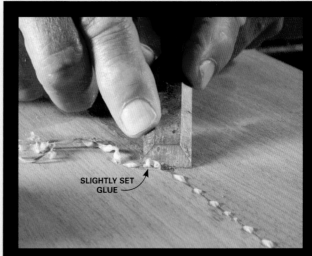

Removing glue squeeze-out

The best time to remove glue squeeze-out is when it's starting to set up and slightly rubbery–about 20 minutes or so after clamping. Just scoop it off with a chisel and wipe off the excess with a damp (not wet!) rag. If you wait until the glue is dry, you'll have to scrape it off, which is a lot more work and can damage the wood.

Avoid sunken joints

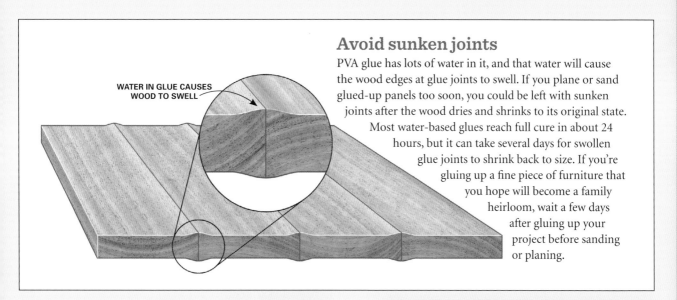

WATER IN GLUE CAUSES WOOD TO SWELL

PVA glue has lots of water in it, and that water will cause the wood edges at glue joints to swell. If you plane or sand glued-up panels too soon, you could be left with sunken joints after the wood dries and shrinks to its original state. Most water-based glues reach full cure in about 24 hours, but it can take several days for swollen glue joints to shrink back to size. If you're gluing up a fine piece of furniture that you hope will become a family heirloom, wait a few days after gluing up your project before sanding or planing.

SAWDUST FROM SANDER BAG

Glue + sawdust = wood filler

When you need wood filler that matches the color of your project, mix some fine sawdust and glue together until it forms a paste, which you can use to fill small gaps and cracks. For best results, use sawdust from the same species of wood as your project; you can get some from the bag on your electric sander. Just don't try this trick for large gaps or patches—they'll stick out like a sore thumb.

Water finds hidden glue

Once squeezed-out glue has been removed, there's still a chance that some is hiding. And if you don't find it now, you'll see it later when you apply stain or finish. Spray some warm water near glue joints to make hidden glue more visible. The water will also soften the dried glue, making it easier to scrape off.

HIDDEN GLUE

Spray painting

And flawless wood finishes, too

Do it right, and a sprayed-on coat of paint is absolutely flawless. Do it wrong, and you've got a sloppy, spattered mess. The same goes for clear wood finishes like lacquer or spray-can polyurethane. Whether you're painting or clear-coating, here are some tips to avoid trouble and achieve perfection.

Overlap the spray pattern

If you overlap just a little, you'll get narrow bands of heavy coverage. Instead, overlap the spray about halfway over the previous pass. That way, the entire surface will get the same coverage.

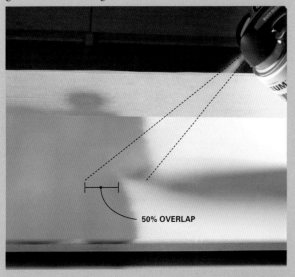

50% OVERLAP

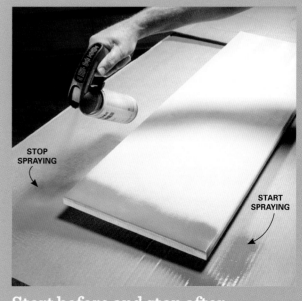

STOP SPRAYING

START SPRAYING

Start before and stop after

Spray nozzles tend to spit out a few large droplets when you start spraying and spit again when you stop. To keep sputter splatter off your project, pull the trigger before you're over the target and release the trigger after you're past the edge.

Make a spray booth

Take a tip from pro finishers and contain messy "overspray" with a spray booth. Yours can be a simple cardboard box. Cut a hole in the top to let in light. The hole also lets you suspend items from a coat hanger and spin the item so you can hit all sides.

Get a handle

If you've sprayed a project that required a few cans of paint, you already know about finger strain and pain. For less than five bucks, a trigger handle not only prevents the pain, but also gives you better control of the can.

Don't swing an arc

It's the most natural motion for your arm, but it gives you heavy buildup at the center of the surface and poor coverage at the ends. So instead, move the can parallel to the surface. Concentrate on straight, steady motion for even coverage.

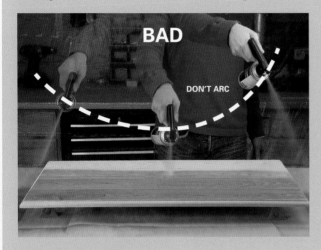

BAD

DON'T ARC

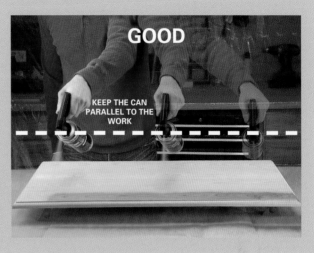

GOOD

KEEP THE CAN PARALLEL TO THE WORK

Wear a respirator

Spray cans fill the air with a fine mist and solvents. Open windows and doors to provide ventilation and wear an organic vapor respirator to protect your lungs. Working outside is the most effective way to avoid breathing fumes, but wind can blow away your paint before it reaches the surface, while bugs and falling leaves wreck your finish.

Go light on vertical surfaces

You've probably heard this many times before, but it's true: Several light coats are better than one heavy coat, especially on a vertical surface where heavy coats mean runs. Nobody has ever regretted going too light, but every experienced spray painter knows the agony of drips and sags.

Unclog a nozzle

When you're done painting, hold the can upside down and spray for a few seconds until only propellant comes out. That almost always works to blast paint out of the nozzle, leaving it clear and open for the next job. If it doesn't, or if you forget, there's a fix: Soak the nozzle in nail polish remover. It may take a few hours to unclog the nozzle.

Spin and spray

On some projects, you'll walk miles circling the item to spray all the surfaces. So pick up a lazy Susan turntable at a discount store and save some legwork.

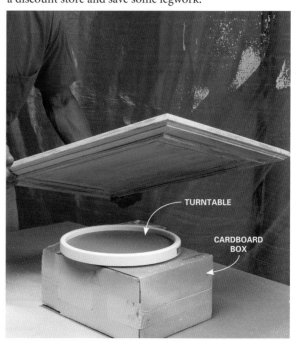

Elevate to avoid sticking

If your project is sitting directly on a workbench or newspaper, it's impossible to paint it without also gluing it to the work surface. So whether you're spraying paint or brushing, find some way to raise the work. Screws driven into furniture legs work great. Scraps of plywood with protruding screws also solve the problem.

Caulk like a pro

Anyone can seal a crack—making it look good is the challenge

Laying a smooth bead of caulk is like playing the piano: You can learn to do it well, but don't expect applause for your first efforts. It's best to start where perfection is less important (exterior window trim, for example), and then move on to high-visibility work like a tub surround.

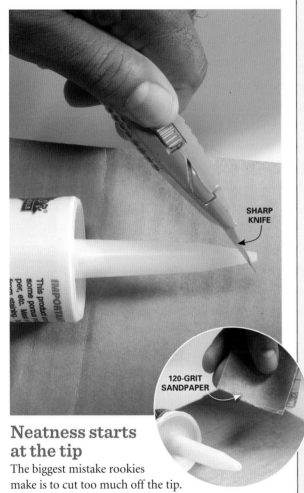

SHARP KNIFE

120-GRIT SANDPAPER

Neatness starts at the tip

The biggest mistake rookies make is to cut too much off the tip. That allows too much caulk to flow out, which leads to a mess. So cut near the end at a sharp angle. You can always trim off more if needed. Smooth and round the cut tip with sandpaper.

Clean the tip

Start every bead with a clean tip. Plan to muck up two or three rags over the course of a caulking project.

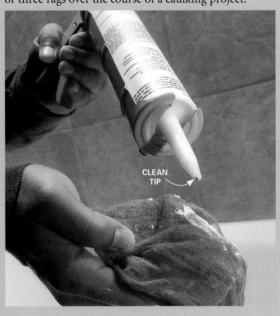

CLEAN TIP

WET RAG

SMOOTHED CAULK

Smooth it with your finger

Immediately after laying the bead, drag your finger across it. In order to slide smoothly, your finger needs lubrication. For acrylic/latex caulk, dip your finger in water. With silicone, slip on a surgical-style glove and use alcohol.

Don't use your wrists

Every golfer knows that the best way to control a putter is with the upper body. The same goes for caulking. Use your upper body, or even your legs, to move the tube, not your wrists.

Nix the squeeze tube

Squeeze tubes are OK at first, but as they empty, it's harder and harder to squeeze out a steady, consistent flow. That means a lumpy bead. Better to spend a few bucks on a caulk gun and use gun tubes.

Meet in the middle

When you have a long bead to run and can't get it done in one pass, don't start again where you left off. It's hard to continue a bead without creating a glob. Instead, start at the other end and meet in the middle.

Patching walls

With a little patience, you can get pro results

Fill small holes

For holes smaller than 1/8 in., use spackling compound. If you have a mix of hole sizes, some larger than 1/8 in., some smaller, you can use joint compound for all of them. Whatever you use, expect shrinkage as the compound dries (no matter what the label promises). Don't be surprised if you have to coat the hole two or even three times to compensate for shrinkage.

Choose lightweight compound

At the home center, you'll find premixed joint compound in plastic containers and powder in bags. Unless you want to take on a messy mixing job, buy the premixed stuff. And choose one that's labeled "lightweight." Lightweight compound shrinks less and sands easier than the standard version.

Fix nail pops—and keep them from coming back

Nail pops happen when drywall nails or screws break through the surface, usually due to shrinking and swelling of the wall studs. If you just pound them in and patch them, they'll be back. Here's how to fix them permanently:

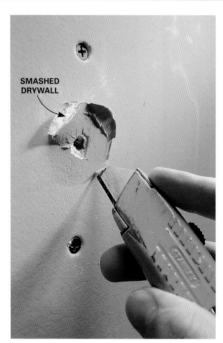

SMASHED DRYWALL

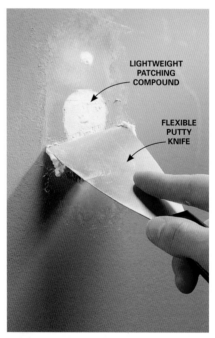

LIGHTWEIGHT PATCHING COMPOUND

FLEXIBLE PUTTY KNIFE

1 **Prepare for patching.** Drive drywall screws into the stud above and below the pop. Don't use nails. If the drywall has puckered around the pop, slice it out. If the area is flat, leave it alone. Remove the popped nail or screw.

2 **Patch the holes.** Fill the depressions with joint compound. Let the compound dry and coat it again (and probably again!) until the patch is flat. Smooth the patch with 100-grit sandpaper, then prime and paint.

Patch a big hole

The usual way to cover a large hole (such as a doorknob disaster) is to cut out the damage, insert new drywall and reinforcing tape, then smooth it over with joint compound. But here's a shortcut: Home centers carry adhesive-backed metal patches in various sizes. They're cheap and save a few steps. Here's how to use one:

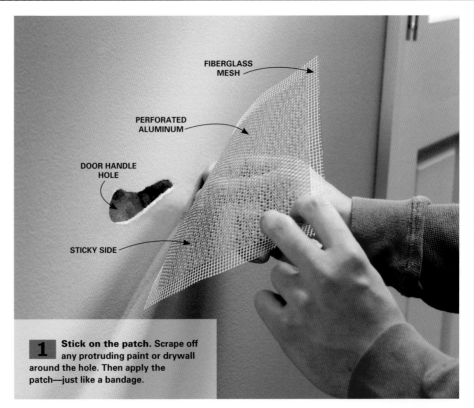

FIBERGLASS MESH

PERFORATED ALUMINUM

DOOR HANDLE HOLE

STICKY SIDE

1 **Stick on the patch.** Scrape off any protruding paint or drywall around the hole. Then apply the patch—just like a bandage.

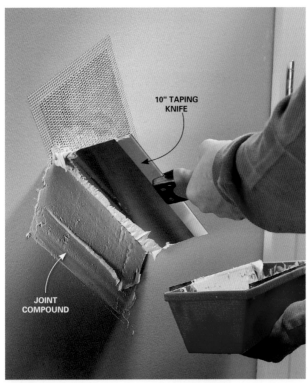

10" TAPING KNIFE

JOINT COMPOUND

2 **Coat the patch.** Spread joint compound over the patch with a wide knife. Smooth out the compound, let it dry and add another coat. Keep the coats thin and smooth; it's better to apply three or four coats than to create a thick buildup. Extend each coat a few inches beyond the previous coat to form edges that gradually taper.

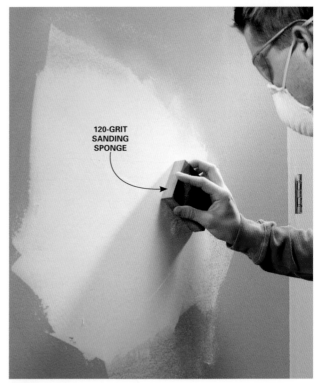

120-GRIT SANDING SPONGE

3 **Sand the compound.** Smooth the dried compound with a sanding sponge. If you did a good job of smoothing and tapering the compound, this will take just a few minutes and the slight hump on the wall will be invisible after priming and painting.

Building face frame cabinets

A classic way to make cabinets is to build plywood boxes (aka carcasses) and cover the front with a hardwood face frame. Cabinets like this are strong and handsome and relatively easy to build. And we have the experience to prove it. Some of our editors have built dozens of face frame cabinets; a couple of us have built hundreds. We all recently sat down to compile a list of tips that we felt could help experienced cabinet-makers as well as those just starting their first one.

Don't settle for what's in the home center

Home centers and lumberyards typically have only a few cabinet-grade plywood options in stock, but almost all of them can order what you need. You can order sheets with more plies for stability; pick the orientation of the wood grain; buy sheets with hardwood on one side and melamine on the other; choose marine-grade plywood for outdoor projects ... the options go on and on.

It takes a little planning ahead, and ask about minimum orders, but don't limit yourself to oak if you really want cherry.

Build the cabinets, buy the doors

Building cabinet doors is doable but can be tricky. It sometimes requires powerful and expensive wood-shaping equipment. And if you have a bunch to build, you'll need a lot of clamps and even more space. Unless you have unlimited free time, consider building your cabinets but buying your doors. You'll find many door makers online (search for "buy cabinet doors"). Cabinet doors can be ordered in a variety of styles and in increments as small as 1/16 in. It's always nice to be able to see and touch, so check out your local cabinet shop as well.

Label your face frame parts first

Dry-fit face frame parts so the best side of all the boards will be seen, avoiding stark grain color variations at joints. Label all the pieces with a pencil so the frame goes back together the same way you laid it out. The pencil marks also come in handy when you're ready to sand the assembled frame. You'll know you have flat joints when the pencil marks disappear.

Gang up on your components

Even with a high-end table saw, it's difficult to reset the fence to exactly replicate previous cuts, so plan ahead and cut all your face frame parts at the same time. Gang-planing your stiles and rails will save time and ensure all the parts are exactly the same width and thickness. Gang-sand board edges by clamping them together. That not only speeds up sanding but also keeps you from rounding over edges. And *always* make more parts than you need. It's better to have a couple of pieces left over than to have to cut, plane and sand one replacement board if you make a miscut. Also, having extra allows you to choose the best boards of the lot.

Assemble the face frame with pocket hole screws

Pocket hole screws are a fast and easy way to join a face frame. You don't need a lot of clamps or wood glue. A mortise-and-tenon joint may make you feel like a true craftsman, but only you will know you spent all that extra time. An entry-level pocket screw jig is inexpensive, but if you plan to build several face frame projects, spend more to get a top-of-the-line jig.

POCKET HOLE SCREW

Trim some face frames flush

Face frames on furniture look best when they're flush with the cabinet sides. But it's still better to build the face frame a little bigger (about 1/16 in.), and trim it off with a flush trim router bit. Adjust the bit depth so the cutting edges are only slightly deeper than the face frame.

FLUSH

Leave off the back until you apply finish

If you plan to finish your project before you install it, leave the back off until after you've applied the finish. It makes getting into all those nooks and crannies a lot easier, especially in deeper cabinets. Wood glue won't stick to finishes, so if you want to glue on the back, use polyurethane glue.

Build individual boxes

Moving and installing long one-piece cabinets can be a tough job, and it may not even be possible to get the assembly into the room. Instead of creating such a monster, build individual cabinet carcasses. Add the face frame after they're all in place.

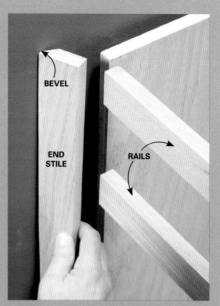

Leave the end stile off to scribe

Leave one end stile off when you install cabinets that butt against walls at both ends. With a complete face frame, you won't be able to push the cabinet into place or scribe and adjust the stile to fit. Cut that last stile a bit oversize to leave room for scribing, and rip a 45-degree back bevel for easier planing to your scribed line. The bevel also makes it easier to twist the stile into place.

Assemble the whole face frame on your workbench with pocket screws, then remove the last stile. That way you'll be guaranteed a perfect fit when you reattach it after planing. Or attach it with a bit of glue and a few brads.

Build face frames larger

A main function of a face frame is to hide the exposed plywood laminations. A face frame does a better job of this if it overlaps the box edges a bit. Making the face frame run past all the plywood edges provides a little wiggle room and hides not-so-perfect saw cuts on the plywood. Face frames on sides of kitchen cabinets should overlap 1/4 in. on the outside edge. This makes room for adjustments when installing them next to one another. Build the face frame so that the bottom rail ("rails" are horizontal boards and "stiles" are vertical boards) projects 1/16 in. above the bottom shelf of the cabinet.

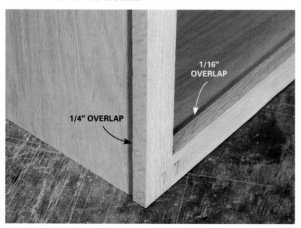

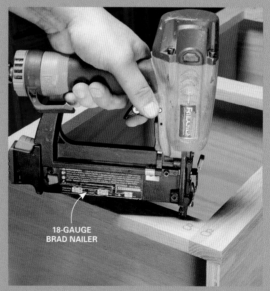

Nail the face frame to boxes

One of the easiest ways to attach face frames to carcasses is with a thin bead of wood glue and an 18-gauge brad nailer with 2-in. brads. Be sparing with brads; their main duty is to hold the frame in place while the glue dries. A couple per side and wherever there's a void should do the trick. A little putty will make the brad holes almost invisible.

Build a separate base

Most factory-built cabinets have a recessed "toe-kick" that's typically about 4 in. high and deep. But you can also make a separate base that's the total length of the cabinet assembly and build shorter cabinets to make up the difference. With this method, you won't have to mess around with figuring out and cutting toe-kick profiles on your cabinets.

This is also a handy technique when you have an uneven floor because you need to level and shim only one base instead of several individual cabinets. It's important to use dead-straight wood for bases so it'll be flat for setting the cabinets. Once your cabinets are installed, finish off the base front with a strip of 1/4-in. plywood that matches the cabinets.

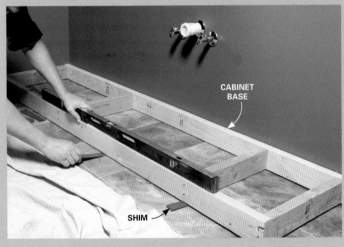

CABINET BASE

SHIM

Cap end cabinets

If you cap the end cabinet with 1/4-in. plywood, you don't have to hide the fasteners you used to build your boxes. That means you can use large, sturdy screws without worrying about ugly putty-filled holes. You'll also need an end cap if you choose to build a separate base. Use construction adhesive and a few small brads to fasten the panel in place, and make sure you extend the outside face frame stile an additional 1/4 in. to account for the thickness of the plywood.

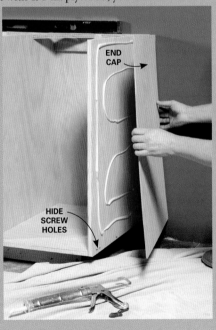

END CAP

HIDE SCREW HOLES

BACK OF CABINET

SIDE OF CABINET WON'T BE SEEN

Don't cut rabbets if they're not needed

It's common practice to cut a rabbet (a notch to receive the 1/4-in. back panel) on the back edge of cabinet carcasses so the back panel will be recessed. But that's not necessary if the cabinet sides won't be visible—the back panel edges won't be either. Save yourself some time and just tack on the back panel with a brad nailer. Make sure to take into account the overall depth of your cabinets—they'll be 1/4 in. deeper if you go this route.

Edge-banding plywood

With a roll of wood veneer edge banding and a few simple tools, you can cover raw plywood edges so the plywood is nearly indistinguishable from solid wood. Iron-on edge banding is wood veneer with hot-melt adhesive preapplied to the back. You simply hold the edge banding in place, run over it with a household iron to heat the adhesive, let it cool and trim the edges flush. Here you'll learn the best way to do it, plus tips for getting perfect results every time.

You'll find edge banding in common species like birch, oak and cherry at home centers and lumberyards. For exotic species and a greater variety of widths, search online or visit a specialty woodworking store. Rolls of edge banding come in lengths of 8 ft. to 250 ft. and widths of 13/16 in. to 2 in. For typical 3/4-in. plywood, buy 13/16- or 7/8-in.-wide edge banding.

7/8" OAK EDGE BANDING

120-GRIT SANDPAPER

Clean up the edges

Saw marks or other roughness will prevent a strong bond between the edge banding and the plywood. To avoid loose edge banding, sand the edges of the plywood smooth before you apply it. To keep from rounding edges while you sand, wrap a quarter sheet of 120-grit sandpaper around a small block of 3/4-in. plywood and screw another scrap to it as a guide. When the sandpaper starts showing signs of wear, remove the screw and reposition the sandpaper. After sanding, vacuum the edge to remove any dust.

Press it while it's hot

Make sure the edge banding is fully adhered by pressing it down with a block of wood while it's still hot. Go back and forth over the edge a few times while the glue is cooling. Look for any areas that are raised. Heat those spots again and press them again with the block.

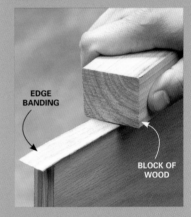

EDGE BANDING

BLOCK OF WOOD

Iron on the edge banding

Use your regular clothes iron if you wish, but be aware that you may get adhesive on the soleplate. To be safe, buy a cheap iron from a thrift store or discount retailer. Empty the water out to avoid any steam and move the heat setting to "cotton." Use scissors to cut a length of edge banding about 1 in. longer than the edge you're covering. Starting at one end, center the edge banding with equal overhangs on each side and set the preheated iron at that end. Move the iron along the surface, keeping the edge banding centered with your other hand. Move the iron along at a rate of about 2 in. per second. The goal is to melt the adhesive without scorching the wood.

Don't sweat it if you scorch or misalign the banding during application. Just run the iron over it again to soften the glue so you can peel the banding away. Cut yourself a new piece and start over.

"COTTON" SETTING

ROLL OF EDGE BANDING

Slice off the ends

The easiest way to remove the overhanging ends is to simply slice them off with a utility knife. Place the edge banding on a work surface and lightly score it a couple of times. Don't worry about cutting all the way through. Just lift the plywood and bend up the banding to snap it off.

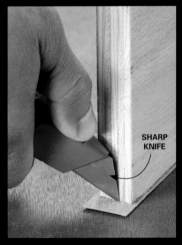

SHARP KNIFE

Use a trimmer on edges

The quickest and easiest way to trim the edge banding flush to the plywood is with a special edge banding tool, such as the FastCap trimmer shown here (No. 836877 at Woodcraft stores or online at woodcraft.com).

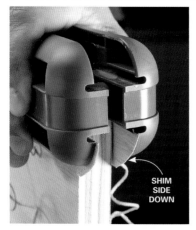

SHIM SIDE DOWN

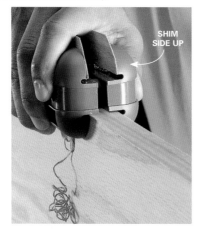

SHIM SIDE UP

Make a shallow pass first

Trim with the shimmed side first (see below for how to modify the trimmer with shims). Since less veneer is being removed with this side of the trimmer, the likelihood of runaway splits is greatly reduced. Start at one end and squeeze the trimmer until the shims are against the plywood. Then press down and slide the trimmer along the edge. Thin strips of veneer will peel away from both edges.

Flip the trimmer for the final pass

Flip the trimmer over and use the unshimmed side for a final trimming. When you're through, the edge banding should be almost perfectly flush with the plywood. If you missed any spots, just make another pass or two with the trimmer. The final sanding will remove the sharp edge and any remaining overhang.

SANDPAPER

WOOD BLOCK

EDGE BAND

Touch up with a sanding block

After you trim them, the edges will be sharp. Ease them with 150-grit sandpaper on a sanding block. Hold the sanding block at a slight angle and smooth out the edge. Sand gently and inspect the edge often to avoid sanding through the thin veneer.

Modify your trimmer

Trimming the overhanging edges flush to the plywood without damaging the edge banding can be tricky. If the trimming blade catches in the wood grain, it can split the thin veneer and you'd have to start over. Prevent that headache by shimming one side of the trimmer with strips of edge banding so that it doesn't cut as deep. Just "tack" the shims on with the iron, making sure to leave a gap where the blades are. Since this trimmer has two cutting sides, you can leave the shims on one side to make the initial pass, and then just flip it over to make the final pass.

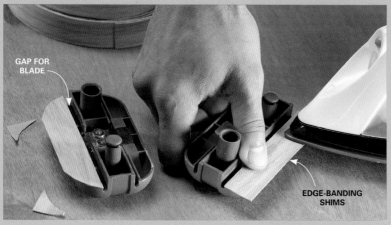

GAP FOR BLADE

EDGE-BANDING SHIMS

SPLICE

Don't

Don't leave a splice where it'll show

Splices can be hard to see on raw edge banding, but they may be highly visible after stain is applied. Inspect the edge banding before you cut it to length so you can cut around splices and avoid surprises later. Avoid waste by using spliced pieces in less visible areas.

Installing cabinets

Kitchen cabinets aren't cheap, and while you shouldn't be afraid to install them, you don't want to screw them up, either. We asked Jerome Worm, an experienced installer, to show you what it takes to install basic box cabinets successfully. His tips can save you time and help you avoid costly mistakes on your next installation.

Mark up the wall first

Every good cabinet installation starts with a good layout. Jerome calls it "blueprinting" the wall. Here's how to do it: Measure from the highest point in the floor (see "Raise the Cabinets for Flooring," p. 266), and draw a level line marking the top of the base cabinets. Measure up 19-1/2 in. from that line and draw another line for the bottom of the upper cabinets. Label the location of the cabinets and appliances on the wall. Draw a vertical line to line up the edge of the first cabinet to be installed. Finally, mark the stud locations.

Shim extreme bows

Most of the time you can shim the cabinets as you go, but if there's an extreme bow in the wall (more than 3/8 in.), shim it out before you hang the cabinet. If you don't, you may accidentally pull the back off the cabinet while fastening it into place. Hold a level across the wall, and slide a shim up from the bottom (go in from the top when you're doing the top side) until it's snug. Then pin or tape it into place.

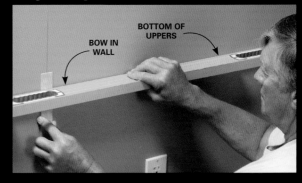

BOTTOM OF UPPERS

BOW IN WALL

MEET THE PRO

Jerome Worm has installed cabinets in hundreds of kitchens. These days, he can hang them in his sleep. Here are some of his best tips.

Remove the doors and drawers

Removing shelves, doors and drawers makes installation easier and prevents damage. Mark the location of the doors on painter's tape, and make a pencil mark at the top of the hinges so you have a good starting point when you reinstall them. Remember that many upper cabinets have no designated top or bottom. They can be hung either direction depending on which way you want the doors to swing. So decide that before you mark the hinges.

TOP OF HINGE

24 30 LEFT SINK

Mark the stud locations on upper cabinets

Jerome prefers to predrill the screw holes from the inside of the cabinet so the drill bit doesn't "blow out" the wood on the inside where it can be seen. Do this by marking the stud locations on the inside of the cabinet and drilling pilot holes. Start by finding the distance from the wall or adjacent cabinet to the center of the next stud. For 1/2-in.-thick cabinet walls, subtract 7/8 in. from that measurement, and measure that distance from the inside of the cabinet. Make a pencil mark on both the top and the bottom nailing strip. The outside of the cabinet walls are not flush with the rest of the cabinet; that 7/8 in. represents the thickness of the cabinet wall and the distance the walls are recessed.

Use good screws

Jerome prefers GRK's R4 self-countersinking screw, which he calls "the Cadillac of screws" (available at home centers or online). You'll pay accordingly, but why scrimp on screws when you're spending thousands of dollars on cabinets? Whatever you do, don't use drywall screws—they'll just snap off and you'll end up with an extra hole.

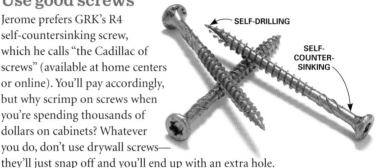

SELF-DRILLING

SELF-COUNTER-SINKING

Start with the upper cabinets

It's easier to hang the uppers when you're not leaning way over the base cabinets. Rest the uppers on a ledger board—it'll ensure a nice, straight alignment and eliminate the frustration of holding the cabinets in place while screwing them to the wall.

LEDGER BOARD

Clamp, drill and fasten

When connecting two cabinets to each other, line up the face frames and clamp them together. Both cabinets should be fastened to the wall at this point, but you may have to loosen one cabinet or the other to get the frames to line up perfectly. Jerome prefers hand-screw clamps because they don't flex, and less flex means a tighter grip. Predrill a 1/8-in. hole before screwing them together with a 2-1/2-in. screw. Choose the less noticeable cabinet of the two for drilling and placing the screw head.

FILLER STRIP

SCRIBING BLOCK

Use a block of wood for scribing

Find the largest distance between the outside of the cabinet and the wall. Take that measurement and make a pencil mark on your filler strip (measure right to left in this case). Clamp the filler onto the cabinet flush with the inside of the vertical rail. Measure from the wall to your pencil mark and make a scribing block that size. Use your block to trace a pencil line down the filler strip. Masking tape on the filler strip helps the pencil line show up better and protects the finish from the saw table.

Fasten the back, then shim

Line up the base cabinets with the level line on the wall. Fasten the back of the cabinets to that line. Once the backs of the cabinets are level, use shims to level the sides. Take your time on this step—nobody likes to have eggs roll off a slanted countertop.

Use 2x2s to secure cabinets to the floor

Cabinets that make up islands and peninsulas need to be secured to the floor. Join the island cabinets and set them in place. Trace an outline of the cabinets on the floor. Screw 2x2s to the floor 1/2 in. on the inside of the line to account for the thickness of the cabinets. Anchor the island cabinets to the 2x2s with screws. If needed, place flooring blocks under the 2x2s (see "Raise the Cabinets for Flooring," at right).

2x2

FLOORING BLOCK

Raise the cabinets for flooring

If the kitchen flooring is going to be hardwood or tile, and you're installing it after the cabinets, you'll have to raise the cabinets off the floor or the dishwasher won't fit under the countertop. Use blocks to represent the finished floor height, and add those distances to the guide line for the base cabinet tops. Hold the blocks back a bit from the front so the flooring can tuck underneath. Your flooring guys will love you for this.

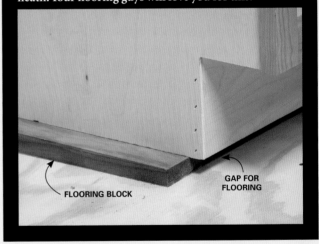

FLOORING BLOCK

GAP FOR FLOORING

Cut oversize holes

Cutting exact-size holes for water lines and drainpipes might impress your spouse or customer, but such precision is likely to result in unnecessary headaches for you. Cutting larger holes makes it easier to slide the cabinet into place and provides wiggle room for minor adjustments. No one's going to notice the oversize holes once the cabinet is filled with dish soaps, scrubbers and recycling bins.

Hanging shelves

F rom leveling to anchoring, here are 10 tips to make sure your next shelf-hanging project is quick, easy and strong. We'll show you tips for hanging and installing everything from store-bought display shelves to DIY closet shelves. And even if you don't have any shelf projects in the near future, you'll find leveling and anchoring tips here that you can use on other building projects.

Mark the tape, not the wall

The first step in any shelf-hanging project is to locate the studs so you can anchor the shelf to the studs if possible. Here's a tip that allows you to make marks that are clearly visible without the need to repaint the wall.

Use a level and draw a very light pencil line where you want the top of the shelf to be. The shelf will hide the line. Apply a strip of masking tape above the line. Use "delicate surface" masking tape to avoid any possibility of messing up the paint. Locate the studs and mark the centers on the tape. Electronic stud finders are the go-to tool for this task. Now you can plan your shelf-mounting project to hit as many studs as possible and use the tape as a guide for leveling and attaching the shelf.

STUD MARK

MASKING TAPE

STUD FINDER

Figure-eights simplify the job

These nifty little fasteners are actually designed to attach table and desktops to aprons (the vertical skirt around the perimeter), but they're also a handy solution for hanging shelves. You can buy a pack of eight at woodworking stores or online.

The only caveat is that the top of the figure-eight shows above the surface of the shelf, so it may be visible if you hang the shelf low. Try to position the figure-eights where there are studs if possible. You can use good-quality hollow-wall anchors if the studs don't line up with the figure-eights.

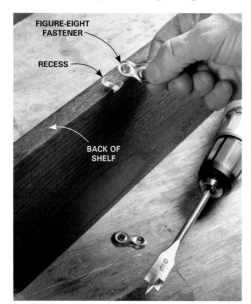

FIGURE-EIGHT FASTENER

RECESS

BACK OF SHELF

Drill a recess for the figure-eight

Use a spade bit or Forstner bit to drill a slight recess in the back of the shelf to accommodate the thickness of the figure-eight. Then chisel out the remaining wood until the figure-eight sits flush to the shelf. Attach the figure-eight with a screw.

Simply screw it on

Mount the shelf by driving screws through the figure-eights either into hollow-wall anchors or into studs.

Dead-on leveling with a laser

Got a lot of shelves to level? A laser level is the perfect tool. We're using a self-leveling laser, but any laser that projects a horizontal level line will work. The tip is that you don't have to mess with getting the laser line at the height of your shelf. Just project it anywhere on the wall, and use it as a reference by measuring up from the line. This is especially handy if you're mounting several shelves at different heights, since you never need to reposition the laser. Pick up a self-leveling laser and use it for many interior leveling tasks.

SHELF LEVEL

LASER LINE

SELF-LEVELING LASER

Super-sturdy closet shelves

Here's a fast, strong and easy way to install closet shelves. Paint a 1x4 to match your shelf. Then draw a level line and locate the studs or use our masking tape trick (p. 267). Nail the 1x4 to the studs with 8d finish nails. Run the strip across the back and ends of the closet. Then put blocks in the locations where you want brackets. Now you have solid wood to attach the brackets and the closet pole sockets to. And the back of the shelf is fully supported to prevent sagging.

HOOK STRIP

LOW-QUALITY FREE ANCHOR

Throw away the free anchors

Most of the hollow-wall anchors included with shelves or shelf brackets aren't worth using. If you can't attach your shelf to studs and must use hollow-wall anchors, make sure to choose one that will support your shelf in the long run.

For light-duty shelves, we like the type of anchor shown here. You'll find them at any hardware store or home center. Make sure you know how thick your drywall or plaster is before you head to the store, though. Then match the anchor to the wall thickness.

To install the anchors, check the instructions and drill the right size hole. Then fold the wings so the anchor will fit and press it into the hole. You may have to tap it with a hammer until it's fully seated. Finish by pressing the included red tool through the hole to expand the wings behind the drywall or plaster. And make sure to use the screws included with the anchors, or ones that are the same diameter.

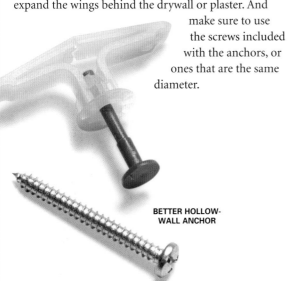

BETTER HOLLOW-WALL ANCHOR

Build in a hanging rail

Whether you're building a shelf or modifying a store-bought unit, including a hanging rail is a great way to add strength and allow for more flexible positioning while anchoring to studs. The rail strengthens the shelf and lets you anchor the shelf by driving screws anywhere along the length of the rail.

If the shelf isn't too heavy, you can hang it with finish-head screws that are easy to hide with wood putty. For heavier shelves, drill recesses for wood plugs to hide the screws.

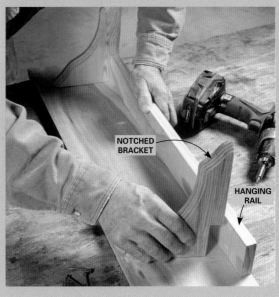

NOTCHED BRACKET

HANGING RAIL

Self-plumbing standards

The next time you install metal shelf standards, remember this tip. Rather than use a level to plumb the standards before you attach them, simply hang them loosely from the top with one of the screws and let gravity do the work. The standard will hang plumb, and all you have to do is press it to the wall and drive in the remaining screws. If you're using hollow-wall anchors, hang the standard from the top screw and use an awl to mark the screw locations. Then take the standard down and install the anchors.

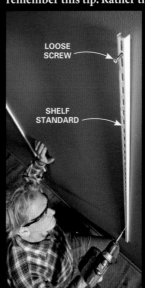

LOOSE SCREW

SHELF STANDARD

The key to keyholes

Keyhole slots on the back of shelves are a common way to hang shelves or brackets on hidden screws, but you have to get the screws perfectly aligned or you'll have all kinds of trouble.

Here's one foolproof method for transferring a pair of keyhole locations to the wall for perfect screw placement. If you're lucky, you may be able to line up the screw locations with studs. Otherwise, use this method to mark the center of the hollow-wall anchors you'll need.

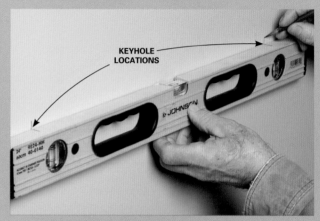

Mark; don't measure

Place a strip of masking tape on one edge of your level and mark the center of each keyhole on the tape.

Transfer to the wall

Hold the level against the wall at the height you want the shelf. Remember that the top of the shelf will be above your marks. Adjust the level until the bubble is centered, and mark the keyhole locations on the wall. Then install anchors or drive the screws into the studs and hang the shelf.

A better anchor for heavy shelves

Of course it's always best to fasten heavy shelves to studs, but if you can't, there's an anchor that's almost as good. If you've used standard toggle bolts, you know they hold well. But they're a hassle to work with, and they leave an oversize hole that may show. And if you ever need to take the shelf down to paint, the toggle falls into the wall and you have to repeat the whole tedious process when you reinstall the shelf.

Snaptoggle anchors solve these problems. After installing the toggle according to the instructions, you'll have a threaded opening in the wall ready to receive the included bolt. You can simply screw the shelf to the captured toggle. And you can remove the bolt and the toggle will stay put, ready for you to reinstall the shelf. You'll find Snaptoggle anchors in hardware stores and home centers alongside the other wall anchors.

French cleats for fast, solid hanging

Pairs of beveled strips that interlock to support shelves, cabinets or pictures are called French cleats. They're great for hanging any shelf or cabinet and have a few advantages in certain situations.

First, the cleats work well for heavy cabinets because you can easily mount the wall cleat and then simply lift the cabinet and "hook" it on. There's no need to support a heavy cabinet temporarily while you drive screws to anchor it.

Another common use for French cleats is to create a flexible system of shelves or cabinets. You can screw one or more lengths of wall cleats across the entire wall, and then easily relocate shelves, or add more shelves at a later date. Make cleats by ripping strips of 3/4-in. plywood with a 45-degree bevel on one edge. Screw one strip to the wall and the other to the back of the shelf or cabinet.

Clamping tips
Pro lessons for the weekend woodworker

MEET A PRO

In 30 years as a professional woodworker, Dave Munkittrick has tried just about every clamping technique imaginable. Some of them are his own inventions; some are borrowed from other woodworkers. As for the rest, he's been doing them for so long that he can't remember where they came from.

Tape those hard-to-clamp jobs

Every woodworker occasionally uses masking tape in place of clamps. But we prefer electrical tape because it's stretchy and lets you put the pressure exactly where you need it.

A dry run is a must-do

If you skip this step, you end up regretting your impatience. Don't make this mistake. Take the time to rehearse your glue-up. That way you'll know all the clamps you need are at hand and there won't be any nasty, unexpected misfits in your joinery to ruin your glue-up and your day.

Cauls keep glue-ups flat and flush

As you squeeze boards together with pipe clamps, they sometimes arch or slip out of alignment. Pairs of upper and lower cauls are the solution. I lightly squeeze the cauls with bar clamps, then tighten the pipe clamps, then tighten the cauls a bit more... I continue this back-and-forth process until the boards are joined flush and flat.

My favorite cauls are made from 2x4s. I carefully select ones that have a slight bend or "crown" along the 1-1/2-in. edge, but no twist or warp. The crown is an advantage because it creates extra pressure in the middle of the caul. I label all my cauls with an arrow marking the direction of the crown and the length of the caul.

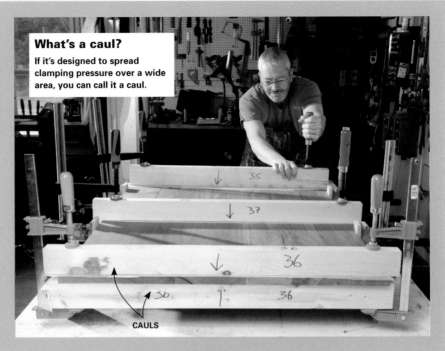

What's a caul?
If it's designed to spread clamping pressure over a wide area, you can call it a caul.

CAULS

Prevent clamp stains with wax paper

Moisture in glue triggers a reaction between iron and chemicals in wood (called "tannins"). The result is black stains on the wood, especially with tannin-rich woods like oak or walnut. A strip of wax paper acts as a barrier between the clamp and the wood. I also use wax paper to keep glue off my cauls.

Water pressure

Some woodworkers keep a stack of bricks in the shop for those times when weight is better than clamps. But I think plastic buckets make the best weights. Filled with water, they provide a lot of weight. When empty, they're light, easy to store and handy for other jobs.

135 LBS. OF CLAMPING POWER!

Give clamps a lift

Homemade clamp jacks raise your pipe clamps off the bench so the handles turn freely and there's plenty of room underneath for alignment cauls and clamps. The jacks also act as pads to keep clamps from denting the wood. These jacks are 8 in. tall and made from 1/2-in. plywood.

CLAMP JACK

Shift clamps to square

To check the squareness of a cabinet frame or box, take diagonal measurements. If the measurements aren't equal, shift the positions of the clamps. In this photo, we exaggerated the shift for clarity. In most cases, a slight shift will do the trick. Sometimes, shifting just one clamp will pull the assembly into square.

Hold it square

When you're clamping cabinets together, getting a square assembly is half the battle. These simple blocks, made from three layers of 1/2-in. plywood, pull the cabinet into square and keep it there. After the squaring blocks are in place, use pipe clamps to squeeze the joints tightly together.

CORNER BLOCK

Iron out veneer-clamping problems

Gluing down veneer is tough. You have to apply flat, even pressure over every square inch. There are fancy tools for this, but for small veneer jobs, try this nifty trick: Apply a thin coat of wood glue to the substrate and the back of your veneer. Let the glue dry. Then position the veneer and use a hot iron (no steam) to reactivate the glue and press it into place. The bond is almost instant and very strong. I love it.

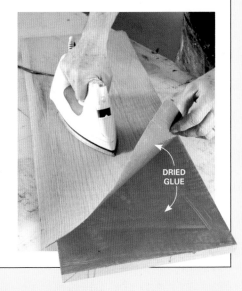

DRIED GLUE

One caul instead of many clamps

Thin, flexible parts require lots of clamps to create a consistently tight fit. Or you can use a caul. This solid-wood edging on plywood, for example, would have required a clamp every few inches. But with a stiff caul to spread the clamping force, I was able to use fewer clamps, spaced far apart.

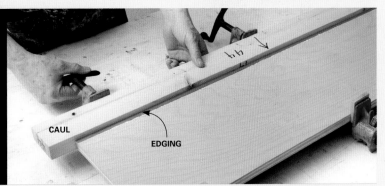

CAUL

EDGING

Long-jaw hand screw

Extend the reach of your hand screw clamps with a couple of lengths of scrap wood. Screw the jaw extensions to the side of your hand screw and away you go. Works great and couldn't be easier.

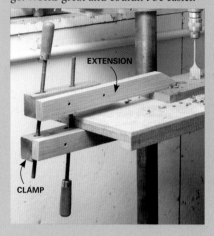

Put the pinch on miter joints

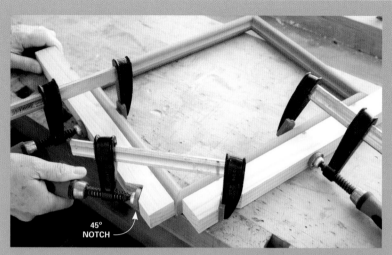

A pair of notched "pinch blocks" puts clamp pressure right on the miter joint. This approach is especially good for picture frames because it lets you deal with one joint at a time rather than all four at once. Position the blocks shy of the mitered ends so you can see how the joint lines up.

Magnetic clamp pads

Instant on and instant off. You can't beat the convenience of these wooden clamp pads. Best of all, they don't leave oily stains like the plastic ones do. To make these pads, drill shallow holes in 3/8-in.-thick blocks of softwood. Then drop in dabs of epoxy and insert rare earth magnets. These magnets were 1/2 in. diameter and 1/8 in. thick. Make sure the magnet is flush or slightly below the pad surface.

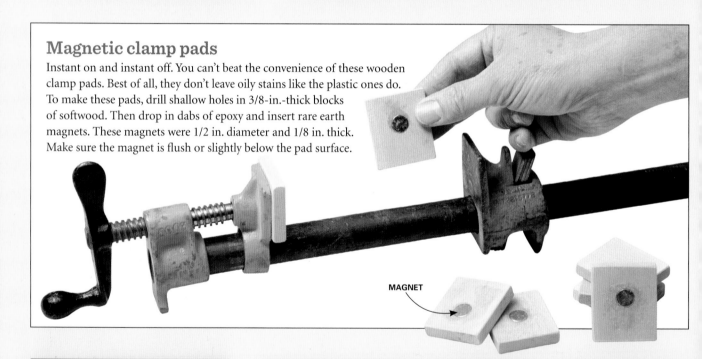

Slow down

Glue-ups can be a frenzied, nerve-jangling activity. So why not slow things down a bit? Take the edge off your glue-ups with a slow-setting glue such as Titebond's Extend. The extra 10 minutes of open time can be a real lifesaver and nerve calmer.

Anti-slip tip

Wet glue is like grease, allowing parts to slide around while you're trying to clamp them. But a few strategically placed brads or pins prevent that frustration. I like to use a 23-gauge pinner because the heads are almost invisible. But a standard brad nailer works too.

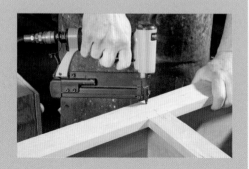

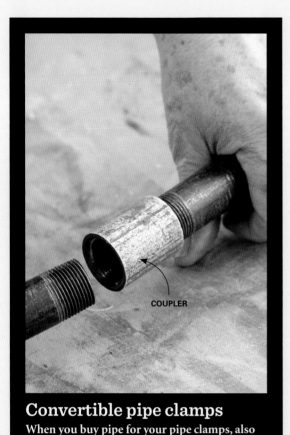

COUPLER

Convertible pipe clamps

When you buy pipe for your pipe clamps, also pick up some couplers. That way, you can join pipes to make longer clamps.

Overhead hold-down

Sometimes, a 2x4 wedged against overhead joists is better than a clamp.

When routing a tabletop, for example, you can rout all the way around without stopping and shifting clamps. This trick is also handy when you need to apply pressure where clamps won't reach: gluing down bubbled veneer in the middle of a large tabletop, for example.

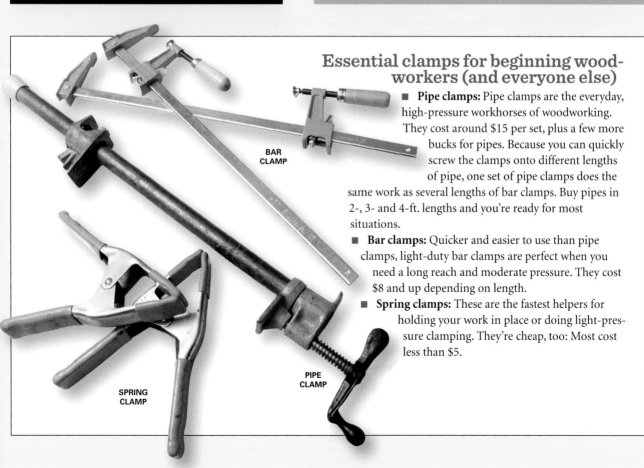

BAR CLAMP

SPRING CLAMP

PIPE CLAMP

Essential clamps for beginning woodworkers (and everyone else)

■ **Pipe clamps:** Pipe clamps are the everyday, high-pressure workhorses of woodworking. They cost around $15 per set, plus a few more bucks for pipes. Because you can quickly screw the clamps onto different lengths of pipe, one set of pipe clamps does the same work as several lengths of bar clamps. Buy pipes in 2-, 3- and 4-ft. lengths and you're ready for most situations.

■ **Bar clamps:** Quicker and easier to use than pipe clamps, light-duty bar clamps are perfect when you need a long reach and moderate pressure. They cost $8 and up depending on length.

■ **Spring clamps:** These are the fastest helpers for holding your work in place or doing light-pressure clamping. They're cheap, too: Most cost less than $5.

Driving screws

For such a simple task, it's surprising how many things can go wrong when you drive screws. Stripped screw heads, split board ends and broken screws are just a few common problems. We'll show you how you can avoid all the frustration just by using the right screws and a few special tools.

Look for Torx-head screws

Torx-head screws have been common on automobiles for a long time, but now they're available for general construction use too. Star-shaped Torx bits fit tightly into the star-shaped recess in the head of the screw, providing a firm grip that rarely slips out or strips the screw head. It's easier to drive these screws because you don't have to press down as hard to maintain good bit contact. Plus, most Torx-head screws are premium-quality fasteners available with other features like self-drilling points, self-setting heads and corrosion-resistant coatings.

Torx-head screws require star-shaped bits that are labeled with a "T" followed by a number. Some screw packages include a driver bit, but if yours doesn't, check the package to see what size is required. If there's a downside to Torx-head screws, it's the price. You wouldn't want to use them to hang drywall.

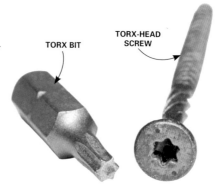

TORX BIT

TORX-HEAD SCREW

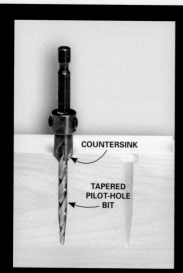

COUNTERSINK

TAPERED PILOT-HOLE BIT

Buy a set of countersink bits

Drilling a pilot hole for the screw and then creating a recess, or countersink, for the screw head is standard practice on cabinets and furniture projects. The pilot hole bit creates a hole that reduces friction to make screw driving easier, and the countersink allows you to set the screw head flush with or below the surface. With a set of countersink bits like these, you can complete both operations in one step. Even though they cost a little more, we prefer the combination pilot/countersink bits with the tapered drill bit.

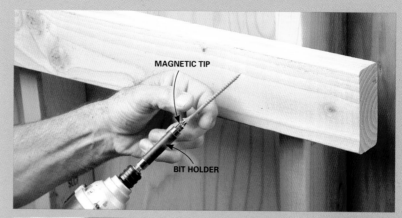

MAGNETIC TIP

BIT HOLDER

SLIDING SLEEVE

Use a magnetic bit-tip holder

If you're new to driving screws with a drill, you may not know the many benefits of using a magnetic bit holder. First, and most obvious, is that it holds any driver bit with a standard 1/4-in. hex-shape base, making it super quick and easy to change bits. But there are other advantages too. The bit holder extends the length of the bit, making it much easier to get into tight spots. The magnet in the bit holder magnetizes the tip, allowing you to hold ferrous-metal screws in place on the end of the bit for easier driving (top photo). And if you buy a bit holder with a sleeve, like the one shown here, you can use it to hold long screws upright as you drive them in (bottom photo). Look for a magnetic bit holder that's at least 3 in. long and includes the sleeve.

Ditch the lag screws

The next time you build a deck, gazebo or fence that requires lag screws, consider using a modern version instead. These new structural screws are just as strong but skinnier, and they have specially designed tips and threads to make it easier to drive them in. You don't even have to drill pilot holes. And you can drive them with a standard drill, impact driver or strong cordless drill. They cost a little more than conventional lag screws. But if you've got better things to do than waste time with lag screws, they're worth every cent.

STRUCTURAL SCREW

Trim-head screws aren't just for trim

Trim-head screws are slender screws with very small heads. Originally they were designed to attach wood trim to walls built with steel studs. But now you can go to the fasteners department in any home center or full-service hardware store and find trim-head screws in several colors, long lengths, corrosion-resistant finishes or stainless steel, which make them perfect replacements for nails in many situations. When sunk slightly below the surface, the heads on these screws are small enough to be covered easily with wood filler or color putty.

Here we're using trim-head screws to connect a fence rail to a post. But you can also use them in place of galvanized casing nails to install exterior doors and windows, or to attach exterior trim. Trim-head screws have several advantages over nails. They hold better and are easier to install in tight areas. Plus, if you're not an experienced carpenter, they allow you to install trim without worrying about denting it with an errant hammer blow. Keep a supply of trim-head screws of various lengths on hand and you'll be surprised how often you reach for them rather than nails.

Get a cordless impact driver

Nothing beats impact drivers for driving screws easily. Impact drivers combine hammer-like blows with rotation to apply plenty of torque to the screw head. The hammer action means you don't have to press down hard to keep the bit in contact with the screw. This allows you to drive screws one-handed in spots that would be hard to reach otherwise. But beyond this advantage, the extra torque makes it simpler to drive any screw, especially long ones.

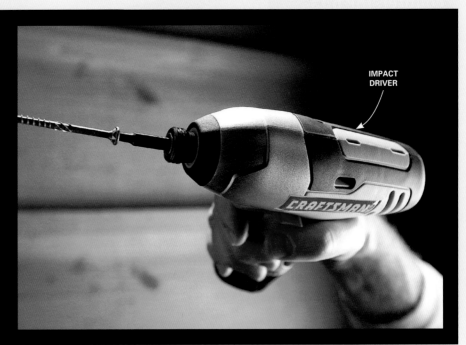

IMPACT DRIVER

Install drywall with special tools

If you're considering driving drywall screws with a cordless drill and a regular Phillips-bit driver, don't. Drywall screws have to be driven to exactly the right depth. Too shallow, and you won't be able to cover them with joint compound; too deep, and you'll break through the paper face of the drywall, which will give you ugly drywall screw pops later. It's nearly impossible to drive screws quickly and accurately without special tools.

Here are your choices. If you only have a few sheets of drywall to hang, you can buy a special tip for your cordless drill that limits the depth you can drive the screw. These drywall screw tips cost just a few dollars and work well if you're careful. A better option is a driver drill that's built to drive drywall screws. You can buy a time-saving auto-feed version (center photo below) that uses special collated screws, or a dedicated drywall screw gun (left) that drives regular drywall screws. Both versions have adjustable nosepieces for precise depth control. If you only need the tool for one drywall job, consider renting one for a day or two.

DRYWALL SCREW GUN

CORDLESS AUTO-FEED DRYWALL SCREW GUN

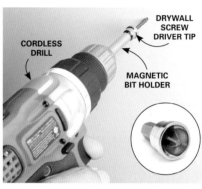

CORDLESS DRILL

DRYWALL SCREW DRIVER TIP

MAGNETIC BIT HOLDER

NAIL GUN

CABINET BACK AND SIDE

COUNTERSINK BIT

Tack first, then drive screws

It can be frustrating and time consuming to try to hold parts in place while you drill pilot holes and drive screws. Here's a trick that solves the problem and speeds up assembly too. Tack the parts together first with a brad or finish nail gun. That enables you to align the parts with one hand while you tack with the other. Once everything is held in the right position, it's simple to drill the pilot/countersink holes and drive the screws.

Center starter holes with a self-centering bit

When you drill pilot holes for hardware mounting screws, it's tough to keep the hole centered. That's where self-centering pilot bits come in handy. Just choose the right size self-centering bit, press the nose into the hole in the hardware, and the cone-shape guide keeps the bit centered while you drill the hole. You can buy a set of bits that work for screw sizes Nos. 6, 8 and 10.

SELF-CENTERING PILOT-HOLE BIT

Adjust the clutch to avoid stripped screw heads

Most cordless drills come equipped with a clutch. If your drill has a clutch, try it out the next time you use the drill to drive small brass or aluminum screws that are easily damaged. Start with the lightest clutch setting and increase it until the proper driving depth is reached. The clutch will prevent you from accidentally stripping the screw heads.

CLUTCH ADJUSTMENT

Using a hot-glue gun

If you think hot glue guns are just for school projects and holiday decorations, discover just how useful hot glue can be in the workshop, and your glue gun will become one of your favorite tools.

MEET THE EXPERT

Travis Larson, our senior editor, has been a builder, remodeler and woodworker for more than 30 years.

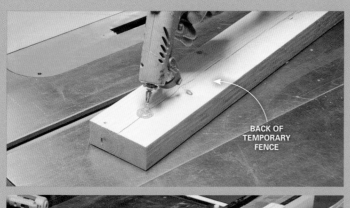

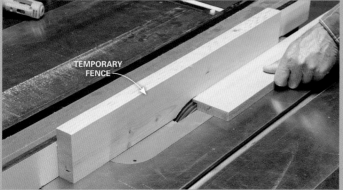

BACK OF
TEMPORARY
FENCE

TEMPORARY
FENCE

Fasten a temporary fence

When you're woodworking, you often need a temporary fence or stop on a table saw or router table or other power tools. Clamps aren't always an option because they can get in the way, and you probably don't want to drill holes in the machine's fence or table for bolts or screws. Instead, use a few dollops of hot glue to hold your temporary fence in place.

Hot-glue parts together for shaping and sanding

When you have several identical parts to make, hot-glue them together and work on them all at once. This will save you lots of time, and all the pieces will be exactly the same. Don't use too much glue—just a little dab will do. Use too much and it can be nearly impossible to separate the parts. Apply glue near edges so you can easily cut it with a putty knife later.

Cut and twist to separate

Hot glue is a tenacious fastener. If you just pry apart the wood, you're very likely to tear out some of the grain along with the glue. Instead, cut through the glue blob at one end with a putty knife. Then twist the boards apart to free the other end. That'll break the bond without damaging the wood.

CUT THE GLUE
AT ONE END

TWIST THE
BOARDS APART

Remove leftover glue with a chisel

If possible, place glue dabs where they'll be trimmed off later, such as along edges or on ends. Then you won't have to deal with glue residue. But if you do have glue dabs to remove, shave them off with a sharp chisel held flat to the board. Get as much as you can without gouging the wood, and then sand off the residue. Be sure to get it all—leftover glue won't accept finishes.

Glue small parts to a pedestal

Sometimes it's impossible, impractical or downright dangerous to hold small pieces in your hand while you shape or sand them. So just hot-glue them to a temporary pedestal and clamp that in a vise while you work on them.

Hard-to-clamp repairs call for hot glue

When you need to glue parts that can't be clamped together, hot glue is the answer. Hot glue will set in just a few seconds while you hold the pieces together.

FAST FIX

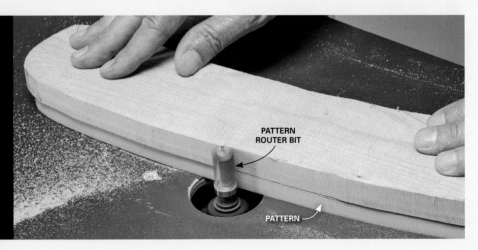

Hot glue for pattern routing

The best way to make multiple identical parts is to first create a perfect pattern from 1/2-in. MDF. Then cut out the parts slightly oversize, and final-shape them by using a router and a pattern bit to transfer the shape to the part. The best way to temporarily attach the pattern is with hot glue.

PATTERN ROUTER BIT

PATTERN

DABS OF
HOT GLUE

Stick stock to your workbench

If you need your workpiece to be stationary but clamps would be in the way, use a few dabs of hot glue to hold it in place.

Position drawer fronts

When you're installing new cabinet drawer fronts, apply hot glue, align the fronts perfectly in the cabinet opening and hold them against the drawer box until the glue sets. Then pull out the drawer and fasten them permanently with screws from the back.

DRAWER
FRONT

DRAWER
BOX

Secure mirrors or glass in cabinet doors

Swivel clamps are typically used to hold glass in cabinet door rabbets. But hot glue is a quick, rattle-free alternative. Just don't skimp on the glue or the glass may fall out. If you ever need to remove the glass, just heat the back with a heat gun to soften the glue.

Building cabinets with biscuit joints

Of all the ways of joining wood, biscuit joinery is about the easiest. You'll need to invest in a biscuit joiner (aka plate joiner) to cut matching slots in both boards. Then it's just a matter of gluing the football-shaped biscuits into place and clamping the boards together for 20 minutes or so.

The trick to successful biscuit joinery is cutting the slots in exactly the right spot so that the parts will line up correctly when they're joined. Biscuit joiners have an adjustable fence that can be used to align the slot, but here we'll show you a different technique. Instead of referencing the slot from the fence, we'll show you how to reference the slots from the base of the tool. This method has a few advantages. It's simpler to make an accurate slot because the tool is steadied against the workbench rather than the tool's fence. Another advantage of this method is that you don't have to readjust the fence for every cut. Here we'll show you how to use the bench reference method to join cabinet parts. We'll show you how to join cabinet panels, face frames and 1/2-in. drawer material. You can use the same technique for any biscuit joint.

Join plywood with the bench reference method

Photos 1 – 5 show the steps for joining 3/4-in. plywood without using the fence. On most biscuit joiners, the slot will be pretty close to centered when you use this method. But even if the slot is a little off-center, it'll still work fine as long as you orient the biscuit joiner and pencil marks as we show in the photos. Here are a few tips to ensure perfect joints:

- Work on a flat surface. The top of a table saw or a solid-core door is a good choice.
- Clean sawdust off your work surface before each setup.
- Hold the base of the biscuit joiner and the workpiece tight to the work surface as you cut the slots.

BISCUIT LOCATION

1 **Mark for the biscuits.** Align the two parts to be joined end to end. Then number the parts and draw pencil lines where you want biscuits. In our example, the lines will be inside the cabinet.

2 **Rest the base of the joiner on the bench.** To cut accurate slots, rest the biscuit joiner on the workbench instead of the fence. It's more stable and doesn't require any setup.

RIGHT ANGLE SUPPORT

3 **Hold the panel up with a right angle support.** The support keeps the panel steady and at an exact right angle. Then use the same method of resting the base of the biscuit joiner on the benchtop to cut the slots.

FLUX BRUSH

4 **Glue and biscuits make strong joints.** Brush glue into each slot. Then slide biscuits into the slots. Brush glue into the slots on the second panel before you joint the two.

5 **The panels will fit together perfectly.** The base of the biscuit joiner and the panels were against the bench top when the slots were cut, so the joints will line up perfectly.

Support narrow face frame parts against a block

It's tricky to cut slots in the ends of narrow parts using the biscuit joiner fence. The small surface area makes it hard to hold the biscuit joiner stable. But it's easy to cut accurate slots in narrow parts using the bench reference method. The photos here show how. We also show how to cut the biscuit slots off-center so the biscuit will protrude on one side only. This is handy if you want to join narrow parts and the biscuits are too large.

1 **Use a template to align the slot.** Cut a biscuit slot in a scrap of wood and mark the center and the size of the slot, in this case No. 0. Now use the template to position the biscuit mark. We offset this slot to the top where the protruding biscuit can be cut off and the slot won't show.

MARKING TEMPLATE

CENTER OF BISCUIT SLOT

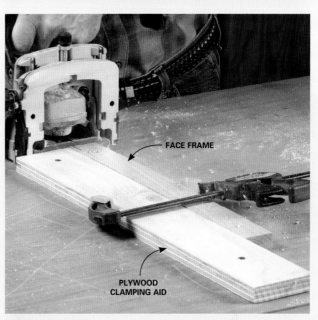

FACE FRAME

PLYWOOD CLAMPING AID

2 **Screw plywood to the bench as a clamping aid.** Line up the end of the part with the end of the clamping board and clamp the two together. The wide end makes a stable surface to press the biscuit joiner against.

FACE FRAME

3 **Cut the side slot.** Align the center marks and cut the biscuit slots. The clamping block makes a solid surface to push against.

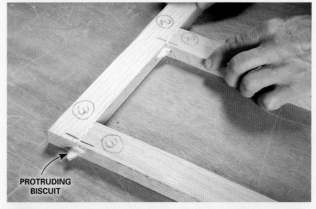

PROTRUDING BISCUIT

4 **Assemble the face frame.** Spread glue in the slots and insert the biscuits. Align the parts and clamp them. When the glue dries, cut off the protruding biscuits.

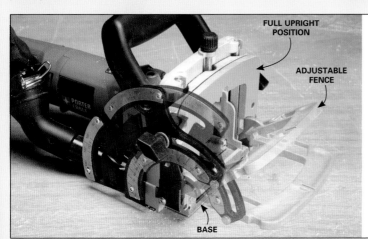

FULL UPRIGHT POSITION

ADJUSTABLE FENCE

BASE

Cutting slots without the fence

All biscuit joiners feature a fence that can be adjusted up or down and pivoted at varying degrees for cutting slots in beveled edges. Some woodworkers prefer not to use the fence when cutting slots. Instead, they use various spacers and jigs to cut accurate, consistent slots every time with far less hassle. For most of the tips we show, the adjustable fence is simply locked in the upright position.

Biscuits in thin material

You can use the same bench reference method to cut slots in material thinner than 3/4 in. by placing spacers underneath. Subtract the thickness of the material from 3/4 in. The difference is the spacer thickness. We show cutting slots in 1/2-in. plywood drawer parts. Without the spacer, the slots would be too close to the edge. But with the spacer, the slots are nearly centered. Photos 1 – 4 show how.

1 Label the parts and mark the biscuit locations. Avoid confusion by carefully labeling all the parts. Then mark where you want the biscuits.

1/8" SPACER

2 Don't adjust the fence—use spacers. Instead of adjusting the fence to cut slots in thinner material, add a spacer underneath. You'll get great results as long as you use the same spacer when you cut the slots in the adjoining panel (see Photo 3 below).

1/8" SPACER

3 Place the spacer under the end of the panel. Make sure the spacer doesn't protrude past the face of the panel. Then rest the base of the biscuit joiner on the workbench when you cut the slots.

4 The outsides will be perfectly aligned. Since both parts were held up the same amount by the spacer, the parts will line up exactly when you assemble them with biscuits.